BILL ALEXANDER

Bill Alexander was introduced to Shakespeare by a brilliant English teacher, John Binfield, who also directed an annual production of a Shakespeare play. Bill's first role was Perdita at the age of twelve, and his last, aged eighteen, was Prospero. At Keele University he created an experimental theatre group called Guerilla Theatre. After acting with another avant-garde group, The Other Company, he joined the Bristol Old Vic as a trainee director, where he attempted *Twelfth Night*, his first professional Shakespeare production.

In 1977 he joined the Royal Shakespeare Company with a brief to develop new plays for their studio theatres in London and Stratford. His first Shakespeare for the RSC was a touring production of both parts of *Henry IV*, after which, as an Associate Director, Bill staged productions of *Richard III* (in which Antony Sher won the Olivier Award for Best Actor), *The Merry Wives of Windsor* (which won Bill the Olivier for Best Director), *A Midsummer Night's Dream*, *Cymbeline*, *Much Ado About Nothing*, *The Merchant of Venice*, *Twelfth Night* and *The Taming of the Shrew*.

In 1992 Bill became Artistic Director of the Birmingham Rep, where his Shakespeare work included *Othello*, *Macbeth*, *Hamlet*, *Twelfth Night*, *The Tempest* and *The Merchant of Venice*. On leaving Birmingham he returned briefly to the RSC to direct *Titus Andronicus* and Corin Redgrave in *King Lear*. At both the RSC and the Rep he also directed a mixture of new plays, classic revivals and a variety of lesser-known works.

He has directed four Shakespeares in America and, more recently, has taught Shakespeare at three drama schools – LAMDA, Bristol Old Vic Theatre School and Drama Studio London. He lives in rural Gloucestershire with the artist, children's author and actress, Juliet Harmer.

Bill Alexander

EXPLORING SHAKESPEARE

A Director's Notes from the Rehearsal Room

NICK HERN BOOKS
London
www.nickhernbooks.co.uk

A NICK HERN BOOK

Exploring Shakespeare
first published in Great Britain in 2023
by Nick Hern Books Limited,
The Glasshouse, 49a Goldhawk Road, London W12 8QP

Cover photograph: Antony Sher as Richard III,
Royal Shakespeare Company, 1984, directed by Bill Alexander
(© Donald Cooper/Photostage)
Author photograph: Juliet Alexander

Designed and typeset by Nick Hern Books, London
Printed and bound in Great Britain by Severn, Gloucester

A CIP catalogue record for this book
is available from the British Library

ISBN 978 1 84842 981 9

CONTENTS

Preface

Anyone reading this book should be aware of three basic assumptions that underpin it but are not necessarily discussed at any length within it.

The first assumption is that actors are at the centre and are the soul of theatre. Everything a director does should be about them. They are not puppets to be fitted into a director's 'concept'. They are not there to be shaped, manipulated or instructed. Every aspect of a production – the design, the sound, the lighting, the music – should serve them, support them and enable the focus to be on their creativity, their art. Shakespeare knew this; he was an actor himself as well as a playwright, and each one of his plays was written with specific actors in mind: actors such as Will Kemp, Richard Burbage or Robert Armin. These were people whose personalities, skills, strengths and weaknesses he knew and understood as well as his own. His plays involved completely new challenges for an actor as the old medieval theatre was replaced by one of infinitely greater psychological complexity.

Stage acting is a unique, and uniquely brave, form of creativity. It demands that a human being give themselves openly and honestly to a room full of strangers for about two or three hours while making an alchemical transformation – becoming someone else; or rather, a peculiar fusion of themselves and someone else; and usually someone else who doesn't really exist except as words on a page. Hamlet is the actor and the actor is Hamlet. The encounter that is live theatre, where the unprepared (the audience) meet the prepared (the actors), is forged in the rehearsal room, a laboratory of psychological exploration. Throughout rehearsals the director's job is to organise, guide, challenge and encourage the process of changing from one human being into another. The director's duty is to protect the actors from the mental stresses these journeys of exploration sometimes entail, and never to exploit that responsibility with power games and fantasies of control. 'No guru, no method, no teacher,' as Van Morrison sang. If ever the rehearsal room becomes a place of fear and insecurity, creativity withers away. When it is a place of laughter, trust and mutual endeavour, creativity will flourish. The process of rehearsing is never easy, but when it works well it can create the conditions for an encounter between spectators and performers that is without parallel in any other form of art. Truthful acting, honest, present and informed, can make an audience feel glad to be alive, more sure of who they are, knowing themselves better, and grateful for the existence of live theatre.

Any director who fails to understand and respect the courage it takes to act, who treats actors as mere materials for their own creativity and sees their own 'vision' as more important than Shakespeare's play, seeking to divert praise due to actor and writer onto themselves, is betraying the meaning and purpose of one of the greatest bodies of work ever left to posterity.

The players at the Globe had to close their theatre and stop performing many times because of the plague, and the visitation of Covid recently left our theatres dark for months on end. If that were to happen permanently, part of what it means to be human would be lost.

My second assumption is that any argument about whether there is a right or wrong way to cast Shakespeare's plays is long over. There is nothing more to debate about a Black actor playing Henry V or a female actor playing King Lear. It's extraordinary how long it's taken to get there, and how long it's taken to realise that it's nothing to do with political correctness – it's about the wonderful revelations and excitements there are to be found when casting is completely gender and colour blind. Elizabeth Powell became the first woman to play Hamlet in 1796, and one of the most famous interpretations of the role was by Sarah Bernhardt in 1899. Over the last twenty or so years the whole casting palette has opened up in an almost limitless way revealing an array of new possibilities. Nothing now is out of bounds.

The third assumption is that the reader should have access to a text of the plays discussed here: to be able to read a scene in full so as to establish context, or a play that is unfamiliar in order to get the whole story. In rehearsal I usually work from an Arden edition because they have the best and fullest notes, and often the best Introductions too. Simply reading them before rehearsals begin can make any director seem a lot cleverer than they are. But the edition doesn't really matter so long as the reader at any moment is able to have their own direct relationship to the text. I didn't want to clog this book with lengthy or elaborate descriptions of the plots and tell readers stories they would be better off reading for themselves; it simply tries to explore how actors and directors together make choices – choices about broad areas of meaning, and choices about the small but crucial moments that colour the performance and engage an audience. In short, how to reveal the purpose of the play.

Part One

DIRECTING
SHAKESPEARE

The Rehearsal Room

On the first day of rehearsals I always try to be in the room at least an hour before anyone else. Excitement and nerves are twisted together, and I find it calming to sit there alone taking in the empty space, making it my own. This is a place where I need to lead, to set a tone, to create a sense of possibilities. Every rehearsal room I've ever worked in, from small wooden Scout huts to purpose-built modern studios, has plenty of chairs. Slowly I arrange some of them into a circle. I place a table with a single chair just outside the circle for the stage manager – I think they prefer it that way, they like to be a little bit detached, just beyond the emotional currents that are about to be stirred, and they need a big table, most importantly for 'the book', the precious record of everything that happens, the bible of what will emerge from the rehearsal process. I try to make the circle as perfect as possible, each chair exactly the same distance from the next, the circumference dictated by the number of actors. For a while I move about inside the circle, then outside, visiting every part of the room, seeing it from all angles. The next people to arrive are, invariably, the stage management team, usually three of them. They see the circle, and I feel a little guilty. This should be their job: they are used to asking the director how they want the room arranged and then arranging it. Some directors like no chairs because they will begin with physical exercises, and some have rows of seats for the actors facing a long table behind which sits the 'creative team', which at the most might consist of the director, the set designer, the costume designer, the lighting designer, the sound designer, the movement director and the voice coach. The actors become the audience in this scenario, and may well be outnumbered! So why do I make the circle myself? I suppose it relaxes me, and allows me to make my mark on the room, a gesture towards how I want things to be: egalitarian, focused, an image of the perfection we aim for but can never achieve. An image of togetherness and of common purpose, a sign that we are there to make something with each other, to turn Shakespeare's words on a page into a play on a stage. When the actors start to arrive, the room gradually fills with the hum and crackle of meeting, of something beginning, threads of nerves, laughter, talk, anticipation, weaving themselves clumsily into camaraderie. We all settle, and I begin to talk. Of course, by now my perfect circle has been comprehensively disrupted – chairs moved to make way for baggage, rearranged so old friends can be together, set back a little out of modesty, the one next to the director always the last to be occupied as no one wants to be seen to be currying favour. I talk about the play, about the structure of the days to come, and at some point ask the designer to show us the model of the set. This will usually have been assembled and covered with a drape before any of the cast arrive – the idea being to increase the dramatic impact of its revelation. The physical chemistry of the room shifts as actors leave their seats and gather round the model. I watch faces as the designer explains and demonstrates how it will all work, looking for reactions. Do they like it? Is it making sense? What mood is forming? Then the costume drawings are produced, and a new intimacy begins to emerge around the actors' relationship to the production: these are the clothes they will wear when they step on stage in front of an audience as a character that has not yet even begun to exist.

Coffee break. The focused mood fragments into a multitude of conversations creating a party-like scene where old relationships are being renewed and new ones are taking root. The chatting over, the room resettles. The work begins. There is a long way to go.

Some directors begin with an uninterrupted, straightforward reading of the play from start to finish. I've never found this particularly useful. Others begin with physical exercises, games, improvisations around characters, and situations from the play. I've never done that. I favour a long, slow reading of the text, stopping after every scene, discussing, going back, reading some sections again, sketching in possibilities, talking about alternative ways of looking at the relationships, and all the time trying to start understanding the implications latent in the text. This might take two or three days, with the full company getting acquainted with the totality of the play, regardless of which scenes they are in. We break the text down into 'blocks' (usually about forty), which are shaped by the coming and going of the characters; basically whenever someone leaves the action or someone arrives. So by the end of the first few days, the play will have been numerically restructured, and we will talk about, say, Blocks 12–16, not Act 2 Scene 3. It's a way of making the rehearsal process focus on small units of action, encouraging detailed analysis, not generalised feeling. From then on, only the actors involved in a particular block will be called for rehearsal, not the whole cast all the time.

Once the play is broken down into smaller sections, we begin to explore movement, and that, along with digging deeper into the text, helps the learning – suiting 'the action to the word, the word to the action', to quote Hamlet. I always want actors to learn their parts gradually through the discoveries they make about their characters during rehearsal – never to come with the lines pre-learnt. Bit by bit, blocks of action come together, making bigger blocks, giving an increasing sense of how the whole narrative hangs together, until eventually we are able to attempt the whole play in one seamless arc of storytelling.

Sometimes at this stage – maybe just before or just after the first full run – we go back to the circle with which we began. The chairs are reassembled as on the first day, but now the words have been absorbed into that mental space where actor and character meet. I tell the cast to forget about the movement we have added and to improvise if they feel the need to move, in order to concentrate purely on the text, with one strict rule: every time they speak the name of another character they must look at them, wherever in the circle they may be and regardless of whether that character is in the scene or not. Other people are in our minds an amazing amount of the time, even when not physically present. We exist in a web of self-defining relationships. Others are in us and part of us all the time. Shakespeare understood that, and it is constantly there in his plays. It's remarkable how this exercise, after rehearsing in fragments, brings the whole together, and how it helps the actor move out of their part and into their role. The cast becomes a choir, hopefully singing in tune. We live caught in the net of other people's feelings and expectations about us. We are constantly aware we can never, quite, see ourselves as others see us. Rehearsing Shakespeare is primarily concerned with applying what we instinctively know about life in this respect to Shakespeare's world of inter-relationships. As Bassanio describes Portia to Antonio, is he seeing her in his mind's eye as she really is, or as he wants Antonio to see her? When Viola says, 'My father had a daughter loved a man,' is she trying to conceal from Orsino that it's herself she's talking about, or trying to reveal it? The rehearsal process is the gradual accumulation of decisions about these kind of questions, the weaving of a network of tiny, subtle moments that will suck the audience into a world of complex feelings and motives; the ever-changing chemistry of human interaction.

The rehearsal room is the Petri dish for experimentation and discovery.

Rehearsing

Virtually single-handedly, Shakespeare invented an art form through which human beings could look at themselves, think about themselves, and potentially change themselves. This had never been done before. He was operating in a sympathetic environment. Late Renaissance England was a place full of enquiry, curiosity and adventure. Hamlet calls it holding the mirror up to nature, human nature in all its strange complexity and unpredictability. Every member of his audience was being invited to understand by witnessing vivid examples of how, for instance, a man might smile a lot yet still be a bad person. Individuals almost certainly knew this from their own private thoughts and experiences, but the stage could give them electrifying reflections of their intuitions and could make them concrete, clear and exciting – could make them feel less alone with their fears.

In example after example Shakespeare revealed publicly just how strange and familiar men and women could be. This gave those who saw his plays the possibility of real self-knowledge, of acquiring mental tools with which they could understand, challenge and maybe reshape themselves and their passage through the world. Much about the way the world was changing in his time was generating a thirst for self-contemplation that went beyond the ideas and instructions offered by religion. The suggestion that a principal purpose in life was to know yourself – an idea born in the Classical world and re-born in the European Renaissance – echoes through the plays:

I am I.

(Richard III)

I have much ado to know myself.
(Antonio in *The Merchant of Venice*)

This above all: to thine own self be true.

(Polonius in Hamlet)

He hath ever but slenderly known himself.

(Regan in King Lear)

To know my deed, 'twere best not know myself.

(Macbeth)

The choices were stark and brutal in the medieval world: follow the Church all the way to heaven, or go your own way to hell. This choice had shaped the thinking of generation after generation of women and men from all classes of society and at all levels of intellect. The proposition was simple – your body might die but your mind remained alive, forever, in one of three possible places: Heaven, Hell or Purgatory. The last was the place for those who had been neither all good nor all bad; in other words, the vast majority. The prison term was flexible according to God's assessment, but the punishments were beyond brutal. Hamlet's father tells him all about it. The priests of the day told their congregations all about it – graphically – once a week. Fire and much more for unimaginable stretches of time. What effect must this have had on the human mind? Was it really like that? Everyone must have thought about it a lot, so to go to a theatre, a very new kind of place and very different from a church, and hear Hamlet think about life after death as an 'undiscovered country' must have been astonishing. The Reformation, by consigning the idea of Purgatory to the realms of superstition, was opening minds to a huge range of speculative possibilities regarding the nature of life and death. Hamlet is the child of the reformed philosophy, and in the new theatre you went to hear him thinking. A clever man's brain is made audible to enrich our own thoughts, to take us beyond the grip of doctrinal fear.

The fundamental truth about acting Shakespeare is that thinking and speaking are the same thing. When an actor first realises this and understands the significance, it can be transforming. The sound of a word coming alive in the air triggers other words that begin to explain the individual to themselves. This is the process of knowing yourself. Whoever the character is, cynical or innocent, ambitious or humble, angelic or brutish, they face revelations about the world with a kind of constant incredulity, and these moments of comprehension, whether in dialogue or soliloquy, force a complicit response in the listener. This was all new at the time, and it always needs re-discovery. No two soliloquies in Shakespeare work in quite the same way because no two people are quite the same. This is the creation of character in its modern sense; personal and inimitable. In rehearsing we always have to ask if such a thing as character actually exists, because the deeper we dig into our characters and ourselves, the more we realise we are all actually several people: we don't just have one character. We try to have, but mood, circumstance, place, time and especially other people mean that we are always changing, always in a state of flux – like nature itself. Shakespeare's examination of people and their inter-relationships, the constant triangulation of mixed desires and thwarted loves, pulses through all the plays like an iambic heartbeat. Young lovers, middle-aged lovers, husbands and wives, brothers and sisters, fathers and sons, sons and mothers, form the first detailed kaleidoscopic examination of the human mind and heart. His plays stand today as a blueprint for understanding ourselves. Heart and Brain, Body and Soul, Wit and Will, Reason and Emotion, are the raw material of conflict that makes the Shakespearean rehearsal room one of the most exciting places on earth.

Texts

If a director told me they were preparing to rehearse a new production of *Hamlet*, the first question I'd ask would be, 'Which *Hamlet*?' There are three distinct texts of the play and they vary substantially from each other. They are known to students and academics as Q1, Q2 and F. Q stands for Quarto and F for Folio. Quarto basically describes an Elizabethan paperback, and Folio a modern 'coffee table book', but without the glossy illustrations. I would hope the director answering the question 'Which *Hamlet*?' would not reply either 'the Folio' or 'the Quarto' or 'the Arden edition', but 'my *Hamlet*', indicating that they intended to put together a rehearsal text from all the available sources. This is a big task of preparation, but worth it because by comparing all the available texts you are taking a journey into Shakespeare's mind and into the company of the other actors with whom he first rehearsed the play.

The Quarto texts were mainly printed during Shakespeare's lifetime, and some plays come down to us in different Quarto versions, which has given academics many happy hours discussing which of these are authentic renderings of the author's intentions and which of them are in some ways bastardised or corrupt scripts. Some are claimed to be 'memorial reconstructions' put together by actors remembering their own lines from productions they were in and the lines of others less well – or just plain making them up. But the gold standard text of all the plays is known as the First Folio, published in 1623, seven years after Shakespeare's death, by his friends and fellow actors John Heminges and Henry Condell. Around half of the plays in the Folio (which was reprinted several times) also have surviving Quarto versions – but half don't, and without the First Folio we would not know that they had existed at all: they would have disappeared from history like the vast majority of plays written between 1590 and 1610, the two decades of Shakespeare's working life. There would be no *Twelfth Night*, no *As You Like It*, no *Tempest*, the first play in the book. We would never have watched *Measure for Measure*, *The Two Gentlemen of Verona* or *The Comedy of Errors*, though we would have tantalisingly heard of them through contemporary references. We would never have to discuss whether *The Taming of the Shrew* is a sexist play or whether *All's Well That Ends Well* is a comedy, a tragedy, a dark satire on sex or a moral muddle. No director would ever have to struggle with plays as demanding as *Coriolanus*, *Cymbeline*, *Antony and Cleopatra* or *Timon of Athens*. No one would ever ask if *King John* is worth doing, discuss whether to double mother and daughter with the same actor in *The Winter's Tale*, or wish their theatre company had enough actors for a real crowd in *Julius Caesar*. There would be no *Macbeth*.

The men who put together the First Folio did so because they believed all the plays their friend and colleague wrote deserved to be preserved for posterity, because they were special, and because they wanted to set them down exactly as he had written them. They were not happy with many of the versions that had appeared in Quarto publications and wanted to create a definitive record: a text as close to the author's intentions as it was possible to be.

Hamlet is a rather special case because a lot of academics think Heminges and Condell got it wrong and that their Folio text is actually not as close to their partner's original thoughts as the second Quarto, though it may well represent his final thoughts. However, everyone agrees that the first Quarto is certainly not up to scratch, which is why it's known as the 'Bad Quarto'. One advantage it does have is that it's considerably shorter than either of the other two. I say 'advantage' because I'm thinking as a practitioner, not an academic, someone who knows, through the experience of a theatre seat as opposed to a study armchair, that *Hamlet* uncut can easily run to the best part of five hours. Which brings us to the question of cutting Shakespeare, and its central importance to actors, directors and, at the sharp end of their decisions, audiences. With *Hamlet*, which has no definitive text, I would expect the director, working closely from Q1, Q2 and the Folio, to put together a rehearsal-room script that runs no more than three hours and which therefore entails a lot of cutting. As the director rolls their sleeves up and gets on with this, it is bound to occur to them while they're at it that the word 'fardels' (in 'To be or not to be…') is a bit obscure (which is also true of literally thousands of words in Shakespeare no one uses these days), and that maybe it could be changed to a word that everyone would understand; 'bundles', say? 'Who would bundles bear?' Doesn't sound quite right, does it? What about 'burdens' – 'Who would burdens bear?' Better than 'bundles', definitely. The Folio reads 'Who would these fardels bear'. The addition of the word 'these' significantly changes the rhythm of the line. The notorious 'Bad Quarto' reads simply 'Who would this endure?' which implies that it isn't just modern audiences and directors who found fault with 'fardels'. The director has a nice little group of textual choices to chew on. These choices are of course entirely personal. My guidance would be this: change as little as possible, because once you start, you are on course to simply rewriting Shakespeare, which isn't against the law, but nevertheless risks producing a script that the audience will hear as a modernised version of the play, therefore implicitly a criticism of Shakespeare's text, and, by extension, a claim that the director knows better than Shakespeare. Obscure words can of course become clear through context, their meaning explaining itself within the overall meaning of the line, the perceived mood of the speaker, the broader narrative situation and the way it is said. Sometimes a line has historically seeped into the national consciousness even amongst those who neither read nor see much Shakespeare, so that changing a word that is familiar, like 'fardels', even if odd and not completely understood, could strike an uncomfortable note of dissonance in the listener. Let us take another line from *Hamlet*, one far less well known:

> Perhaps he loves you now,
> And now no soil nor cautel doth besmirch
> The virtue of his will…

This is Laertes to his sister, warning her to stay away from Hamlet on the grounds that, being Prince of Denmark, his choice of wife is a matter of state, not of personal preference; he may love Ophelia, but wouldn't be allowed to marry her. The word 'cautel' meant a trick, or what we'd call an 'ulterior motive', so he is for a moment giving Hamlet the benefit of the doubt concerning his sincerity. It's an important character point: Laertes is intelligent enough to see a range of possibilities and argue around them. It's also an important narrative point: it makes the audience wonder about the exact nature of Hamlet's feelings and intentions. But these points are in danger of being lost because of one word. I would change it (possibly to 'motive') whereas I wouldn't change 'fardels'. I just think you have to be incredibly careful, and only change a word when you think that something about the play is at stake; a nuance of character, a twist of plot, a really good joke!

There are no rules, you just have to develop good instincts, but there is one area of preparing a rehearsal-room text that can really put the cat among the pigeons. In Act Five of *Hamlet* a minor character appears to deliver a message. His name is Osric, and he has come to say that the King would like to see a fencing match between Laertes and Hamlet: 'My lord, his majesty bade me signify to thee that he hath laid a great wager on thy head.'

Osric speaks in an affected and stilted manner throughout the ensuing dialogue and is one of those tiny parts that Shakespeare's genius bothers to make real and interesting rather than leave them as a one-dimensional plot server. You never know whether he is exceptionally arrogant or pathetically nervous. Depending on how he's played, you could feel repulsed by him or truly sorry for him. But more to the point, you are unsure purely from the text whether he's being polite or rude. The line that I just quoted above sounds Shakespearean, doesn't it? Actually it isn't. In both the second Quarto and the Folio it reads: 'My lord, his majesty bade me signify to you that he has laid a great wager on your head.'

A lot of people, asked to say something Shakespearean, would probably invent a sentence with a lot of 'thee's', 'thy's' and 'thou's' in it; they likely wouldn't use the word 'you'. I've never sat up all night counting how many times 'thou' or 'you' are used in the entire canon, and I'm sure there's some App that could tell me, but my rough guess would be it's about 50/50. What dictated the choice between using 'thou' or 'you' was the context: 'thou' was informal, and 'you' was formal. So Osric is being polite; at least, superficially polite. For a mere courtier to use 'thou' to a royal prince would have been exceedingly rude. You would use it to someone you loved or who was an intimate in some way, or to a favourite servant, but never to someone you'd either never met or didn't know well, and never, ever to a social superior (although the ultra-intimate is also used as an ultra-condescension). The Elizabethans cared about these things. However, if you were angry or upset with a person you would normally address as 'thou' you might well use 'you' to underline the estrangement of that moment, or even to indicate to them how you were feeling; so 'you' could either be respectful or cold. I know this, and now you know this – if you didn't already – but I doubt if more than 5 per cent of any modern audience would know it unless you were playing to a house of English teachers. I have never changed 'thou' to 'you' all the way through the script in a professional production. I did do it in a drama school production of *The Two Gentlemen of Verona* a few years ago and, interestingly, no one noticed; or no one mentioned it, at any rate. I think it's an important issue.

The various shades of meaning that adhere to these two words (and other related words such as 'thine', 'canst', 'mine' and so on) are shades that can be discussed in the rehearsal room and understood almost as subtextual notes which actors can play, using the information in the way they inflect a line with a particular thought and interpretation. The old terms can also be seen as a kind of antique patina that hovers around the language like the darkening of an old painting that can be cleaned away to reveal vibrant colours underneath. Whether it is right to 'clean' Shakespeare's texts in this way is up to every director to discuss with their cast and come to a coherent decision. There are occasional phrases where it just doesn't sound or feel right, but I think they are in a minority. Because 'you' is as common as 'thou' there is seldom any tonal or emotional shock in hearing 'you cannot' instead of 'thou canst not' or 'your eyes' instead of 'thine eyes', and increasingly over the years I have felt it is better to make these changes than not. It may be that many directors simply don't feel this dilemma one way or the other – that it makes little difference to the overall experience of the play, whichever choice you make, but I would always at least raise the subject in rehearsal to share the issue with the cast, and on the whole encourage the view that it is not 'modernising' the text if the poetic flow, the rhythm of the iambic pentameter and respect for the sound of the language as much as the sense is respected and maintained. If Gertrude says to her son, 'How is it with you?', in place of 'How is't with thee?', it is not damaging; it's simply more moving.

One final thought about the putting together of a text. Shakespeare the actor learnt how to help actors make their character's arguments potent, how to make an idea lodge in the listener's brain. Here is an example from *Hamlet* of the same dramatic moment in the first Quarto (probably a cut, simplified and otherwise distorted version of the original play) and the Folio (the final and, for me, definitive text). It's the moment where Hamlet, determined at last to kill the King, comes across him at prayer and decides that now is not the time to strike. First the Quarto:

> HAMLET. This physic but prolongs thy weary days!
> KING. My words fly up, my sins remain below.
> No king on earth is safe if God's his foe.

Now the Folio:

> HAMLET. This physic but prolongs thy sickly days.
> CLAUDIUS. My words fly up, my thoughts remain below.
> Words without thoughts never to heaven go.

This adds antithesis, where contrasting ideas co-exist and balance each other within the same line, bringing added clarity to the thinking. 'Physic' is contrasted with 'sickly', and 'words' with 'thoughts'. Time and time again, through every one of his plays, Shakespeare uses this simple technique as an aid to the actor who, by stressing the opposing words, helps the audience grasp meaning. By replacing 'sins' with 'thoughts', and repeating the combination of 'words' and 'thoughts' in its final line, the Folio's definitive text throws a far sharper light on Claudius's agonised state of mind, and the actor's job is made easier.

Time

The concept of the 'Unities' of Time, Place and Action was not exactly a rule book for drama, more a set of observations about the way the playwrights of Ancient Greece actually wrote. The Unity of Time meant everything that happened in the play happened within the same amount of time it took to perform the play. A new scene would not start days or months after the scene before, let alone after a gap of sixteen years as happens between Acts Three and Four of *The Winter's Tale*. The Unity of Place entailed everything in the story happening in one location (not divided between, say, Sicily and Bohemia). The Unity of Action demanded that dramatic events (deaths, riots, arson and battles for instance) were described by witnesses, not shown directly on the stage, enabling a sustained, continuous and streamlined plot. The origins of this tight dramatic structure probably lie in the centuries-old craft of the single storyteller. A narrator, surrounded by listeners sitting around an open fire at night or in a town square by day, tells a story: what happened to someone, when and where it happened. The action is moving in time and place only in the imaginations of the audience. Even when a significant change in the craft occurred and the speaker of the tale was joined by a partner – a privileged listener, a questioner, who, unlike the rest of the audience was permitted a voice – what was added was not literal movement in either place or time but simply a deepening of analysis, a curiosity about the meaning of the events being described.

'This happened,' says the storyteller. 'Why?' asks the listener. 'I think it may have been because of X,' says the teller. In that 'Why?' and the subsequent 'I think' and 'may', you have the beginning of character caused by the ingredient of time. The explanation of why a certain thing happened is an individual's interpretation of past events and not merely the events themselves. Different people see things in different ways. If the listener/questioner then goes on to express doubt about the teller's point of view, and by doing so reveals themselves to be a different sort of person with a different way of seeing the world, then you have conflict: you have *drama*.

In the town squares and first theatres of the ancient world it was enough that action was described and meaning debated through the conflict of characters, but it wasn't enough for Shakespeare's audience. In the Globe, dramatic time expanded and created a form of drama that put the whole world on the stage as best it could. The audience watching *The Winter's Tale* even saw Time itself on stage as a character, and they wouldn't have been content with one person telling another about Gloucester having his eyes put out, they wanted to see it; and they did. Theatre in Ancient Greece and Rome was about a desire to get to grips with a world that lay under the control of the gods. Shakespeare's world was hungry to see and understand the consequences of human actions; actions so bewildering sometimes that Viola addresses Time itself: 'thou must untangle this, not I. / It is too hard a knot for me t'untie.'

Eventually Time does just that, but the way he does it can lead to quite an entanglement of thinking in the rehearsal room. In some of Shakespeare's plays, actors and directors are confronted by something called a 'double time scheme', where close study of the text reveals that time is moving at two different speeds simultaneously. The overwhelming sense of time in *Twelfth Night* is that of events moving very fast, sweeping bewildered characters along with it. Right up to the denouement only a few days seem to have passed, yet both Antonio and Orsino clearly state that it has been three months. In *Othello*, when the action moves from Venice to Cyprus, between Cassio, Iago, Desdemona and Othello arriving on the island and the tragic conclusion, a close reading reveals the events as happening in a mere thirty-six hours. This allows no possible time for the alleged adultery to have happened. How do actors and directors aiming for realism and the invention of credible backstories get their heads round this? Iago's invocation of a sexual relationship between Desdemona and Cassio would have to have occurred in Venice before Othello married her, which, although an unpleasant thought, lacks the impact of a post-marital liaison. Is this a problem? Does it matter? In directing both plays I've never really been able to find a way of worrying about it. Nor have any of the actors. More importantly, I've never spoken to a member of the audience that has even noticed the anomaly. As the old saying goes, if there's no solution, then it's not a problem. Shakespeare is playing a trick with time that always seems to work. Sebastian in *Twelfth Night* exists for the duration of the play in a different time frame from his twin sister to make the plot effective. Short time keeps the story moving, and long time provides a background haze of realism that lends credibility to Viola's drawn-out suffering with a love she can't express to a man who may be shocked at her deceit. It makes sense on an emotional level if not on a temporal one. The audience watching *Othello* and being made very aware of the tightness of the passing of the thirty-six hours know that Desdemona cannot have been unfaithful to her husband, so the agonising pressure of Iago's deceit is amplified. And again, to have his cake and eat it, Shakespeare refers to Cassio as having been on the island for at least a week!

So in rehearsals you just have to put it out of your mind and get on with it. Anyway, actors can't act concepts, only actions. Time is too abstract to be played, but what does become a valid and much debated reality – and that most certainly can be played – is Time's humble cousin: Pace.

Comedy and Tragedy
(*Clowns and Fools*)

Think of the two famous masks with their semi-circular mouths: the comic turns upwards like a cross-section of a coracle; the tragic down, a grumpy igloo. A smile for laughter, a grimace for despair. These masks represent the ancient categories of drama, but they do not represent Shakespeare. To say that the comic and tragic are mixed together in his work is a massive understatement verging on cliché. They are inextricably entwined. One of a director's principal goals is to find the tragedy in *Twelfth Night* and the comedy in *Hamlet*, often within the same sentence. It's like our lives, 'a mingled yarn, good and ill together' (as a character in *All's Well That Ends Well* puts it). Without the humour, *Hamlet's* sad and bitter story can become mere bathos, and if you leave the melancholic undertow out of *Twelfth Night*, all that remains is whimsy and superficial laughter reducing the humanity of the characters' inner struggles. The masks of Comedy and Tragedy come from that other black-and-white world that produced the original theatre of Classical Athens. Inheriting this primitive (and powerful) duality, Shakespeare invented the dramatic language of human complexity, which is why we feel so close to him today in our own world of muddy, muddled reality. He replaced the smile and the scowl with the wry grin, the bitter laugh, the ridiculous yet understandable yearnings of the steward Malvolio, and the questioning, phlegmatic attitude of the confused avenger-prince Hamlet. These are people responsible for what happens to them, trying their hardest, trying to understand themselves and their situations. They are not the pawns of the gods or the victims of heavenly astrology:

> The fault, dear Brutus, is not in our stars
> But in ourselves, that we are underlings.

Cassius – in *Julius Caesar* – here speaks with the voice of Renaissance humanism, thinking, acting, failing but always puzzling out a path through life that has nothing to do with Fate or the gods, but everything to do with the choices open for men and women to make at every moment; it is the beginning of our world, the 'invention of the human' (as the title of Harold Bloom's book about Shakespeare describes it). In the rehearsal room an actor should never try to be funny, any more than they should try to be tragic; their contract with their director is simply to find the way to be human.

Trying not to try to be funny is, of course, easier said than done, especially if playing one of Shakespeare's 'comic' characters. It's just a question of remembering that any of us can at times access a sense of humour in ourselves in the right circumstances and any of us can inadvertently deserve to be laughed *at*, whether through incompetence, pride, pretentiousness or a lack of self-awareness in a particular situation.

The distinction between a Fool and a clown is simple. A Fool was paid (the capital letter is important) because it was his job to make people laugh. A clown in the plays is someone who tends to make a fool of themselves, either through ignorance or unsophisticated simplicity, or in striving to be funny in an amateur kind of way because that's their nature, an aspect of their personality, like Launcelot Gobbo in *The Merchant of Venice*; no money need change hands. There should be no confusion with today's Clown (in a circus or at a children's party), who is a paid professional entertainer and the nearest thing we have to an Elizabethan Fool. The word can admittedly be used to describe some politicians, but, generally speaking, who is a fool today and who isn't is a matter of opinion, a subjective assessment we make about someone whose behaviour seems foolish to us; we are all fools to someone. In *Twelfth Night* Feste asks Toby and Andrew, 'Did you never see the picture of "we three"?' This refers to a well-known image of two Fools wearing the cap and bells who are staring out from the picture directly at the viewer with mad grins on their faces. The joke is that the viewer is the third fool.

The job of Fool (or Jester) was a career inherited by the Elizabethan world from the courts of the Middle Ages. Feste, Touchstone and the Fool in *King Lear* are all examples, individuals paid to hang around house, court or palace and amuse people on demand – imagine Eddie Izzard being paid to live in Buckingham Palace. It must have been a strange life, as the expectation of the employer was that their personal Fool should occasionally be wise as well as witty, speaking truth to power, but only if power was in the mood to receive it. Both Lear's Fool and Feste are threatened with whipping and hanging, either for not being on call when they should have been or for coming out with views not acceptable to the sensibility of their paymasters. Eddie would be unlikely to stick around under those conditions, and therein lies the problem with the role of Fool in modern-dress productions.

There was also a less elevated (and less risky) way of earning money by making people laugh: you could be a Tavern Fool, the equivalent of a pub or club comedian today, paid by the owner to entertain the customers while they ate and drank. But there are none of these in Shakespeare. It's incredibly hard to think of ways of making sense of the character of the Fool if the actors on stage are wearing contemporary clothes: no grand houses these days have professional comedians on their staff, whereas in *King Lear*, *Twelfth Night* and *As You Like It* the characters are attached to the residences of a King, a Countess and a Duke. Our current monarch doesn't have a Fool, nor has any British king, queen, duke, earl, count or lord for a very long time, and the more modern the production's historical setting, the greater the strain in making the character fit in. So rationalising exactly why that person is there has to be the starting point for an actor playing a Fool. Establishing a personality beyond the function is central – what is it about them that makes them want to stay in this peculiar servant–master/mistress relationship? Any hints in the text that help establish a psychologically coherent backstory are precious. In an early scene of *Twelfth Night* Malvolio has this speech to Olivia about Feste, whom he clearly detests:

> I marvel your ladyship takes delight in such a barren rascal. I
> saw him put down the other day with an ordinary fool that
> has no more brain than a stone. Look you now, he's out of his
> guard already. Unless you laugh and minister occasion to
> him, he is gagged.

(An 'ordinary' was another name for a tavern, and John Stone was a well-known Elizabethan tavern Fool.) Feste has no verbal response to this; he is indeed 'gagged' and, according to Malvolio, 'out of his guard'. It's an insult, and a comment on his character that clearly stings because he carries the memory of it through the whole play. In the last scene, commenting on Malvolio's humiliation he says to him:

> But do you remember, 'Madam, why laugh you at such a
> barren rascal, an you smile not, he's gagged'? And thus the
> whirligig of time brings in his revenges.

The Fool, who is supposed to be witty and wise, philosophical, clear-sighted and above the fray of human vanity, has been deeply hurt and has waited for his revenge. A professional comedian's worst fear is to be laughed *at*. So there is vulnerability, neediness, the desire to be defined through the laughter and love of the audience. Here is the basis for building a character in whatever period the play is set, and also for avoiding caricature.

The Fools in *King Lear* and *Twelfth Night* can seem like sad, even tragic figures, living permanently under the threat of physical punishment if they transgress. Clowns, on the other hand, rarely come to any harm. Whereas it is incredibly difficult for us now to find the Fools in any way funny (partly because their language is often so obscure), the clowns are basically characters whose peculiarities, obsessions, lack of self-awareness or pure mischievousness were all created by Shakespeare with the express purpose of getting laughs. There is Launcelot Gobbo for his cockiness and opportunism, Dogberry for his pompous self-importance and misconstructions of language, Costard for his pure cheek, Parolles for his boastfulness, Thersites for his bitter, black, caustic cynicism, and Bottom the weaver for his epically misplaced belief in his acting ability. With all these characters (and many more) the director has to free the actor from the pressure to be funny: they all fit seamlessly into the narratives they are part of; they all have a role in the scheme of the play, as well as a personality. Their place in the text guarantees that if the actor plays their situation honestly, and allows the script to reveal who they are, and has imagined a credible, useful and unobtrusive backstory, then the laughs will come without funny voices, funny walks or 'comic business' unconnected to the words.

While I think all this is true, I need to pull back a bit lest I begin to sound like Malvolio: dour and puritanical. Of course, there are brilliant comic actors who would find these thoughts, if not ridiculous, then at least repressive to the spirit of comic invention. It may just be that as a director I've never been any good at physical comedy and so have built an approach based on an over-reverential deference to the text as the only source of viable comedy. If the audience are splitting their sides with laughter, what does it matter whether it's because of what the actor is saying or because of what they are doing? I once worked with an actor who (unaided by me) created such hysterically funny comic business for the 'yellow stockings scene' in *Twelfth Night* that, from the moment of his entrance to the moment of Olivia fleeing the room, the audience were laughing so much and so loudly that it was literally impossible to hear a word he, or the other two actors on stage, said. It was an exhibition of pure comic genius that made Shakespeare's words redundant. No matter how long the actors paused to give the laughter time to die, eventually they had no choice but to speak and their voices became a kind of blurred accompaniment to a ballet of delirious movement. I can't draw any moral from this, and don't know what kind of intervention I could or should have made as the director. But the text is very funny – read it!

If you think of the high tragic moments in Shakespeare, most of them involve death. The orchestrating of stage deaths is a directorial skill that is one of the hardest to master. A good actor can fool an audience about most things – being in love, being afraid, being sad, being angry – but not being dead. Suspension of disbelief is the gods' gift to theatre: without it, theatre wouldn't exist – there would be no point to it. But no adult audience member in any theatre at any time in any place has ever believed that the actor playing Hamlet is really dead after he has said, 'The rest is silence.' It's an artistic precipice on which the skills of actors and directors are tested to the limit. Just as every comic fears being laughed *at*, every actor fears the moment of the 'bad laugh', the laugh you didn't intend when you strive for a tragic effect, or the ripple of laughter that says clearly 'We don't believe you'. These are the moments when the contract between actor and audience dissolves, and the storyteller and the listener part company. There are no worse moments in theatre than these. The key to avoiding them lies in the blending of comedy and tragedy that I described earlier: the establishing of a key signature that reflects back to the audience the reality of life's precarious uncertainty from the moment the auditorium darkens and the light hits the stage. It demands consistency in the control of mood, and the shifting patterns of emotion, right up to and beyond the tragic climax where that control is most tested. It's a hard thing to write about because the processes of the rehearsal room are often non-verbal, and totally dependent on the trust and working atmosphere that have been created between the practitioners face to face. But let's have a quick look at the endings of the four great tragedies: *Hamlet*, *Othello*, *King Lear* and *Macbeth*.

Hamlet has posed as mad for most of the play, and the Elizabethans saw the mad as Nature's clowns and fools. There is a genuine Fool in *Hamlet*, but he is already dead by the time the play begins. He is the old

King Hamlet's court Fool, Yorick, who appears only as a skull, tossed up by a jesting gravedigger (specifically called 'a clown' in Q2) onto the muddy earth of Elsinore's burial ground. Young Hamlet has been both clown and Fool during the action. The tragic conclusion of that action lies in the fact that his haphazard pursuit of revenge has inadvertently brought about his own death. This outcome has an essence of black comedy, as if the iconic masks have blended themselves into a sarcastic grimace. For all Horatio's attempts to eulogise and ennoble the death of his friend, even to mythologise it, the ending of the story tastes more of irony than pure tragedy, and this is a difficult tone to catch in performance. Generally, the climax of a 'tragedy' is harder to make work than the finale of a 'comedy', not only in getting the staging and mood right, but also because you are encountering the human tendency in the audience to prefer happiness to sadness, to want to feel merry rather than glum. Actually, comedy may be a little easier, but essentially the problem is the same: there is absolutely nothing an audience hates more than sensing it is being manipulated into feeling sad or happy. And they are right. The answer isn't to manipulate them without them realising, but simply to find the way to create the spirit of sad happiness at the end of tragedy, and happy sadness at the end of comedy. Denmark has been restored to sanity after the chaotic reign of a usurper, and Illyria contains broken and lonely souls – focus on Fortinbras (not Hamlet) in the final beat; on Antonio (not Viola).

The accumulation of bodies littering the stage at the end of a tragedy can easily seem ridiculous rather than moving, but that's only the director's most obvious problem. How does Othello manage to kill himself when he has already been disarmed? What exactly does Lear die of? (Old age? Grief? Exhaustion?) And why, after all his murderous acts, should we feel any pity for Macbeth as his decapitated head is brandished by Macduff? And if we don't, how can we call his death tragic? Why is the play even called a tragedy? The classic definition states that a tragic hero is a potentially great man who falls because of a fatal flaw in his nature. I don't buy that. These four men have a multitude of flaws, and if you pick on one – indecisiveness, jealousy, senility, ambition – you will have squeezed the scope of the central character to the point where a mixed response of conflicting feelings becomes impossible for an audience. Final stage moments are perilous emotional balancing acts for director and actor, and the path towards them must be meticulously detailed in rehearsal. Perhaps it's better to forget the terms Comedy and

Tragedy; I don't think Shakespeare really thought in those terms anyway. In the collected volume of his plays in 1623 it was the editors who
listed them by category (along with Histories), not the writer. They are
restrictive labels that can only get in the way of exploring Shakespeare's
complexity, labels that he was prepared to ridicule in Polonius's
announcement of the arrival of the players:

> The best actors in the world, either for tragedy, comedy,
> history, pastoral, pastoral-comical, historical-pastoral,
> tragical-historical, tragical-comical-historical-pastoral, scene
> individable, or poem unlimited.

Elizabethans

They were like us. They were not remotely like us. They loved and hated and feared, laughed and died like us, but they also believed profoundly different things about the nature of human existence. They were confused too, like us: their most fundamental beliefs were being challenged, they feared chaos both in the social and cosmic realms, and this fearful uncertainty is a drumbeat through Shakespeare's plays. Tapping into it is the heartbeat of the life of rehearsal.

The other day I heard an astronomer say that science can only tell us what 10 per cent of the universe is made of – stars and planets and other material left over from the Big Bang – but the other 90 per cent is a mystery: they call it 'dark matter' and know nothing about it at all. Well, the Elizabethans who either read or heard about the astronomer Nicolaus Copernicus were being told something far more mind-blowing than that. He was suggesting that they should discount the evidence of their own eyes and the centuries-old teaching of their Church. They were invited to forsake the idea that the earth was the still and constant centre of the universe, that the sun, moon and planets circled around us, that the stars were fixed points of light embedded in a revolving transparent sphere on the other side of which was Heaven, the realm of God and his angels. Copernicus said this was not the case after all: rather, the sun was the motionless object around which we revolved along with the planets and the moon and, yes, that meant we were moving, the earth was moving under our feet travelling in a vast circle through the sky and spinning too, like a child's top, even though we couldn't feel it. The huge majority of Elizabethans refused to believe this of course, despite Galileo and his telescope. Instead they continued to believe what generations before them had believed and what the Church, whether Protestant or Catholic, taught: that the earth was the centre of God's creation, with Hell deep within and Heaven beyond the stars. The challenges posed by

Galileo and Copernicus caused a mental crisis in the Elizabethan world which is perfectly expressed in a poem by John Donne, Shakespeare's contemporary. Here are lines from 'The First Anniversary':

> And new Philosophy calls all in doubt,
> The element of fire is quite put out;
> The Sun is lost, and th'Earth, and no man's wit
> Can well direct him where to look for it.
> And freely men confess that this world's spent
> When in the Planets and the Firmament
> They seek so many new; they see that this
> Is crumbled out again to his Atomies.
> 'Tis all in pieces, all coherence gone.

This was from about the same time that Shakespeare was writing *The Tempest*. Donne was eight years younger and would have been in his early twenties when the older man was gaining attention with his first successful plays. He was a passionate theatregoer and a friend of rival playwright Ben Jonson. He knew Shakespeare well and respected him deeply. Imagine the three of them – Donne, Jonson and Shakespeare – talking late into the night in the Boar's Head or the Cardinal's Hat. Did they believe the globe of the earth was travelling through space spinning like their heads after too much talk, too much wine, too much thought? Whether they personally did or not, the hugeness of the idea transfused itself into their work – especially Shakespeare's.

Elizabethan sensibilities in some ways barely make sense to us now. Many of them would have been to an animal-baiting show or a public execution in the same week they saw *Hamlet* or *Twelfth Night*. They lived in a world where, without electricity, the dark of night was truly dark, in rooms where you could not see your hand in front of your face unless you lit a candle. Rehearsing once with the actor playing Juliet I asked her, when she got the chance, to watch the shadows a candle makes on a white plastered wall and then think about Juliet's line imagining the naked Romeo:

> Come, night, come, Romeo, come, thou day in night,
> For thou wilt lie upon the wings of night
> Whiter than new snow upon a raven's back.

The new snow, his skin; the raven's back, the darkness; but the wings? Why 'the wings of night'? That is the flickering effect of the light that only a candle makes on a bare wall. Every Elizabethan would have recognised the appropriateness of that image instantly, so we have to find a way of making a modern audience see it too; but first the actor must see it.

They were like us; they were not like us. They accepted that justice might involve being part of a crowd watching a man having his guts cut out on a platform stage in a public square, believing torture was a valid part of punishment; then, on a day *Much Ado* was playing at the Globe, applaud with relish as Benedick says about the villain Don John: 'I'll devise thee brave punishments for him. Strike up, pipers!' He is talking about torture, then calls for a dance. The cruel and the merry within the same thought. You can't shy away from this kind of paradox in rehearsals; you have to embrace it. You can't rationalise the moment by saying Benedick doesn't really mean it, that he's only joking. To do that would be to evade the truth that for the Elizabethans viciousness and laughter co-existed in a way we find difficult to understand. There is tragedy lurking in the comedy, and comedy roguishly present in the tragedy.

Many of the comedies include a kiss between lovers towards the end. This would involve a young man in his mid-twenties to thirties kissing a young boy aged between twelve and fourteen full on the lips in a portrayal of eroticism that would now be illegal.

The cold was colder, the dark darker, journeys that now take hours would take days or weeks. Medicine was random, unimaginably inadequate by our standards, death frequent and constantly anticipated at any age. The fear of death was generated anew every Sunday by the sermon that you would be fined for not attending. The message was crystal clear; if you followed the Church's rules you stood a chance of going to heaven, if you strayed you would go to hell. Virtually everyone believed in the doctrine of sin and salvation, and the reality of an individual's continued existence after death. Everyone understood a reckoning was coming.

Throughout Shakespeare's twenty-year career the theatres were closed roughly every two years for some weeks or months because of the plague. In *Twelfth Night*, after her first meeting with Viola, Olivia, realising she has fallen in love, says: 'Even so quickly may one catch the plague?' Everyone in the audience was afraid of the plague, everyone knew the authorities closed theatres because the tightly packed gatherings there were known to be one of the principal ways in which it spread. In the rehearsal room director and actor have to find a way of showing that Olivia is frightened as well as excited; that's the point of the image. Love was sometimes depicted as a disease that gained entrance into the heart through the eyes; that's why women were encouraged to keep eyes lowered to the ground in male company.

The realities of life and the social and religious belief systems of the period thread their way inextricably through the texts, and we must try to react to them in rehearsals, not pretend they don't exist. Portia, in *The Merchant*, is overjoyed at Bassanio making the right choice of caskets, winning her in the bizarre marriage lottery invented by her father. She speaks about her happiness to her future husband and in front of witnesses saying this:

> Happiest of all is that her gentle spirit
> Commits itself to yours to be directed,
> As from her lord, her governor, her king.

This was simply the received wisdom of the age with its passion for order: the world was a better place if women obeyed their husbands, were 'directed' by them, just as subjects obeyed their monarch. You can find this belief stated over and over again in Elizabethan literature. But to us the implications of this idea are at least as indigestible as the casual anti-Semitism that runs through the same play. Given my basic thesis that to distance yourself from the language by using modern irony or turning a blind eye to the actual meaning is to rip the heart out of the thought, my approach in rehearsal has been that Portia means what she says in that precise moment with every fibre of her being and doesn't care who knows it. This is as achievable in modern dress as in Elizabethan. It's what she feels, and we can decide not to like her for it if we choose. They are on the front foot all the time, the Elizabethans, and we should not dampen their passion with a wink. They were physical; they thought their feelings were in their blood not their brains. Coursing through their veins, they believed, were substances called 'humours'. To be at ease with yourself these liquids needed to be in balance. There were four of them: blood, which controlled the characteristics of happiness and positivity; yellow bile, which made you angry; black bile, which made you sad; and phlegm, which offered passivity and acceptance. They didn't think a person had simply to strive to be happy all the time any more than we should. What would we do without anger in the time of Trump, without the capacity for sadness in the face of suffering, or the ability to accept the inevitability of disease and death? We know these things are in our minds, but the Elizabethans thought they were in their bodies, and their behaviour and language reflect exactly that.

In the rehearsal room we have to discover ways of expressing this, to feel the rawness of life as they did, without the cotton wool of modern comfort.

When we are acting Shakespeare we can be like us, but we have to be like them as well.

Age

We know from the text of *The Tempest* that Prospero's daughter is fifteen years old. A betrothal happens during the play of a kind Jacobean audiences would have been familiar with. Miranda is pledged to Ferdinand, overseen by her father, in an improvised ceremony involving just the three of them. Imagining beyond the end of the play we can assume, once everyone is back in Naples, there will be a full wedding. Maybe by then Miranda will have passed her sixteenth birthday, a perfectly acceptable age for marriage in that society. Not, however, the average age, which has been estimated at between twenty and twenty-three. Rosalind, Viola and Portia, all of whom head towards marriage in their respective plays, would seem to be about that age, though no one mentions it. By contrast, Miranda is very young, which means she is both vulnerable and malleable. Her manipulation into a union that neatly fits the schematic demands of the play – old enemies reconciled through dynastic bonding – is not a comfortable idea if you are trying to look at the play naturalistically and through modern eyes. The issue in the rehearsal room is how old she should be played: do you cut the text that refers to her exact age? Or just ignore it?

The situation for Juliet is different, and *Romeo and Juliet* is a much less schematic play, which carries within it a far more complex approach to age and marriage. She is – again according to the text – thirteen. In the early part of the play, before she's even heard of Romeo Montague, she is being set up in an arranged marriage against her will. But here her father seems to make it clear that he regards thirteen as too young to get married. There is disagreement between her parents; her mother is all in favour and, rather shockingly, points out that she herself was thirteen when she gave birth to Juliet. Lady Capulet could be played no more than twenty-seven, which would make her a lot younger than her husband, who from the characterisation of his speech, its rhythms and repetitions, seems closer to sixty than forty. However, there are other references that could imply she is older. This matters in rehearsal because the ages of Miranda and Juliet are important narrative elements. They are significantly more innocent people than the shrewd Viola, the witty and sophisticated Rosalind or the confident, clever and well-educated Portia. Shakespeare's intention is partly to explore their vulnerability within the different circumstances of each story. Originally both Juliet and Miranda would have been played by actors who were exactly the right age for the parts. Not the right sex, but definitely the right age. The boy players tackling these roles just before their voices broke would have naturally placed an emphasis on the importance of the characters' extreme youth to the two storylines. This is why casting the parts now is notoriously difficult. Coming out of drama school these days, most actors would be, on average, somewhere between twenty-one and twenty-six, depending on whether they had gone straight from school to college or taken a university course first; potentially they could be ten years too old for either character. Several years of training will, hopefully, have equipped them to handle the language, but there is a huge psychological difference between thirteen and twenty-six. That's a massive acting challenge.

This raises a bigger question about age and casting in Shakespeare. The average life expectancy in the late sixteenth century (given the huge rate of infant mortality) was forty-seven years. In London, where most of the theatres were, it was thirty-five years in the wealthier parts of the populace and twenty-five years in the poorer. The vast majority of people in Shakespeare's London were young. The average age of Francis Drake's crew on the *Golden Hind*, during his first circumnavigation of the globe, was twenty-five. The implication is simply that most of Shakespeare's characters were conceived of as considerably younger than we tend to think of them. Because of our longer lives we fill up a casting gap. If we didn't, no actor over fifty would ever get to play a part. Burbage, Shakespeare's leading actor, was under forty when he played King Lear, textually eighty. Of course, he did write older people; as well as Lear, there's Polonius, Justice Shallow, Falstaff, and so on, but the age was acted, not real. In certain plays, perceived old age is the subject of tragedy or satire or pure comic ridicule, but we need to be aware that Beatrice and Benedick, for instance, were not intended to be in their mid-forties, as they now tend to be played.

I believe our re-imagining of many key characters as middle-aged (or what is now middle-aged) has profound implications for the way we tend to see and do Shakespeare today. It is because we are older and more sophisticated, and more ironic – more cautious, self-conscious, and more self-aware – that we sometimes find it hard to access the untempered, unsophisticated, incredulous passion and anger, joy and fear that surge and eddy through the plays, and are an aspect of the characters' youth. Furthermore, it is bound up with the totally non-naturalistic device of endowing characters with powers of speech beyond the normal; putting exquisite poetry into the mouth of a thirteen-year-old girl or beautiful imagery into the mind of a murderer. We moderns value irony and understatement so highly that it is hard to get into the heads and capture the spontaneity of personalities less ironic and less understated than ourselves. What we most fear is that the language, and hence the acting, will seem 'over the top'. This is certainly the problem many English actors have with Shakespeare. The instinct to use our modern sensibilities, prejudices and habits of thought as a guide to the behaviour of an early modern individual is so strong because we fear appearing ridiculous. It may well be just an English condition. There is something wry and undemonstrative about the English character now that wasn't the case in the sixteenth century, when we were looked on by our European neighbours as particularly volatile, unstable and over-emotional. They put it down to too much beef in our diet. Sir Andrew says: 'I am a great eater of beef, and I believe that does harm to my wit.' 'Wit' meant reason.

Every day in the rehearsal room is a search for how to combine the subtle with the fiery, the understated with the emotional, and how to blend the modern mind with the Renaissance mind, which valued the cultivation of manners and gentility precisely because brutality and suffering were so much closer to the surface of life.

Backstory

The rehearsal room is the place where actors and directors relate their own lived experiences to the imagined experiences of the characters in the play. Key to this is the notion of 'backstory'. Its usual meaning is the history of the characters before they enter the play, or at least a glimpse of that history. There is the kind of backstory that can be purely the invention of the actor; but also there are the glimpses provided by Shakespeare. These hints are delicate brushstrokes in the writing which some people argue had little significance to Shakespeare and shouldn't have for us, either as readers or interpreters. But in rehearsal they are pure gold dust. For actors they work as a currency of engagement with the characters and clues into the ways of bringing them to life on stage. They can help shape personality, motivation and attitudes to those others who become involved in their stories. These little shards can be used as the basis for building quite complex backstories.

For instance: the text of *Macbeth* tells us that Lady Macbeth had a child that she breastfed: 'I have given suck, and know / How tender 'tis to love the babe that milks me.' But there is no hint as to whether that child is still alive or what became of him or her if they are. Was it a boy or a girl? Did it die as a baby or a little infant or grow up to be an adult? If the baby she loved and nourished at her breast died, what effect might that have had on the person she has become? No one playing Lady Macbeth could avoid thinking of this and not letting it in some way shape their feelings about a woman who urges her husband to commit murder. What depth of emotion might there be behind that line?

In *Much Ado About Nothing* we learn from the text that Beatrice and Benedick have for a long time conducted a 'merry war' with each other, and there are several hints about what lay behind it. These hints need to be carefully analysed in the rehearsal room. Was an expression of love rejected or misunderstood? These are two intelligent and proud individuals who tell the world they loathe each other but must already be in love. It's vital to create their backstory.

In *Twelfth Night*, when Sir Toby boasts to Sir Andrew that Maria 'adores' him, the weak and gullible Andrew says, 'I was adored once too.' Toby ignores this simple but heartbreaking statement. Who adored him? How long ago? Most importantly, why did they adore him? In the same play we will never know the circumstances in which Olivia and Fabian fell out over a bear-baiting, but the actors playing them have to know, because that will inform the way they speak to each other in the final scene. These touches of backstory can be seen as the delicate colouring of a great artist adding depth and interest to his narrative, but for actor and director they can also illuminate the way to interpret a character, or trigger an idea that can be developed in rehearsal and deepen a performance.

- Does the death of her baby make Lady Macbeth more callous about life?

- Did Benedick and Beatrice come close to having an affair?

- Is there more to Sir Andrew than Sir Toby understands?

- Was Olivia disgusted by Fabian's enjoyment of bear-baiting?

There is, of course, a line to be drawn. An actor's job is not to write imaginary biographies of imaginary people, it is to be a presence on stage that an audience want to spend time with. Too much immersion in background might lead to an alienating self-absorption that detracts from being completely in the moment; and 'being in the moment' should be the constant state of performance. This vital balance between knowing all about your character and being your character lies at the heart of the director/actor relationship. Acting is a blend of subjectivity and objectivity. The subjective part is immersion in the needs, motives and desires of your character; the objective part is playing your role, your part in the story, understanding the function of your character within the bigger picture of the whole play.

One of the principal jobs for a director is to be always seeing the events on stage from the audience's point of view – an audience that hasn't spent several weeks preparing to be there. So the director needs to help the actor extract from their identification with their character only that which is useful in communicating with the audience.

But this is not an absolute. It may well be that even something that can't be understood helps a performance anchor itself in reality. I once worked with an actor playing Emilia in *Othello* who had convinced herself that Emilia and Othello really had had a sexual relationship, as Iago casually hints in an early soliloquy. That this was caused by Iago's jealous nature, which Emilia herself speaks of, and that it made no sense of the plot, was neither here nor there – it helped her. Watching the performance it was hard for me to decide whether her decision added an enigmatic and interesting depth to some moments or whether it was simply confusing.

Acting is a mysterious process, and sometimes the intimate decisions that actors make about backstory, although unobservable, help them access parts of their psyche that generate depth and fascination.

Subtext

How can rehearsals help an actor ingrain the idea of being in the moment in performance? How do you prepare for spontaneity? That seems paradoxical. This is where the concept of subtext comes in, and it's an idea that can lead to passionate debate. Most people understand subtext to mean thoughts that lie beneath the text but are not expressed directly by the words – words that, if interpreted in a particular way, convey the true intentions and real meaning of the speaker. For instance a character might say in response to information, or the expression of a point of view about someone or something, 'I really can't believe that,' but at the same time imply, by a subtle inflection, the precise opposite; to say, in effect, that they can believe it only too easily. We call this irony (or sarcasm)! But this way of speaking is related to a very modern frame of mind and a way of expressing ourselves that didn't really exist in early modern writing, or indeed thinking. In Shakespeare's plays, characters tend to use language to say exactly what they mean with as much detail and precision as their command of words allows. Irony is seldom present, nor is concealment. There is usually no 'subtext' in the modern sense. When Iago deludes Othello about the relationship of Cassio and Desdemona, he is lying, as he told us he will do. That's not subtext; that's pure deceit, which he has already given us the key to. The same applies to Richard of Gloucester, and to Sir Toby's dealings with Sir Andrew.

This is one of the reasons Shakespeare's text can often seem dauntingly dense. It is crammed with meaning, often nuanced and qualified at length, and strongly imbued with rhetoric and imagery. This elaboration, as opposed to distillation, of language was one of the principal subjects taught in the grammar schools of the day. It had a profound influence on the literary and dramatic art of the late Renaissance. There was simply no space for subtext except in very particular circumstances.

Elaboration was the pursuit of clarity, of argument, of persuasion, of thinking out loud.

A kind of subtext is, however, present in situations involving disguise. A good example of this is in *Twelfth Night* where Viola, a naturally honest person but disguised as a boy and consequently deceiving everyone she meets, is forced by her situation to give roundabout and evasive answers to direct and simple questions. There is a powerful narrative reason for her being unable to say exactly what she thinks, because she is trapped in maintaining the illusion of maleness. The comedy comes from her efforts to stay as close to the truth of her own feelings as possible while maintaining her disguise. Pretending to be someone else, or pretending to believe something you don't believe, as with Viola and Iago, is the only type of subtext in any of the plays.

It may seem odd trying to define something while claiming it doesn't exist, but the absence of subtext is one of the keys to getting under the skin of the text. When an actor tries to supply a subtext to Shakespeare's lines, as opposed to letting the words speak for themselves as thought in action, then a deadening layer of psychological fog will clog the airwaves between their mouths and the listeners' brains. The art of rhetoric, a word we regard with suspicion as implying shallowness and pomposity, was central to Shakespeare's education and to his thinking and development. Rhetoric (the formal, elaborate and pictorial use of words) was essentially the art of persuasion, of getting your point of view across. Better than seeing it as poetic for its own sake is to see it as a method of getting your own way, either practically or emotionally.

In rehearsal the question should be: 'What is the character's argument here?' It's extraordinary how much time the people of Shakespeare's world spend arguing with each other, or with themselves. As an actor, you should always ask 'What is my argument?', not 'What is my emotional state?'; 'What am I thinking?', not 'What am I feeling?' Clarity of argument makes the emotion happen to you and makes the audience empathise. It connects them to their own experience and helps them identify with you rather than being showered in generalised angst. The words themselves *are* the emotion.

Cutting

Ben Jonson records actors who had worked with Shakespeare telling him one of the things they most admired about their house dramatist was that they always received their new scripts without a 'blot' in the lines. This didn't mean he had neat handwriting and that there were no messy blobs of ink, but that the manuscripts were free from any crossings-out, rewritings crammed between the lines, or alterations in the margins. In other words, the lines flowed from him without need of correction; that what they read was his first thought, not the second or third attempt. Jonson's slightly caustic comment on this was: 'Would he had blotted a thousand.' He went on to make clear that, despite being a great admirer of the man he seems to have considered a close friend, in his opinion Shakespeare wrote too much. Jonson implied Shakespeare could have said what he wanted in fewer words; that his imagination was astonishingly fecund but his discipline in controlling it was weak. Anyone who knows Ben Jonson's own lengthy and verbose work could be forgiven for thinking this was a major case of the pot calling the kettle black. Perhaps that's a little unfair, but try reading *Catiline*!

In the opening speech of *Romeo and Juliet*, spoken by the Chorus, the mention of 'the two hours' traffic of our stage' implies that either the actors must have spoken incredibly fast, or that they regularly cut the texts for performance, the full text being retained only in the printed versions. The editors of the First Folio, published seven years after Shakespeare's death, make the claim that only there can be read the complete and definitive record of the plays as their author intended them. It's also clear that the scripts evolved in performance. Shakespeare was an actor, and it is vanishingly unlikely that he didn't let his fellow actors have their say. It's fascinating to compare in the rehearsal room the different versions of *Hamlet* and *King Lear*, for instance; how adjustments both small and large indicate debate and experimentation during the rehearsal process. Are the mechanicals preparing their performance in *A Midsummer Night's Dream* a gentle satire on the discussions that took place in Shakespeare's rehearsals? And in our own rehearsals, how do we identify what to cut and what to change in the text?

It's no good denying that some of Shakespeare can be obscure, so the first thing to do is identify the nature of the obscurity. Can the meaning be made clear by its context within the whole sentence? Does the situation at that moment in the story provide clarity? Can physical action of any kind help the sense? Has every possible way of saying the line – involving phrasing, inflection, and attitude – been fully explored? All this assumes prior agreement about the actual meaning of the word, phrase or sentence under question; the debate concerns the communicating of that to an audience. In both the director's preparation before rehearsal and in the rehearsal room itself the analysis of meaning must be word by word, phrase by phrase, and sentence by sentence, constantly asking the question: 'Are we certain the audience will understand?' But the answer to this question, and the question about what it means in the first place, is inevitably subjective: there is no absolute right or wrong any more than there is about the right way to say it. Honesty is the most important element because it is so easy in the excited atmosphere of the rehearsal room to persuade yourself that you can make an audience understand something, something that will actually always remain incomprehensible whatever you do, however you say it. You have to remember that the audience haven't been in the room with you; they haven't heard your discussions or been part of your experiments. Actors and director might have spent hours talking about the meaning of a line, but the audience are hearing it for the first time. Performance is an encounter between those who have prepared for the occasion and those who haven't. If in doubt – CUT.

So far, so straightforward; but if, after removing obscurity, the play (or scene, or speech) still feels too long, cutting becomes harder. You may have become attached to sections of the text that provide emotional and narrative continuity, form bridges between different moods, or that you love simply for what they are, their own beauty, their own drama. Sometimes you just have to accept that asking an audience to spend too long in your company, however brilliant and necessary you may feel every moment to be, may be counterproductive. You may have to lose something you cherish, but the audience won't feel that loss the way you do. For better or worse, they don't know what they're missing.

I once prepared a text for *Hamlet* that left out every reference to the war between Denmark and Norway and consequently removed the character of Fortinbras as well.

That's a big chunk of *Hamlet*.

The production was still three hours long.

Blocking

I'm not sure where the term 'blocking' to describe the organisation of stage movement comes from. Perhaps from a time when there was such a thing as weekly rep. Repertory theatres throughout the country knew that the size of their audience was limited. They knew that to maximise that audience it was necessary to put on a new show about once a week. This meant that the turnover had to involve playing at night while rehearsing the next show during the day, usually with the same group of actors. This rhythm would apply whether the play was a Noël Coward or *King Lear*. There was little time, so deep discussion about character motivation and complex meanings was limited. Often a director's primary function amounted to little more than telling the actors where and when to move and which entrances and exits to use: blocking out the physical action of the performance like a traffic policeman. Not knocking over the furniture was a higher imperative than debating why Lear is so emotionally illiterate. Still, it's worth remembering that Shakespeare's company may often have been putting on several plays a week. In the days of British provincial weekly rep an actor asking their director about motivation might receive the reply, 'Just do it!' I've often thought it revealing that the Nike advertising team who came up with that as a slogan clearly thought it a bracing and inspiring injunction, unaware of what a deadly phrase it can be on the rehearsal-room floor. I was assistant once to an old-school rep director on a production of *Henry IV*. It was a deeply conventional production in Elizabethan dress, and at the technical rehearsal he was busily moving a group of small-part actors around the stage for Prince Hal's coronation scene just before the famous rejection of Falstaff, when one had the temerity to ask: 'How did I get here?'

'You took a fucking taxi!' came the reply.

These days the amount of rehearsal time you have varies greatly, but less than three weeks is unusual – it can be much more – and the movement of actors around the performance space is as fundamental a part of rehearsing as the text. Obviously, different kinds of stage require different approaches: a proscenium arch asks different questions from a theatre-in-the-round. I think directing for an end-on proscenium stage is the hardest. Any actor will tell you the best place to be is near the front and in the centre. There they are most present for the majority of the audience; there they can best command the space of the whole room. So the character with the most to say and whose role is most important to the scene should stay there while the others approach and withdraw in turn. Right? Clearly not. The result would be static, predictable, unreal and utterly dull. You don't need two years on a drama school course for directors for this to become apparent. Ten minutes would do. But it requires a surprising amount of ingenuity to create a constant flow of alternatives. Theatre-in-the-round is in some ways much easier because, as there will always be some of the actors with their backs to the audience, constant movement is essential. At any one moment there are as many different stage pictures as there are watchers, so even random, unplanned movement is better than none. Other types of stage space have their own special challenges, but whatever the geometry between actor and audience, you are contriving a manipulation of movement that seems both natural and interesting, bringing clarity and focus to each evolving moment of the story.

Imagine an empty space. If an audience are looking, it's probably a stage. Put a chair in it, or two chairs, or twenty chairs, and the space changes its nature. The range of possibilities for movement in that space changes according to the number of chairs. Imagine you add walls, doors, or just gaps in the walls. Then if you carry on adding objects – tables, bookshelves, sofas, windows, rugs, a telephone, a cocktail cabinet – you have a naturalistic interior that's at the other end of the spectrum from the empty space. Many scenes in Shakespeare can be performed either in an empty space or a room filled with furniture, but each will dictate the nature of the movement.

Take an example from *The Merchant of Venice*. Bassanio and Antonio are talking to Shylock about a loan. They could be on their feet in the open air, by a canal, in a square – no furniture in sight, not even a bench or bollard. They move around each other with nowhere to sit; that shared space dictates their body language, which needs to be as precise and meaningful as the inflections in their voices. Now imagine them in a room – let's say Shylock's office, with tables and chairs. The body language changes, conveying similar meanings in different ways. How do they sit down? Why do they sit or stand? How do their bodies behave in a private as opposed to a public space? There are now props through which they can send each other signals about their attitude and intentions. This stage room might be detailed or purely representational, depending on the design, but the furniture and the privacy create different impulses in the characters from when they were in an open and public space. Consider these images: feet on a desk, a knocked-over chair, a man spitting on a moneylender's account book as he makes his calculations with ink and pen. Furniture, and the idea of a private interior, provide a rich range of opportunities for physical behavioural choices related to the world we know. On the other hand, a space empty of such objects as chairs, desks and ink is more demanding for both directors and actors. It needs more imagination to motivate a move. However, it can also be liberating, because, although the vocabulary of movement is restricted, the actual flow of activity can be more beautiful and interesting when unshackled from the comforting but restraining presence of furniture. Some directors feel more confident with solid objects around the actors so that they can bang their fists on a desk or break a chair; in this way the objects can provide the subtext that modern actors crave but that is frustratingly absent from the text! But other directors like to embrace both the constraints and freedoms of emptiness. A lot of rehearsing is about finding out how physical activity enriches the text. It's also about locating the need to move, what makes an individual sit or stand at any particular moment. Movement for its own sake will be seen through, if only subconsciously, by an audience.

Of course, the limits of stage movement are pre-set by the design before rehearsals begin. I've done productions without a stick of furniture from beginning to end and also ones that have used quite a lot. There's no right or wrong – both have their pluses and minuses – but the choices the director and designer bring into the rehearsal room massively affect the impulses of the actors and the physical style of the production.

When you begin the 'blocking' is a big issue! Some directors start by sitting round a table reading and discussing the text for days or even weeks. Others get the actors on their feet from the word go, developing speech and movement simultaneously. There are even some directors who expect the cast to have learnt their lines before rehearsals begin.

My own belief is that you need to work on the text first and have a reasonably good understanding of it before you begin to move, because, vital though movement is, the words come first, especially with Shakespeare. Only once you have got into the meaning and flow of the thought through the language, and the inter-play of the characters' minds, will the blocking flow – naturally, meaningfully, easily.

Costume
(*Tights and Trousers*)

Robin Hood: Men in Tights is a zany comedy film by Mel Brooks, whose very title seems intended to get a laugh. Any male actor who has been made to wear tights in a Shakespeare production probably wouldn't find the thought funny. Why should that be? Male ballet dancers wear them with pride and grace and no one even smiles. But when was the last time you even saw an image of an actor playing Hamlet, or Orsino, or any male character in tights? Possibly in black-and-white photos from the 1950s but probably not on a stage. Yet in Elizabethan prints, paintings and engravings, tights are what most men are wearing, commonly referred to as stockings or 'hose' (from which we get the modern term 'hosiery'). Along with doublets (jackets) and breeches (sort of padded shorts reaching to just above or just below the knee), tights were one of the three most common items of male clothing. Buckled shoes, capes and many types of elaborate hat made up the full wardrobe. Elizabethan-style dress on stage these days usually transforms the slightly comic combination of short breeches and tights into leg-wear consisting of baggy three-quarter-length trousers that meet the tops of long boots leaving not even a glimpse of stocking. Of course, it's no surprise that for a male dancer the wearing of tights is a display of exuberant pride as they have far better legs, on the whole, than actors. In movies and on stage a version of male Elizabethan fashion that avoids tights can look ravishingly sexy and feel great to wear, but the question I've never been able to resolve is whether it changes the way you think.

Elizabethan-style clothes created for the actor (with the adjustments mentioned) are in tune with the text in a way that modern dress is not; but does it, can it, should it affect the actor's inner processes? I have never had the chance to sit down in a room and discuss this with a group of actors who have had experience of both. That's because such occasions never arise in professional theatre. The actors turn up on the first day of rehearsals and are told what they will be wearing: Elizabethan, Jacobean, Restoration, Victorian, Early Twentieth-Century, Mid-Twentieth-Century, Contemporary or Star Trek. Or any combination of the above – Martian/Victorian perhaps? From then on, the thinking they put into rehearsals has little to do with the clothes they will wear: it can only be about the human being inside those clothes. Sometimes an actor will request an item of clothing to practise with in rehearsals that more closely resembles the feel and weight of what they'll wear on stage to help with physically getting into the part, or they'll ask for a hat because their character has a particularly uneasy relationship with hats (like Osric); but aside from these practical aspects there is no way they can prepare for the full impact of wearing the clothes of another time and another place. That is why you will often hear an actor say that they never really felt at home in their character until they put the costume on. For an actor, wearing the clothes of today implies a radically different body language from the postures, gestures and ways of walking suggested by the clothes in sixteenth-century paintings and engravings. The holding of gloves, the flicking back of cloaks, the way of standing, turning and greeting all demand a different way of being in your own body – and this way can feel false and profoundly unnatural to the edge of awkwardness. But give a man a cool, beautifully cut, modern two-piece suit where the hand can slip casually into the trouser pocket to indicate relaxation or glide effortlessly to the inside jacket pocket to retrieve a cigarette case, then into the outer pocket to produce the lighter and… though come to think of it, I'm probably describing a production set in the 1930s and any stage business involving smoking is, I think, now illegal whatever the period. But I hope you get my point. We (men) simply can't imagine what it must have been like to go around wearing tights all day. The only men that do so apart from ballet dancers and cyclists are likely to be greeting customers on a Tudor-themed open day at a National Trust stately home.

When Shakespeare was writing, men's legs were clothed to emphasise their natural shape and be admired by women. It was utterly unthinkable that women should expose their legs in the same way, to the same end. Isn't that a strange thought? The good news is that this aspect of the language of clothing is as irretrievably lost to us as the distinction between 'thou' and 'you', and the banishing of stockings from the male stage wardrobe does no damage to the text, because there are so few references to them, with the notable exceptions of Malvolio's yellow stockings and of Sir Andrew's appraisal of his own stockinged leg: "Tis strong, and it does indifferent well in a flame-coloured stock.'

Once the director and designer have eliminated a literal, historically accurate imitation of Elizabethan clothing from the spectrum of choices around how to clothe the actors, and they've settled on a comfortable, adapted version as a possibility, the question 'period or modern?' still remains, and in a play like *Twelfth Night*, which has a text deeply embedded with multiple assumptions about class, marriage, social hierarchy and sexual morality, any director needs to make a very careful cost-benefit analysis before opting for modern dress. Tights may be out of the question, but trousers are not always the answer.

Design

It's the first day of rehearsals, and the red electrician's tape used by stage management to mark out the set has been stuck to the rehearsal-room floor. The tape may simply outline the dimensions of an open space – square, rectangle, circle etc. – into which actors and objects will come and go. Or it may be a more complex pattern on the floor with angled and dotted lines marking where doors and windows will be. Possibly the red tape will be overlaid with other colours – blue, yellow, orange – in different patterns, each one representing a different set for different parts of the play. The cast are gathered around a model of the set (or sets) while the director and designer explain their thinking, the reasons for the choices they have made, and how the scene changes (if there are to be any) will work.

The most obvious decision a director, with the collaboration of a designer, has to make when planning a production of Shakespeare is the visual world of the play – Roman, Elizabethan, Victorian, modern, a purely invented world, or whatever. When I say 'world', I'm not just talking about the set and costumes, but the entire world of class structure, religious belief, social etiquette, and attitudes to political justice and the law: in other words the total socio-historical context that informs the mindset of all the characters. Without question the best fit for the text of a Shakespeare play is the Elizabethan/Jacobean world in which all his plays were written – roughly between 1590 and 1610. But Shakespeare's plays looked at in these terms are all hybrids. To a large extent, the pasts in which he sets his stories are always overlaid with the shadow of his own time. And this liberates us to invent worlds of our own, since his worlds are themselves inventions. All his plays are really about his own time, although set in another era and usually another place. With the exception of the History plays none of them is set in London (Windsor was a long way from London then), the place in which he lived and worked. Perhaps this is what Ben Jonson meant when he made the famous observation that Shakespeare was 'not of an age, but for all time'. The play may be set in Ancient Rome, Renaissance Italy or medieval England, but the issues, ideas and emotions examined were those of the Elizabethans or, after 1603, the Jacobeans. We empathise because the way Shakespeare's world thought was the beginning of the way we think now, and his plays played a major part in cultivating it. That's why academics call the period 'early modern', as so much of the thinking anticipates our own time. But so much is different, too, that the created stage world is bound to be hybrid. The choices made by director, designer and actor invariably co-exist with choices made by the writer and simply add another stratum, another shadow. We are always in 'all time', never 'an age'. But here is the paradox: the play is *Hamlet*, the clothes the characters are wearing are completely modern, but the words they are speaking were written four hundred years ago. Hamlet speaks of bodkins and believes in life after death, but he's wearing T-shirt and jeans. If you, the director, are insisting every single word counts, as you should be, and the words the actors are saying are contradicted by the world you are wearing, isn't the dissonance unbearable? Well, strangely, no. It's a paradox.

Design can create a multitude of different worlds for Shakespeare, provided they are created with an integrity of purpose, a desire to express the play's meaning and essence, and not to show off the director or designer's brilliance.

Deciding on the visual world is harder for some of the plays than others, but whatever world you create in whatever period (or combination of periods), one very elementary decision is crucial. How much stuff – walls, doors, windows – do you put on stage? As I've said, this significantly affects the mood and movement of the production. On the one hand it's wonderful for the first line of a scene to be able to follow the last line of the previous scene in a heartbeat, rather than having to wait for a load of stuff to be shifted. On the other hand, scene changes can be spectacularly interesting – some directors enjoy them more than working on the text – and whereas a bare space may seem visually dull unless filled with human intensity, too much to look at can detract significantly from the text; depriving the audience of spectacle can be a good thing, focusing their attention on the pictorial quality in the language, helping them see with their ears. This is the injunction of the Chorus in the first speech of *Henry V*. Shakespeare paints landscapes with language; he builds sets for you with words.

In striving to find the right balance it's helpful to consider whether the play's action is intensive or extensive: does it stay mainly in one place, as in *Hamlet*, where we are seldom outside the walls of Elsinore, or does it move from heath to castle, from battlefield to the English court, as in *Macbeth*? From the point of view of design the most difficult for me are the ones that alternate between just two prime locations. For example, in *The Merchant of Venice* we have the constant shifting between Venice and Belmont, and in *Troilus and Cressida* we go back and forth between Troy and the Grecian camp outside its walls. Of the two basic types of design discussed so far – naturalistic sets with ingenious scene changes, or an empty but protean space that can change many times – neither can quite solve the problem for me. With the naturalistic style, a revolve might be the answer, but only on a large, well equipped, proscenium stage, because it needs a big budget and strong nerves, as machine-driven revolves can break down halfway between Belmont and Venice! The open space is probably the better option and allows you never to visit the same part of Venice or Troy twice, and always be in a different part of Belmont or visiting another Greek tent. I suppose you could achieve that with a revolve too, but you'd need a very quiet stage crew. And in fact this option (changing the part of the set that is invisible to the audience) is much used in well-resourced productions.

The ways of designing Shakespeare are infinite. I've not done a scientific study of this but I would guess the majority of productions over the last twenty or thirty years have been in some sort of modern dress. For a long time at the RSC, Victorian was a very popular choice but Regency less so. The 1920s always got a lot of outings, but I think my own *Merry Wives of Windsor* might have been the only production set in the 1950s. Actual Elizabethan was reasonably common but not as popular as Edwardian. Mixed period or purely invented worlds, such as Peter Brook's famous *Dream*, were always cropping up. In the last few years the post-apocalyptic look is a favourite for *Macbeth*, but I still think pure modern dress would come out on top.

That category you can divide into two: with and without mobile phones. I always opt for the latter. Mobile phones make me nervous – they can implicitly ruin the plots of most of Shakespeare's plays, written as they were in an age when the quickest way of communicating news was a man on a horse.

Character and Language

He can be exotically poetic or as clipped, dry and natural as if writing yesterday. Shakespeare's language has remarkable variety, not only in the movement between verse and prose but also in the use of rhyme, song, parody, the twists and turns of rhetorical tropes or spontaneous sonnets shared in the act of falling in love, and of course in the exquisite delineation of character. This last element is something he became better and better at throughout his writing life and today lies at the centre of the rehearsal process – the revelation of character through language.

In many ways his writing is as different from modern texts as Renaissance cosmology is from astronomy today. The characters don't use language in the same way we do. However, the spectrum of psychological types is strikingly familiar. That is why we love Shakespeare despite the alien nature of his language. The characters are expressed – and explained – through their individual use of words. Speech may be heightened but is always revelatory.

If an actor ever finds themselves thinking, *My character wouldn't say that*, then they are missing the point: their character *does* say that. They are in danger of insinuating what they want the character to be into what the character actually is. In a sense, there is no character in the abstract: only what they say. I was once working with an actor who was having problems with Hotspur's dying speech in *Henry IV, Part 1*. He felt that Hotspur, being a far greater warrior than Prince Hal, wouldn't have lost the fight, and would therefore not be about to become 'food for worms'. Although all acting is about seeing the world and everything in it from your character's point of view, he was failing to distinguish between his character and his role; between subjective and objective thinking. He had been possessed by Hotspur's spirit, but not his function. Hotspur dies because his death serves the narrative. However subjectively you feel, in the end the character is not 'yours', it is the story's, a spirit within a bigger picture, a soul within the verse. Shakespeare's most vital skill was to link complex human feelings with language operating on a higher level of expression, so that those feelings take on a vividness beyond the human brain's usual capacity to explain itself. An actor's role resides in their character's interaction with all the larger currents of life beyond their control, understanding or even contemplation.

It is part of rehearsal to talk about the way the verse and prose are structured, how their rhythms work, how the imagery is working within the flow of thought, and how freshness, clarity and being in the moment are compatible with going with that flow. Being real is being real *within this context*, and is never achieved by wallowing in subjectivity while breaking up the language into awkward chunks of inarticulacy that somehow sound modern.

In the verse sections the underlying iambic pentameter is the skeleton that shapes the passage of the thought through the words, and the words contain the character within themselves. There should be no imposition. It's never about what the actor can do to the verse, it's about what the verse can do to them.

There's a word I use when rehearsing Shakespeare: INCREDULITY. A lot of the time characters are using words that reflect their amazement at what the world is, at what the world does to them and others. Words are their only way of expressing this astonishment. The potency of this idea of incredulity in speaking Shakespeare is that it is a way of finding spontaneity and immediacy; a way of being in the moment. To ask an actor to simply be spontaneous is as unhelpful as asking them to be quicker or louder or more energetic. These things are too generalised to mean anything. But the quality of incredulity (whatever form it takes in a particular moment) is that it puts the actor in touch with how language (especially poetic language) new-mints itself into thought in the instant of speech. Language *becoming* thought seems a counter-intuitive idea; surely thought *precedes* language, and indeed is the basis of language? But it isn't helpful to see it that way when acting Shakespeare. With text this dense, this pictorial, this complex, the act of speaking has to be the act of thinking. The two things are virtually simultaneous, but the words are actually explaining to the speaker the reasons for their feelings of astonishment, their incredulity. This is the experience of seeing the world explained by the medium of language. As each word passes through their lips, the speaker is being transformed, and the world will never be quite the same again to them. Feelings are translated into thoughts through speech, then more feeling is generated by the arrival of the newly articulated thought.

So what is character? Where is it hiding? Sometimes you will hear an actor say that they can't 'find' their character, as if he or she had gone missing and is perhaps hiding somewhere in the rehearsal room waiting to be found, like an excited child in a game of hide-and-seek. Once found, the 'character' can then be examined and imitated. But models or avatars of 'characters' don't exist. All that exists is the actor, the text and the other actors. Character is a relative concept. In life we meet people in whose presence we feel good about ourselves, and others who make us feel bad, awkward, inadequate, stupid, ugly. People change each other constantly. Personality is just a series of interactions, always fluid, never solidifying into 'character', a word that derives from a Greek word meaning something engraved, stamped or moulded – an indelibly solid thing. In this respect acting Shakespeare is no different from acting any other dramatist or, for that matter, simply existing as a human being in real time and place. Sir Andrew, in *Twelfth Night*, was a different person to his mother than he is to Toby Belch. He was 'adored once too'.

Character and Narrative

There is another way of looking at character: not in relation to language but to narrative, to storytelling. Drama students are taught that narrative is character in action, that it's the things characters do and why they do them that make stories. This way of looking at acting as storytelling means that character is shaped by circumstances of birth and life experience, and that people acquire certain mental characteristics which lead them to behave in certain ways. So language turns into narrative because it is the way characters seek to discover the meaning of what made them, their backstory, and to reveal or conceal themselves to other people.

In *Twelfth Night* Sir Andrew wants Sir Toby to know that he was once adored, just as Toby says Maria adores him. It gives them something in common; they can compare experiences – after all, they are friends, aren't they? What would happen if, at that moment in the play, instead of ignoring this invitation to learn more, Toby were to say: *Tell me about it. Sit down. Let's talk about you for a moment, it's not all about me.* He doesn't because he's too selfish; he's only interested in having his own ego fed. But if he did, just for a moment, let kindness intrude on his plan to milk Andrew for every penny he can, then the story would develop in a different way. But most people are not like feathers in the wind of every passing moment. Personalities tend to be stuck in grooves, compelled by needs and desires. This is how character drives narrative. The art of rehearsal is to capture moments of potential change, when the direction of life hangs in the balance, when a character might behave or react in an unexpected way. For instance, after Andrew has said, 'I was adored once too,' Toby might pause for a second, look at the man he is conning and think: *Does he deserve this?* Curiosity and sympathy for another could visit the vain knight just long enough for his gull to sense an openness into which he could pour out his heart to his friend. He might begin to speak... but the moment passes, the hunger for money shifts the con artist back into his groove. So all we get is: 'Let's to bed, knight. Thou hadst need send for more money.'

In Shakespeare's four great tragedies the stories are propelled by the principal character being possessed by a side of themselves that over-whelms everything else about them. With Macbeth, his ambition, a smouldering ember, is blown into raging fire by his damaged wife. Othello's jealousy, which he never knew he had, is brought to the sur-face by an envious and lying 'friend'. Lear's pride becomes enraged by the innocent honesty of his youngest daughter. Hamlet's intellect makes him his own tormentor. We all have these characteristics latent within us – ambition, jealousy, pride, self-doubt – but narrative thrives on them becoming enlarged by encountering the crosswinds of other per-sonalities with different backstories and competing passions. Shakespeare took drama to another level by taking types from the medieval morality plays who actually went by names like Pride, Jeal-ousy and Ambition, and turning them into complex human beings almost like you and me.

Fathers and Daughters
(Birth and Class)

Shakespeare was fascinated by the relationships between fathers and their daughters; there are many of them and every one is different. There are Polonius and Ophelia, Lear and Cordelia (and of course Goneril and Regan). There are Capulet and Juliet, Egeus and Hermia, Baptista and his starkly contrasting pair, Bianca and Kate; Titus and Lavinia; Shylock and Jessica; and in the same play Portia and the unnamed father who controls her from beyond the grave. Then there's the solidly middle-class Mr Page, whose daughter Anne runs off with a penniless aristocrat; the furious Brabantio and his Desdemona; Cymbeline and Imogen; Pericles and Marina; Prospero and Miranda; and Leonato, father to the quiet, biddable, obedient and so nearly tragic Hero. How do directors and actors, especially when staging a production in modern dress, come to terms with the huge gulf in societal assumptions about father–daughter relations between Shakespeare's time and ours? The strong presumption in the stories that a father owned his daughter and therefore had the right to tell her who to marry, and the right to be outraged when she begged to differ, is an issue that needs to be fully explored in rehearsal, so that in performance there is no dissonance between the text and the visual and emotional world of the production. Alongside the patriarchal conditions, there are issues of class and birth: treated almost as a law of nature is the view that marriage between two people from different parts of society is not only undesirable and unhealthy but virtually sacrilegious. In *The Merchant of Venice* this is literally the case when Shylock discovers his daughter's flight with a Christian. The underlying belief in the social expectations of Elizabethans is perfectly expressed at the end of *Twelfth Night*. When the Countess Olivia discovers she's married the wrong person, Duke Orsino feels the need to immediately reassure her with the words, 'Be not amazed, right noble is his blood.'

The good news for modern audiences is that these things haven't gone away: fathers are still deeply sensitive about who their daughters marry, and can be jealously possessive and sometimes downright snobbish. Class is still a massive factor in our world, although money has become so important that wealth and birth exist in a blurred and hypocritical embrace; as indeed do love and money – Petruchio and Bassanio, in their respective pursuits of Kate and Portia, appear to barely know where one begins and the other ends. They are hardly men you would call kindred spirits, but they share a common goal: wealth through marriage.

And there is more good news: Shakespeare does not seem to be wholly in tune with the melody of his age. Juliet, holding out for love against patriarchal decree, is absolutely the hero of the story, while her father is muddled, prejudiced and ridiculous. Hermia's resistance in *A Midsummer Night's Dream* likewise has the author's sympathy. Ophelia and Cordelia are characters with whom we feel not just empathy but a sadness and anger at their treatment by fathers who fail to either understand or respect them. So the translational gulf between the world of the text and the world of our stage need not be seen as too great to bridge. There is enough in common to make sense of class, birth and fatherhood without either ignoring the issues and hoping the audience won't notice, or else leaving them discordant and unexplored while distracting the audience with irrelevant directorial inventiveness.

Jealousy

The subject of jealousy – sexual jealousy – is treated as comedy in *The Merry Wives of Windsor*, as tragedy in *Othello*, as a pastoral romance in *The Winter's Tale*, and as history in *Troilus and Cressida*. Four different-coloured lenses applied to one theme suggest, along with the hints in the Sonnets, that this was an emotion Shakespeare knew well. In the first three of these plays it is an unfounded jealousy created by paranoia in Ford and Leontes, and by the manipulations of a malicious 'friend' in Othello. Only in Troilus is the jealousy justified by the real rather than imagined infidelity of Cressida. Shakespeare's vast range of view, expressed through his incredible language, makes the characters possessed by the most agonising and twisted of emotions radically different from each other. As doubt about Desdemona begins to nest in Othello's brain, this noble and proud man explains himself through the imagery of a noble sport, falconry:

> If I do prove her haggard,
> Though that her jesses were my dear heart-strings,
> I'd whistle her off and let her down the wind
> To prey at fortune.

The image of an untamed (haggard) hunting bird being tied to his wrist by leather straps (jesses) shows that his jealousy already exists in embryo because what comes out at its first stirrings in his active rather than subconscious mind is possessiveness and ownership rather than doubt and self-questioning. This is a valuable insight for the actor. It suggests an old-fashioned and conservative relationship to marriage, and hence a vulnerability to any insinuations that come from a cynical but clever language-merchant like Iago.

Leontes doesn't have the excuse of being lied to by a trusted comrade at arms: his own imagination does all the work for him. While Othello lacks a suspicious nature and needs to be persuaded at length and in

detail that his wife in unfaithful, Leontes comes on stage with his jealousy firmly embedded by the evidence of his own eyes, their vision
horrifically distorted by his own insecure and volatile personality. This
is expressed in a very different language from Othello's. When urged by
his senior courtier that there is nothing to his fears, Leontes replies:

> Is whispering nothing?
> Is leaning cheek to cheek? Is meeting noses?
> Kissing with inside lip? Stopping the career
> Of laughter with a sigh? – A note infallible
> Of breaking honesty. Horsing foot on foot?
> Skulking in corners? Wishing clocks more swift?
> Hours, minutes? Noon, midnight? And all eyes
> Blind with the pin and web but theirs, theirs only,
> That would unseen be wicked? Is this nothing?
> Why then the world and all that's in't is nothing,
> The covering sky is nothing, Bohemia nothing,
> My wife is nothing, nor nothing have these nothings,
> If this be nothing.

This is not the innocent soldier who lives in the open air; this is the cor-
rupted thinking of a politician/monarch used to the devious ways of a
court, watching others from concealed places and always fearing the
worst, a mind warped by the constant expectation of duplicity in others.
His speech is rapid and percussive with an angry and frightened sarcasm, and, by the act of speaking aloud, convincing himself of the
interpretation of his wife's behaviour that has been brewing in his head.
The actor here can feel the sensation of jealousy in the choked rhythms
and the words chosen: 'skulking', 'horsing', 'covering' (a word still used
to describe animals copulating), and the word 'nothing' used eight
times in four and a half sentences, a common Elizabethan synonym for
female genitalia.

Troilus is not a middle-aged married man and a father, nor a cynical
and insecure politician/king. He is just an idealistic youth, out on the
battlefield every day fighting for his city and consumed with his first
experience of romantic love and sex. His jealousy is neither provoked
by the lies of malice, nor brought on by marital insecurity: it is caused
by directly witnessing the real thing. When he steals into the Grecian
camp at night and sees Cressida in the arms of Diomedes a mere
twenty-four hours after she has promised to love him 'till time is old
and hath forgot itself' and till 'waterdrops have worn the stones of Troy',
he discovers the language of loathing to try to make himself understand

the betrayal he has witnessed with this bewildering metamorphosis of
love into lust:

> Instance, O instance, strong as Pluto's gates,
> Cressid is mine, tied with the bonds of heaven;
> Instance, O instance, strong as heaven itself,
> The bonds of heaven are slipped, dissolved and loosed,
> And with another knot, five-finger-tied,
> The fractions of her faith, orts of her love,
> The fragments, scraps, the bits, and greasy relics
> Of her o'ereaten faith, are given to Diomed.

If the actor can see the imagery, the remnants, or 'orts', of a meal – the
leftovers of bones and skin and grease smeared on a plate – and feel
how that describes Cressida's movement from himself to another man
in such a short time, it will take them to the centre of Troilus, the disil-
lusioned romantic who heard this promise from the lips that now kiss
the enemy:

> If I be false, or swerve a hair from truth,
> When time is old and hath forgot itself,
> When waterdrops have worn the stones of Troy,
> And blind oblivion swallowed cities up,
> And mighty states characterless are grated
> To dusty nothing, yet let memory,
> From false to false, among false maids in love,
> Upbraid my falsehood! When they've said 'As false
> As air, as water, wind, or sandy earth,
> As fox to lamb, or wolf to heifer's calf,
> Pard to the hind, or stepdame to her son',
> Yea, let them say, to stick the heart of falsehood,
> 'As false as Cressid'.

The last four words had become a common phrase for duplicity, and
here we see Shakespeare imagining the very moment of the phrase's
invention.

Respectable, middle-class, middle-aged Mr Ford speaks in another
language. To discover the truth about his wife and Jack Falstaff, he visits
the latter at his lodgings in disguise. His worst fears are apparently con-
firmed:

> Who says this is improvident jealousy? My wife hath sent to
> him, the hour is fixed, the match is made: would any man
> have thought this? See the hell of having a false woman: my
> bed shall be abused, my coffers ransacked, my reputation

gnawn at; and I shall not only receive this villainous wrong, but stand under the adoption of abominable terms, and by him that does me this wrong... Fie, fie, fie! Cuckold, cuckold, cuckold!

The prose of the common man, Mr Ford, and the poetry of the proud general, Othello, facing the same human crisis – sexual jealousy – come from a different universe of language as an expression of character, and illustrate both Shakespeare's astonishing range and his ability to provide the actor with everything they need to know about the character they are playing.

Soliloquy

Petruchio's house and the soliloquy he delivers from it are the narrative centre of *The Taming of the Shrew* and the place and point at which the most contentious and difficult actions for directors and actors to handle take place. For a moment let's imagine a production without the Sly framing device. The house is a place of abuse posing as tenderness, where a young woman is forcibly changed by a young man from being herself to being what he wants her to be. The constant question at the heart of how to play the scenes is: does the end justify the means? Do things turn out for the best or not? A more sophisticated way of putting that question might be: is it possible that sometimes others know us better than we know ourselves? If the rehearsal-room answer to that is 'yes', and we want the ending of the play to be joyful, not bitter, then we have to work with the assumption that Petruchio is motivated by love, not pride. So what goes on in Petruchio's house can be construed as an act of love based on the twin actions of sleep deprivation and starvation! He keeps her awake by saying the bed's not good enough for her, and hungry by judging the food not well enough cooked. In addition he treats his servants abominably and refuses her new clothes by taking exception to the allegedly poor tailoring. The whole thing, whether an act of love or not, is a total act: there's nothing wrong with the dress, the hat, the food or the bed – it's all pretence. So what exactly is he up to? Fortunately he tells us.

Soliloquies are the secret weapon of Shakespearean psychology. The effect of a character breaking the fourth wall and speaking to us directly is odd, but nearly always powerful, provided the actor *does* speak to us and does not indulge in an interior monologue that happens to be audible, or address the empty air a couple of feet above our heads. In soliloquy the characters never lie to us as they sometimes do to fellow characters, so in this particular and bizarre situation we are taken into Petruchio's confidence and are treated to a full explanation of his methodology. Here's what he says:

Thus have I politicly begun my reign,
And 'tis my hope to end successfully.
My falcon now is sharp and passing empty,
And till she stoop she must not be full-gorged,
For then she never looks upon her lure.
Another way I have to man my haggard,
To make her come and know her keeper's call:
That is, to watch her, as we watch these kites
That bate, and beat, and will not be obedient.
She ate no meat today, nor none shall eat;
Last night she slept not, nor tonight she shall not.
As with the meat, some undeserved fault
I'll find about the making of the bed,
And here I'll fling the pillow, there the bolster,
This way the coverlet, another way the sheets.
Ay, and amid this hurly I intend
That all is done in reverend care of her;
And in conclusion she shall watch all night,
And if she chance to nod I'll rail and brawl
And with the clamour keep her still awake.
This is a way to kill a wife with kindness,
And thus I'll curb her mad and headstrong humour.
He that knows better how to tame a shrew,
Now let him speak; 'tis charity to show.

This speech really sums up the problem people have with *The Taming of the Shrew.*

All Shakespeare's soliloquies assume empathy, even complicity, with the audience. Richard III, Othello, Viola, and many others, all take us, uninvited, into their confidence to share their most secret and private thoughts because they believe that we are just like them. Sometimes this makes them shocking or uncomfortable, and, as here, makes us, perhaps, want to turn away and say, *No, I don't agree with you.* I often think that at the end of this speech it's as if the speaker can hear our unspoken disagreement, to which he replies: *Well, have you got a better idea?*

So the actor playing Petruchio should think of the whole speech as a challenge to the audience, a deliberate provocation. This is who he is and you don't have to like it. He suggests to us that this is the only way to save Kate from herself, to cure her 'madness', by treating her as a wild bird of prey that must be 'tamed' to obedience by her 'keeper'. If the actor can play clearly that he realises the audience won't like to hear this, that it is sexist, insulting, manipulative behaviour, and yet play on the power of the convention that we cannot reply, have no answer to the question he leaves us with, and will eventually have to come to terms with the fact that Kate is a happier person when we leave her than when we met her – if he can achieve all this, then a strange but dramatically effective interaction will have taken place between actor and audience.

The Merchant of Venice has only two soliloquies, neither of them typical. With a soliloquy we are the speaker's friend, or at least a sympathetic listener. We have a role beyond being an audience; like a therapist, we assume the role of one half of a talking cure in which there are no secrets withheld and in which total honesty is expected. When Shylock talks to us, it's in the form of an 'aside', the only form of soliloquy in which another character is present on stage. Shylock expects us to understand that it's the most natural thing in the world that he should hate Antonio. But when it's Launcelot Gobbo's turn to hold our attention with a soliloquy, reality is rearranged, and we become complicit in his plan to escape his servitude to the Jew. Perhaps even more difficult for us to accept is his assumption that we will find him funny. Gobbo is one of the parts written for Will Kemp, in 1597 still the leading comedian in the Lord Chamberlain's Men. His speech, as it's come down to us in print, may or may not be what came out of Kemp's mouth at any given performance of the play during Shakespeare's lifetime. We will never know, but we do know it was his style to be free with whatever was written down for him to speak.

What does Hamlet say on this topic?

> And let those that play your clowns speak no more than is
> set down for them. For there be them that will themselves
> laugh to set on some quantity of barren spectators to laugh
> too, though in the meantime some necessary question of the
> play be then to be considered. – That's villainous, and shows
> a most pitiful ambition in the fool that uses it.

That's written from the heart, I should think; Shakespeare's heart. He'd plainly had enough of the tradition where the Comedian stepped out of the fabric of the narrative to be themselves rather than a character. There's clearly no part in Hamlet for Kemp, who was anyway busy dancing to Norwich and busy being himself.

Quite how Kemp made Launcelot Gobbo's soliloquy funny is certainly not clear from the text. Maybe the strange rhythms and repetitions are the ghost of Kemp's improvisational style? Maybe he had a famous laugh with which he would punctuate the lines to set the 'barren spectators to laugh too'? If Shakespeare himself wrote this bit of text (the first speech of Act 2 Scene 2), the likelihood is that it got expanded by three or four times its length in performance, thereby disrupting the natural pace of the storytelling. Perhaps Kemp picked out individual members of the audience and entered into a scurrilous dialogue with them; maybe he got them up on stage; but the inclinations of a stand-up comic are impossible to square with the intentions of a realistic writer, one who is trying to hold a 'mirror up to nature'.

The rule that speaking a soliloquy is better if the actor directly addresses the audience with the intention of winning their empathy and understanding is tested by Lady Macbeth. Initially we hear her voice reading aloud the letter from her husband that describes his meeting with the witches. The first decision director and actor have to make is: is she reading it aloud to *us*? Reading letters aloud was a common stage convention, for obvious reasons, but as she is alone, she is already within the frame of soliloquy, and so it would make sense if she was reading it to us, because there is less dramatic engagement if we are simply overhearing her reading to herself. This is important because when the letter is finished, she speaks very specifically not to us but to her husband. She addresses him directly in her imagination. She is seeing his face, not ours. Yet is she saying exactly what she would say to him if he was there, or rehearsing a version of it to herself? If she has engaged us by reading to us from the moment she appears, then the act of speaking to him could well be through us, which carries with it the assumption that we know him as well as she does and are part of her preparation. So we become instantly complicit; we are instantly engaged as co-workers in the project of murder:

> Yet do I fear thy nature,
> It is too full o'th' milk of human kindness
> To catch the nearest way. Thou wouldst be great,
> Art not without ambition, but without
> The illness should attend it.

If the actor assumes that we, the audience, are her, then we see Macbeth entirely through her eyes, through her knowledge and estimation of him. This prepares us for the even greater shock of presumed intimacy that follows. A servant enters and tells her that her husband is about to arrive and that, astonishingly, the King himself will arrive shortly afterwards. When alone again, she directly addresses us with the lines:

> The raven himself is hoarse
> That croaks the fatal entrance of Duncan
> Under my battlements.

Then, once more her focus seems to shift, not to her invisible husband, but to the invisible supernatural elements that everyone believed in, the spirits of evil, ever present, always available if approached with energy and commitment:

> Come you spirits
> That tend on mortal thoughts, unsex me here,
> And fill me from the crown to the toe, top-full
> Of direst cruelty.

Should the actor speak to the empty air above the audience's heads, or to the space around her on the stage? She could, if we take 'mortal thoughts' simply as murderous ones. But we are a theatre audience and have the almost supernatural privilege of being able to hear the thoughts of a mortal through the magic of soliloquy. *We* are the spirits, *we* are the entities that have to help her:

> Make thick my blood,
> Stop up th'access and passage to remorse.

Without our will, our desire, she won't be able to perform the act. We have to want it as much as she does or it won't happen. If we are made to understand that we are an essential part of the alchemy, then theatre and life become one and the same thing.

Shakespeare certainly read Montaigne – as I've been meaning to for the last thirty years. All academics agree that he had a lot of influence on Shakespeare's thinking. A little bit of Montaigne that has always struck me as important when exploring the texts is this piece of dialogue between the philosopher and a writer on the art of writing:

MONTAIGNE. To examine the movement of the mind, the poet should penetrate and take over the senses of other men.
WRITER. Are actors merely the ciphers of the story?
MONTAIGNE. The inspiration that stirs you as a poet towards anger, grief, fury and beyond yourself, should, through you, strike and enter into the actor and so to the audience.

The actor is the interpreter of character, but also the conduit through which emotions, harvested from life and shaped in language, flow. Character, and its contradictions, are the key to the relationship between poetry and drama, expressed nowhere better than in Macbeth's soliloquies as he approaches the act of murder. Here is part of the first:

> Besides, this Duncan
> Hath borne his faculties so meek, hath been

So clear in his great office, that his virtues
Will plead like angels, trumpet-tongued, against
The deep damnation of his taking off;
And pity, like a naked new-born babe,
Striding the blast, or heaven's cherubin, horsed
Upon the sightless couriers of the air,
Shall blow the horrid deed in every eye,
That tears shall drown the wind.

When discussing this play's backstories in rehearsal, it is nearly always concluded by cast and director that the Macbeths must have discussed murdering Duncan before the action begins. This seems to be implicit in so much of the dialogue that Macbeth and his wife have when they meet on stage, and why things move so quickly once they are back together after the battle. What has changed is that now, for the first time, they have the perfect opportunity, one that might not come again for a long time; hence their urgency and energy, and for Macbeth the consideration of consequences, and the anticipation of the agony of remorse. Once again, when he soliloquises, we are assumed by him to be in his mind, to share the thoughts not only that he is having now, but ones he has had before. The action is being shaped as he speaks; every moment is a potential turning point as he tries to persuade *us* it is not a good idea to murder this good man. He is making an argument with us against the action that he and his wife have already planned: the imagery is intensely powerful, but the more you read it, the more you see how confused it is; how his emotion is overcoming his reason, as if *we* are propelling him out of control. Pity in the form of a naked baby; angels riding on the wind; that same wind making the eyes of the world smart and weep to the point where the water drowns the wind. These are images of chaos where logic breaks down into pure abstract poetry. And the drama is that the audience and the character are taken to the edge of a cosmic precipice through the actor channelling the words of the writer. Ironically it illustrates what I've said earlier about the argument of the character being more important than the demonstration of feelings: it proves you can argue with your emotions just as much as your reason; through poetic imagery rather than logic.

So all characters who have soliloquies identify with the audience and expect the audience to identify with them. This is very well illustrated in *Othello*, where two men dominated by the disease of jealousy are nevertheless as different as two men can be: Iago, small-minded, bitter, selfish, cruel and cowardly; Othello, open-hearted, at ease with himself,

generous, kind and brave. Yet both succumb to the monster with the
green eyes. This is Iago speaking to us early in the play:

> Thus do I ever make my fool my purse:
> For I mine own gained knowledge should profane
> If I would time expend with such a snipe
> But for my sport and profit. I hate the Moor
> And it is thought abroad that 'twixt my sheets
> He's done my office. I know not if 't be true,
> But I for mere suspicion in that kind
> Will do as if for surety. He holds me well,
> The better shall my purpose work on him.
> Cassio's a proper man: let me see now,
> To get his place, and to plume up my will
> In double knavery. How? How? let's see:
> After some time to abuse Othello's ear
> That he is too familiar with his wife.
> He hath a person and a smooth dispose
> To be suspected, framed to make women false.
> The Moor is of a free and open nature
> That thinks men honest that but seem to be so,
> And will as tenderly be led by th' nose
> As asses are.
> I have it, it is engendered! Hell and night
> Must bring this monstrous birth to the world's light.

Once again, we start with the character's assumption of complicity.
Later in the play, his wife Emilia says he has a jealous nature. That is in
evidence right away, but there's also deep cynicism in the way he talks
about exploiting the 'fool' and 'snipe' with whom he's pretending to be
best friends. But here's the rub: Iago doesn't think there is anything
wrong with jealousy, cynicism and exploitation of the gullible. That's
the way we all are; at least, that's the way the intelligent ones like him
and us – his mates and clones – are, because we understand the reality
of the world: you are stupid if you don't lie, cheat and suspect everyone
and everything. So, given that we know him, it follows that there is
nothing unpleasant about the way he comes across, his casual familiar-
ity with us, his pals in the pub, his straightforwardness. No wonder
Othello calls him 'honest, honest Iago'.

The second time I directed *Othello* was in a tiny theatre in Portland,
Oregon, called The Shoebox. It was really just a small room with a
single row of seats around its four walls, surrounding the actors, close
enough to touch. There was one seat in the centre of one of the rows

that was kept free for Iago to sit on and deliver his soliloquies. He literally became part of the audience, sometimes even speaking directly and confidentially to the two people on either side of him. Of course, the man he torments and drives nearly mad with jealousy is also our friend. I've quoted in the previous chapter what Othello says to us after the seeds of doubt about Desdemona's fidelity have been sown ('If I do prove her haggard...'). We have been befriended by both the villain and the hero, but our role of spectator binds us to the convention of silence. This is how Shakespeare catches us in a web of involvement, and we cannot take sides because we're both villain and hero ourselves.

Anyway, our friend Iago has told us Othello may have slept with his wife and that he's going to lie about Cassio and Desdemona to get even. If the actor playing Iago can make us remember why he's doing what he's doing, then as we watch Othello's suffering, as we see him imagining his wife in bed with another man, we are also seeing what Iago may have felt, may still be feeling. Iago and Othello share their thoughts with us through the dramatic privilege of soliloquy in their own language. But language has no moral value: only we have the dramatic privilege of narrative, of seeing the whole picture that they cannot access, and that allows us a moral perspective on right and wrong, because only we the audience see the full range and consequence of the actions that speak louder than words.

Why does Shakespeare give the gift of soliloquy to some characters and not others? In the four great tragedies Hamlet, Macbeth and Othello all talk to the audience, but Lear doesn't. In *The Merchant of Venice*, there is one aside (Shylock) and one stand-up comedy routine (Launcelot Gobbo), but neither Antonio, Bassanio nor Portia addresses us directly, so this particular love triangle is seen through a slight mist that, to a degree, distances us from the characters' deepest feelings. Maybe Shakespeare wants us to experience levels of uncertainty about all those relationships – to keep them enigmatic and open to interpretation. This is in vivid contrast to one of the love triangles in *Twelfth Night* where Malvolio, Olivia and Viola all look us straight in the face and tell us what they want. What's certain is that in performance this contrast between knowing what a person thinks and guessing what they think, is a big part of what makes the plays seem so real and lifelike.

We always want to know what someone's thinking, don't we?

Performance

Everything that happens in a rehearsal room is focused on what the performance is going to look like, sound like, and feel like to the audience. Performance is the ghost in the room. It is the presence that makes sense of everything we do. Whatever the rehearsal process consists of, performance is the only thing that gives it any meaning. By the time it comes to performance, the cast should be at the point where what happens on stage will explain the play to the audience – engaging them with the play's purpose. It may be a particular group's interpretation of the play, but it has to be an honestly held interpretation of what you have decided was in Shakespeare's mind at the time he wrote it. Whatever the design, whatever shape or size the performance space, on stage the actor has to be the conduit through which Shakespeare's intention flows towards the audience. If it helps to set *The Merchant of Venice* in contemporary Las Vegas rather than Renaissance Venice, that's fine so long as the writer's thoughts about love, money, class and race are made clearer as a result. In that play, where the characters are all a bizarre mixture of good and bad impulses – a play which holds up a mirror and invites us to examine ourselves and understand the reflection better – nothing should intrude between the watcher and the reflection. The danger is that the more gaudy the carapace of the production, the greater the chance of muzzling the meaning of the play. The heart of performance is the revelation of meaning, and that's why theatre is the greatest of collaborative art forms, and Shakespeare its greatest exponent: he used the form better than anyone else ever has to speak truth about the world.

Performing Shakespeare, on whatever kind of stage, an actor has two basic ways of communicating with their audience: soliloquy or dialogue. With soliloquy, the communication is absolutely direct, like an arrow from speaker to listener – provided the actor is not just looking at the audience while actually talking to themselves. But a soliloquy is, in effect, an internal self-enquiry, isn't it? Hamlet is talking to himself, surely? Well, no. Talking to yourself is a sign of madness, and Hamlet is only pretending to be mad! It's a stylistic acting choice. Performing soliloquy as an interior event in which a character is *overheard* talking to themselves is not only self-indulgent but constructs an unnecessary barrier between the speaker and the audience. However, to see the speaker as an orator proclaiming truths about themselves to a roomful of strangers is equally distancing – if easier to hear! To get around this paradox, I ask actors to think of the audience as a conference of 'clones' of the speaker, there to listen to the very latest instant of that person being themselves: as physically separate entities, but all virtually identical to their original – the speaker. If you are Hamlet, Richard III or Othello, everyone in front of you, or around you, *is* essentially *you*. They are outside of you (hence the need for speech), but simultaneously completely of your mind – thinking like you, feeling like you, desiring the same things, sharing your fears, hopes and, crucially, your range of choices. In this way the action of talking to yourself is amplified into a conference, almost a debate, and becomes an arrow of direct engagement one to one.

In dialogue, on the other hand, the danger is abandoning the audience by losing yourself in the other actor (or actors) and failing to find the balance between subjectivity and objectivity that is fundamental to all acting. Here, the image I use in rehearsals is not the arrow, but the boomerang, and basic staging technique is an essential component to make it work. A lot of rehearsal is centred on finding ways to bend the thoughts through interaction with other characters and send them into the auditorium. It is connected to why, in performance, the *argument* is always more important than emotional display. The audience need to feel they are being talked to, constantly being asked by the characters, *Do you know what I mean? Do you know who I am?* Then they will feel the emotion as well, by comparing the arguments of the characters with their own life experiences. That's how you engage an audience – how you make them care.

You may by now be wondering where simple entertainment is in all this? But that's like asking, *What is happiness?* We find peace in absorption, and theatre should have that effect. Successful Shakespeare performances are not about distraction, taking your mind off the fact you're listening to a four-hundred-year-old text by giving you other things to think about: *Don't worry about all these old words – just look at the genius of director and designer and... enjoy!* The production should never be more important than the play; it should never stand between performer and listener.

Rehearsals should have structured the actor within a tight, meaningful framework that, ironically, also gives them the freedom to express themselves in performance. This self-expression derives from being a storyteller who is simultaneously the vehicle for a character. The director should have helped liberate the part of the actor's self that is useful to the story, not trapped them within the suffocating confines of a 'concept', along with a barrage of physically distracting visual 'ideas'. But neither should the director have allowed the actor to see the stage as a shop window for their own magnificence.

A theatre performance is one of the best examples of co-operative enterprise. Theatre is the least individualistic activity imaginable: it is the essence of the art of working together for a common purpose. The mental setting of every actor should be focused on bringing the best out of their colleagues, on how to make each other better. Any hint of *Look at me!* is deadly to live theatre. If, in performance, competition for attention ever manifests itself, the entire point of drama as a collaborative art form is destroyed. After a full and satisfactory rehearsal period, playing together for an audience can be an experience of pure joy, and the very best theatre is usually made by ensembles of equal actors who stay together over an extended period, learning as they go. But... we don't live in a co-operative culture, we live in a competitive one. Or at least one that celebrates competition as an inherent good, where being better than others is seen as an admirable aim. An ambition to be a good actor, along with the desire to understand fully what that means, is vital, but a desire to be a famous one is not. I know that many 'stars' are brilliant actors, hugely exciting to watch live on stage, and I'm not suggesting directors and actors should live like monks and nuns, working only in ensemble companies for minimal pay, but I do remember a time when it was considered uncool to seek fame. When acting becomes entwined with celebrity, it is in danger of losing its soul.

Part Two

EIGHT PLAYS

The chapters in this section are arranged roughly in the same order that Shakespeare wrote the plays discussed. *Titus Andronicus*, dating from the early 1590s, was certainly one of his first – perhaps the very first – and *The Tempest* (1611) is usually accepted as his last, or at least the last one he wrote entirely on his own. There is also good evidence that *Hamlet* and *Twelfth Night* date from 1600–1601, the exact mid-point of his creative life. Of the several imaginative 'arcs' that can be imposed on Shakespeare's total body of work, one of the most noticeable is the movement from the theme of Revenge to the theme of Forgiveness.

The issue of whether or not actors can play 'themes' is discussed below, but directors can certainly be aware of these ideas when working on any of these four plays. Do you want to encourage or discourage an audience from celebrating Titus's revenge on his daughter's abusers? How might you maximise Prospero's struggle to move from a planned revenge on his enemies to his final state of forgiveness? The journey from Hamlet's intense desire to avenge his father's murder to a complex acceptance of his fate is almost the beating heart of the play, while allowing an audience to experience pity for Malvolio, instead of mere contempt, makes the Illyrian 'comedy' a much deeper one. When he breathes out his exit line, 'I'll be revenged on the whole pack of you!', we really should be curious as to how he might go about it.

So in following a chronological order of composition, I'm hoping the reader can follow, if only implicitly, a sense of Shakespeare's moral evolution and his search for meaning.

Titus Andronicus

A HYBRID WORLD

From the moment you, as a director, know for certain the date you are going into rehearsals for a particular play, to open on a particular stage on a particular date, several things start happening in your mind at the same time. It must be researched, cast and designed. Your relationship to it has to become clear to you – you have to know absolutely why you want to do it, and how you want to do it, before you can make anyone else want to do it with you! When you look at the multitudinous ways of conceiving and designing a Shakespeare play, any factor that you can latch on to with conviction and can lead you to a narrowing of focus and a cogent specificity is profoundly welcome. The very act of beginning to imagine a world is so open-ended that it's inevitably insecure as well, so some element of certainty in order to even get to a starting point is vital. For me, confronting *Titus Andronicus*, a notoriously difficult play, the primary conviction was that it was a true hybrid: as much Elizabethan as Roman; as much a pure product of Shakespeare's imagination as a piece of history from the Classical world – and the design had to reflect that. But the inspiration for the look of a production always comes in two stages: first, the broad idea (you can call it a 'concept' if you want), then the detail.

The *Titus* I did was for the old main stage at the RSC in Stratford, a huge proscenium-arch space. Approaching any play on that kind of stage, the first questions to ask yourself (as I have said earlier) tend to be about how much stuff you want to fill the space with, and the basic geometry: the shape of the floor, its depth and width; closely followed by the question of questions: should there be walls? It sounds trivial but it's actually an enormous decision. If there are walls, should they be there all the time or not, and should they have doors in them? How much 'flying' them in and out should there be? How much moving set?

How simple? How elaborate? These choices can begin to be resolved partly by thinking through the narrative of the play, but also by trying to anticipate its atmosphere and aesthetic. What would an invented world that brought together, in harmony, the Classical Roman world of the story with the late Renaissance world of the author look like?

The plot of *Titus Andronicus* is largely invented by Shakespeare. It isn't authentic Roman history and appears to be set sometime around 400 AD, when the outer boundaries of the empire were stretched to breaking point, constantly under attack from northern barbarian Germanic and Gothic tribes. It also seems to be located in a time just after the establishment of Christianity as the state religion, while paganism, in many forms, was still a powerful emotional and theological force. As I began to get to know the play, it was very striking to realise that it had no interest in exploring this conflict of moral perspectives at all. In fact the Christian world is only referenced in one tiny moment, dropped like a tear in a bath of acid, when a character is found hiding with a baby in a ruined monastery. This sliver of anachronism made sense of the Classical/Renaissance palimpsest that underpinned the production's style. The world Shakespeare paints is ruthlessly pagan, just like in *King Lear*. In researching, I read an explanation for this: he simply could not show the horrors these two plays contain as taking place in a Christian world without risking being accused of atheism, or at least of criticism of the Elizabethan state.

Visually, it's a hard act to pull off on stage. An ancient, amoral and bloody warrior world is always in danger of appearing ridiculous. Somehow what the screen can do (in fact these days revels in), the live stage struggles with. Suspension of disbelief is much harder when you can touch an actor's boots than when you are embedded in a cinema's armchair watching panoramas of real landscapes and real horses, or indeed, computer-generated ones. What is even harder is getting inside the heads of characters with radically different belief systems, traditions and values. But then getting into the mind of Shakespeare's age is not easy; it's one of the most difficult aspects of the work between director and actor. A solution is often sought not in the past but in the future. To give contemporary relevance to a play like *Titus Andronicus* a director may go for a post-apocalyptic, dystopian vision, a *Mad Max* brutalism that satisfies the ecological and post-industrial nightmares of modern minds. I've done a *Macbeth* like that. But the irritating thing about art is how quickly fashion lapses into cliché.

Despite being hybrid, imaginary history, *Titus Andronicus* was actually very radical in putting an ancient world onto the stage. Shakespeare's re-imagining of pagan antiquity is extremely convincing, especially when compared to the efforts of other writers of the time. The Elizabethans' grasp of the archaeology of the Classical world was largely inferior to ours, but their understanding of its thinking, its people and its spirit was vastly superior, and, of course, it was one of the bedrocks of their own contemporary culture. A production of any of Shakespeare's Roman plays that blends antiquity with the Renaissance makes complete sense. This marriage, if worked through constructively in the rehearsal room, can create a mental and moral world for the actors to feed on in pursuit of their characters' inner lives. The aim is to construct an alternative social world with its own manners and behaviour extracted from the writings of both periods and filtered through the text's narrative demands. It is about making a social space to feel at home. An actor's prime need is for this kind of concrete reality, whatever overall 'concept' the director might have – a concept, by the way, that they'd best not talk about too much, because actors really can't act concepts. However abstract or naturalistic the design of the production, it's important that the actors don't experience a dissonance between the language they speak, which is their minds stepping into the light, and the physical world in which their characters live. Whatever they look like, it is those characters' preconceptions that matter most. The gods are always in their consciousness, as are received cultural ideas about virginity and honour – this is what illuminates an actor's imagination. Lavinia's virginity is an issue of life and death, and her rape a violation of the sacred, not merely the domestic. After her rape the cultural expectation is that she must die at her father's hands, and whatever the world looks like that the audience see on the stage, they must be made to believe that this is an inevitable and accepted social necessity to the people of the story. This doesn't mean that the actor playing Lavinia has to play her as submitting willingly to her own murder (although the text implies that she does), simply that it is an expectation within her world that family honour can't allow her to live. The truth is that tentacles of belief and practice stretch out over the centuries, and it's not as if our own world is unacquainted with the idea of honour killing. It's facts like this that allow us to make connections and conflations in the creation of hybrid worlds and to understand why sticking to one well-defined historic period is not the only way of giving actors a context in which to think their characters into existence. The challenge that Shakespeare always sets the modern actor is that all his worlds are inventions, all are set in places that exist only on a stage, and all are rooted in an Elizabethan perception of life mingled with elements of the stories' historical settings. Moving the mind to different realities is harder than seeing everything through the lens of our own time, and sometimes contemporary Shakespearean acting can be clogged and weakened by modern conceptions. However, luckily we are talking about the playwright who invented a way of representing psychological truth as the expression of individual identity and who helped create the very idea of what we now call human. He planted the seeds of self-creation, and his insights encouraged the growth of the idea of individual personality.

When I worked on *Titus Andronicus* the design eventually narrowed down to three main physical decisions. The shape of the floor; what else, if anything, to introduce into the space; and whether it was necessary to include an elevated upper acting space as the stage directions strongly imply. (The stage direction '*Enter above*' occurs a number of times in the text, especially in Act One.) There are two other specific design problems which, stated together, sound like a lost short story by Edgar Allan Poe: 'The Pit and the Vault' perhaps? At the beginning of the play, when Titus returns from his wars against the Goths, the action takes place in front of the family vault, and the ceremonial committing of his dead sons to the tomb establishes the importance of ancestor worship as an idea central to the life of a patrician Roman family. It also establishes much about attitudes to death and religion that echo through the play. So, representing this place convincingly is vital. Then there is the pit into which two of his sons fall while hunting in Act Two. But beware: there is something fundamentally comic about someone accidentally falling into a hole on stage. It's hard to explain – but there just is, like slipping on a banana skin: so much physical comedy is based on a person surprised by suddenly losing control of their body. But here this event has tragic consequences, and it highlights one of main reasons this is such a difficult play. The delicate balance between tragedy and comedy in drama was not something that Shakespeare had quite mastered at this stage in his career. *Titus Andronicus* was his first tragedy, and at the time he wrote it he was also experimenting with his first comedies, but at the age of twenty-seven there was still a clumsiness about his movement between the two genres. However, he was trying, which can't be said of any other playwright at the time. Later (from about 1592 onwards) this elusive cocktail, mixing the ridiculousness of human life with its miseries, he achieved brilliantly, and that's a huge part of his revolutionary and unique genius. He developed that touch which enables alert directors and actors to find the perfect balance in which a moment can be both funny and sad. He hadn't got there yet with *Titus*, and it has to be discovered through careful rehearsal, but the design should not slant the key signature too heavily either way.

Many academics believe that Shakespeare did not write *Titus* alone. His co-author is thought to be a writer called George Peele, who was eight years his senior. If true, *Titus*, along with the three parts of *Henry VI* (also thought to be of dual or multiple authorship), would represent a kind of apprenticeship sometime between 1589 and 1592. This sense of Shakespeare feeling his way as a dramatist actually connects with the issue of how to design the play. The author (or authors) clearly had a very specific theatrical space in mind as they wrote, especially with regard to the first section of the play (Act One); and this space fits in with the layout of an Elizabethan playhouse. The whole flow of the action as described in the text implies the use of an upper gallery at the back of the stage, three upstage entrances at ground level, and a trapdoor centre stage. This adherence to the features of a specific playing space, whether at the Rose or the Swan, has always suggested to me either that, as an apprentice and inexperienced writer Shakespeare leant heavily on the physical layout of the stage to help him with the complex dramatic exposition of the opening, or else George Peele, more experienced but less imaginative, did most of the plot-setting for the audience in an inelegant and clumsy way. It is just very noticeable – and even a quick first reading will confirm this – that the shadow of the stage is so much more present here than in any later text. If Shakespeare and Peele wrote the play for the Rose, they would have been writing for a space very similar in layout to the later Globe theatre but with a shallower and wider stage. The effect, in the opening half-hour of the action, would have been almost 'split screen'. So how much should this apparent necessity for an upper acting level affect the choices director and designer make about the basic geometry of the set? There are many ways in which an upper level might relate to the shape of the main floor depending on whether it was rectangular, square, circular or triangular, and this may in turn affect other conceptual and aesthetic choices.

Well, what did affect me was coming across the work of one academic, Brian Vickers, which completely convinced me that George

Peele was responsible for the whole of the first act. In those days I still had qualms about changing Shakespeare but not, funnily enough, Peele. The stage directions for the opening scenes are unusually elaborate for a Shakespeare play and indicate doggedly when groups of characters appear 'above' or 'below'. This has significance in terms of their shifting status and the movement of the plot through the first complicated, and potentially confusing, sweep of the action from the opening moments up to Aaron's first soliloquy. A close reading of these directions seems to indicate that the upper level is meant to represent the Capitol and the lower a public space in front of the family tomb. The confusion lies in the fact that these two spaces have no logical architectural connection with each other yet those 'above' speak directly to those 'below' and vice versa. All the encounters are clearly taking place in public, and, as well as the interactions between tribunes, senators, soldiers and prisoners, from time to time characters seem to be addressing an interested and reactive crowd. This is good news dramatically because it creates an element of 'performance' that drives the tone and motivation of individuals, giving a feel of how they want to appear to the wider public, in other words the electorate, in a world where leaders are chosen by public acclamation.

The problem with any proscenium stage divided between upper and lower acting levels is that it tends to lead the director into creating static groupings. Also, inevitably, the upper level has to be upstage of the lower, meaning that dialogue between characters above and below will always favour those higher and further upstage, while those on the lower level will have to have their backs to the audience. With the first act of *Titus* it seemed to me much better to have the confrontations happening on the same level, enabling greater freedom and fluidity of movement. It also meant changing the text, which is why I was glad that George Peele has never, to my knowledge, been on the schools' English Literature syllabus. We found in rehearsal that, without two levels, almost constant motion was possible, bringing greater volatility to the situation and more direct, face-to-face, physical aggression. Abandoning the need for an upper level by adjusting the script meant the floor shape could become a pure circle, an arena of gladiatorial human conflict.

The actual moment of decision was quite strange. The designer and I were in my kitchen playing around with a rough, white-card model of the set trying out different floor shapes, trying to pin down some element that was quintessentially of the antique world, when our eyes fell on a small round table whose top was made of miniature blue and white tiles arranged in a mosaic pattern. We lifted the table top from its metal base and placed it in the model box, adding some small cut-out cardboard human figures that designers use in their models to show scale. We looked at each other and smiled. We had our design.

ROMANS AND GOTHS

With an acting space and the characters filling it dressed in clothes mixing Classical and Renaissance style, an imagined, hybrid world, the next stage of preparing for rehearsals of *Titus Andronicus* was to identify which areas of research might help us get inside of the heads of the characters. Shakespeare's evocation of this Rome is not period-specific, and, unlike *Julius Caesar* or *Antony and Cleopatra*, the story is not about actual historical figures. There are emperors, rather than a republic, but no clear rule of succession based on blood, and this is significant to both the characters and the plot. Although floating free of history in many respects, the presence of the Goths is central to the human dynamics. Research helped disabuse me of the simplistic notion held since school days that round about 400 AD barbarian hordes swept into Rome, and overnight the Classical period ended and the Dark Ages began. In reality the gradual and complex process of invasion and assimilation over many years in a city that had always been massively multicultural must have led to a cornucopia of intriguing and combustible human relationships, as Romans and Goths mingled, loved and hated.

This research was extremely useful to take into the rehearsal room, and thankfully didn't require reading all six volumes of Gibbon's *Decline and Fall of the Roman Empire* (a book that I keep putting off). Take the relationship between Tamora, captured Queen of the Goths, and Saturninus, the man who becomes Emperor of Rome during the the course of Act One. Although their union is bewilderingly bizarre in its plotting and needs very careful handling from the director to make any sense at all, it becomes during the play a fascinating picture of a marriage between two people of different cultures and one that must have been historically archetypical. It is a relationship, based on opportunism and conflicting motives, in which neither partner can be described as purely 'evil', and as such sets a template for Shakespeare's approach to character in which no one is ever just 'good' or 'bad'. It was new, it was complex, and demanded self-reflection from an audience – the asking of the question: 'Would I behave like that if I was in the same situation?' Despite the horrors that spring from Tamora's desire to avenge the 'sacrifice' of her son, the Goths who side with Lucius at the climax of the play are portrayed as dignified, honourable and composed. Despite the actions of the main Goth characters – Tamora, Aaron (her lover) and Demetrius and Chiron (two more of her sons) – being hard to describe as anything but evil, at least they have some cause, given their treatment at the hands of their Roman conquerors. There is no 'bad Goth' and 'good Roman' opposition, simply the 'mingled yarn' of circumstance, disposition and the opportunity and instincts of the moment. The historical background was essential to the work of the rehearsal room to identifying the things that made the two groups different and that gave an edge to their dealings with each other. The sudden assimilation of Tamora and her two remaining sons into Roman society is more apparent than real and is driven by opportunism in the wake of the new Emperor's extraordinary offer of marriage. The first audiences may have seen the play as a cautionary tale about what happens when you let uncivilised elements inside civilised society, but it retains a historical relevance for our own times. It's a similar fear of disruption that informs the Jack Cade scenes in *Henry VI, Part 2* and the treatment of the restless, insubordinate citizens in *Julius Caesar* and *Coriolanus*. In fact this conflation of the entire history of both republican and monarchical Rome into one imaginary whole, marks the starting point of Shakespeare's career-long exploration of the issue of what makes good or bad government, the nature of what leadership means, and the relationship between the personal and the political. In rehearsal this translates into discovering how a theme is carried in a narrative, and how the narrative is contained in the characters.

The killing of Tamora's son Alarbus is the spark that ignites the furnace of hatred and revenge that drives the narrative. It happens shortly after Titus's return in triumph from ten years of war against the Goths and is a shockingly brutal prelude to a brutally shocking play. Whether we think of this death as sacrifice or murder is a key rehearsal-room question, and worth exploring now. The Romans did not see themselves as a people who indulged in human sacrifice, but on the other hand they would, from time to time, slaughter or mutilate large numbers of prisoners after battle. So in what light should we see the instruction that Lucius (Titus's eldest son) gives to his brothers to 'hew his limbs' and burn them on a sacrificial fire 'whose smoke like incense doth perfume the sky'. They do this to 'appease' the spirits of their dead kinsmen. Lucius has asked his father's permission, and his father has instantly agreed. But in the playing of the scene we found that this sacrifice needed to be an issue amongst the Andronici, conveying a strong feeling of their own confusion about whether it is the right thing to do in moral, religious or traditional terms. I think it should be clear to an audience that the idea of ceremonial human sacrifice creates tension within the Andronicus family; this will heighten its effect on Tamora and her sons, who are well aware that it is they who are thought of as the savage barbarians sunk in a primitive attachment to the principle of vengeance, and yet are deeply shocked by the actions of the supposedly civilised Romans. This sense of a crisis of moral judgement especially applies to the patriarch Titus, whose old age (constantly referred to) may be leaving him vulnerable to the pressure of a new order being chaotically created before his eyes. He may be losing his grip, his authority. The stage mood needs to show the precarious volatility that comes with values being misunderstood and rearranged: by his decision to allow the death of Alarbus he has unleashed forces that he can no longer control.

Shakespeare's three 'authentic' Roman plays – the ones based on real history – are *Coriolanus*, which deals with the foundation of the Republic; *Julius Caesar*, which concerns the last days of the Republic; and *Antony and Cleopatra*, which (among other things) details the foundation of the Empire with the coming to power of Octavius Caesar, later to re-name himself Augustus, first Emperor of Rome.

The idea of the family or clan was important in both Republican and Imperial Rome. It was a system based on wealth revolving around an aristocracy and a senatorial ruling class, in which the term 'liberty' meant primarily the right of aristocrats both to speak their mind and control the machinery of government. In 212 AD the Emperor Caracalla gave citizenship to everyone in the Empire. This included the Goths in the Germanic territories. The text of *Titus Andronicus* suggests that Chiron and Demetrius have had a Roman education, so from that we can assume that Tamora and her family have been to a certain extent Romanised. Their transition into Roman society need not have been too culturally traumatic for them, so the rehearsal-room question becomes: to what extent would a production of the play benefit from emphasising the behavioural, attitudinal and cultural differences between Romans and Goths?

The decisions are complicated because of the huge difference between the ways in which the two distinct groups of Goths are portrayed. The members of the 'Tamora quartet' – a queen, her two sons and her lover – are vicious, scheming and utterly immoral from any perspective, whereas the Goths supporting Lucius at the play's climax are moderate, straightforward and decent. Historical research tells us that the relationship between Goth and Roman was complex, with some Goths embracing enthusiastically all that Rome had to offer, while others were continually in revolt against their occupiers – a situation that finds parallels in nineteenth-century British imperialism in Africa or twentieth-century American hegemony in the Middle East. So Shakespeare (and George Peele, the likely co-author of the play) seem to be describing that ambivalence with some accuracy. In the end, of course, you have to approach each character as an individual shaped by their personal circumstances, but the fact remains that those circumstances are bound to include elements of cultural and racial conditioning. There is the selfish competitiveness of Chiron and Demetrius and their relationship to an adored mother, which is personal, but there is also their somewhat less tender attitude to Roman women, which seems to spring from a racially ingrained prejudice that enables them to justify their actions to themselves. Then there is the particularity of Tamora's scorched pride, that comes from the humiliation of her prisoner status and the ritual murder of her eldest son, and is further fanned by her disdain for the Roman psyche and its manifestations in the family of the Andronici. Shakespeare provides clues to these characters' backgrounds, but the case of Aaron the Moor is different: his backstory needs to be a hundred per cent invented in rehearsals.

What is a Moor doing with these Goths? Where has his 'evil' come from? It seems to have even less motivation than Iago's. If he is to be more than a mere caricature, then what drives him? He has been a first-hand witness to Tamora's humiliation, and, when he is revealed to be her lover, nothing we learn subsequently about either of them suggests anything other than that their love is genuine and mutual. So a starting point for bringing sympathy and complexity into his character is to suppose that his orchestration of Lavinia's rape and mutilation, as well as the death of her husband and brothers, stems from a furiously driven desire to avenge the treatment of the woman he loves. So love is manifest within the generation of evil, and where love exists, pure evil is impossible, however sickening the consequences. There is a fundamental principle about directing Shakespeare here. Every twist and turn of the text and every authentic textually supported element of backstory needs to be excavated to implant understanding and sympathy into the 'bad' characters. The only backstory we have for Aaron (beyond what we might invent) is that he loves Tamora. With Iago it's easier; there's more to go on: he suffers from an excruciating, morbid condition of jealousy, a disease of the mind that he is powerless to escape, and that always has to be the starting point with him. But Aaron is in love – so why not start building from there?

In my own production I eventually decided to re-shape Act One fairly radically. This involved cutting the killing of Mutius by Titus, his own father, and hence the subsequent debate about his burial. I also conflated the confusing timescale in such a way as to make it unnecessary for Tamora and Saturninus to leave the action and reappear only moments later married and in new clothes! I think this greatly improved the flow of the action, and, emboldened by the conviction that it was by Peele not Shakespeare, I didn't feel too guilty about it. Having said that, I've since read very convincing academic arguments defending Shakespeare's authorship. So, there you go.

The killing of Mutius is such an extraordinary act that cutting it has a huge significance for the actor playing Titus. This is a man who has already in a life of warfare seen the deaths of twenty-one of his sons. To kill another with his own hands, in a moment of outrage at being crossed, suggests someone who is on the way to madness. As the story unfolds, one of its most gripping features is the mystery of whether Titus is really being driven mad by events, or only pretending to be. Shakespeare shared his age's fascination with madness, and he took the idea of an avenging hero figure, feigning madness in order to lull his intended victim into a false sense of security, to a peak of dramatic effectiveness in *Hamlet*. Towards the end of this earlier play, in a chilling theatrical coup, Titus is revealed to be terrifyingly sane as he calmly prepares to cut the throats of the rapist brothers. So, as with *King Lear*, the main character's state of mental equilibrium before things start hotting up is a key acting issue. With both Hamlet and Titus you can argue that the emotional effort of pretending to be mad while under the pressure of extreme circumstances could actually send them mad, if only temporarily. Therefore, if you want the story to be about a man's journey from sanity to an apparent madness which is finally revealed to be an act put on to ease the achievement of revenge, then cutting the killing of Mutius helps that narrative line for both actor and audience. Alternatively, however, you may read that early killing as the author's indication that the central character is already seriously unbalanced and carries the seeds of his own tragedy from the moment we set eyes on him. In this interpretation, Titus's journey could be seen as moving from madness to sanity as the horrors engender a process of learning about the iniquity and injustice of the world, which gradually informs his actions with a grim rationality. Both are interesting paths for an actor to follow, and both have pitfalls and rewards. Both can be justified by the text, and both could include at least one moment when you would like the audience to think: 'Maybe Titus/Hamlet only *thinks* that he's pretending to be mad.'

RHETORIC AND REVENGE

Amidst all the horrors of *Titus Andronicus*, its characters speak in a sustained and elaborate poetic language. The translation of passion and grief into poetry was the Elizabethans' way of ordering emotion into words so as to claw themselves back into the state of reason. Even though still relatively young, Shakespeare's ability to create character through language is already beginning to develop in this play, although that language is not yet naturalised in the extraordinary way it was later to be. In his early plays the rules of Classical rhetoric learnt at grammar school still shape the writing, whatever the dramatic context. This use of rhetoric, which was then an admired quality (and in many ways still is), may seem artificial, but it is not obscure. Speaking it is harder for a modern actor if we compare it, say, to the limpid hypnotic flow of the poetry of *Macbeth*, where the dramatic moment is always perfectly synchronised with the imagery and the emotion. In *Titus* it can feel as if the language is suspended in some timeless cloud disconnected from the human situation. But the principle is the same, and with *Titus*, as with any Shakespeare text, the actors' challenge is to find the balance between the rhetorical and the real, between music and meaning: to let the rhythm help motor the thought, and allow the language to create the thought. As the characters find the words, their thinking is illuminated to themselves. What sometimes happens is the equivalent of a movie director using slow motion to explore a moment of drama or pathos. The best example of this in *Titus* is the incredibly difficult scene where Marcus first sees Lavinia after her rape. He speaks at extraordinary length when what he sees is blood pouring from her mouth and

arms, and every human instinct is screaming, *Don't talk - help her!*
What Shakespeare is doing is not naturalistic, but it is, in a poetic way,
completely truthful. Marcus is speaking in order to stop himself
screaming. He is trying to convert the senseless oblivion of emotion
into some kind of reason, some kind of sense. Language was a scaffold
built around chaos in an attempt to contain madness and despair. Read
his speech (Act 2 Scene 3, lines 13–57), and see how it can't be rushed,
it can't be panicked, but, counter-intuitively, it must be slow, controlled,
incredulous, with every single word trying to mend and explain, not
emote and perform.

Telling the tale of *Titus Andronicus* within a world that is both Classical and Elizabethan is actually a notion contemporary to Shakespeare.
Not only is there a surviving sketch of the play on stage in which the
characters are dressed in a style that mixes the two periods (togas and
doublets), but Thomas Heywood, a fellow dramatist, wrote that, in
using stories from the ancient world, the playwright's intention was to
make the audience draw parallels with their modern world. One of the
issues that both cultures fretted over and is explicit in the play is the
relationship between justice and revenge. As a general, Titus has been
a loyal military servant of the Roman state for many years, with a deep
respect for his country, its traditions and its laws. But what do you do
when the law seems unjust? His basic mindset is that the purpose of the
law is to take revenge:

> If they did kill thy husband, then be joyful,
> Because the law hath ta'en revenge on them.
>   Act 3 Scene 1

This play seems to me like a dramatic poem constantly exploring the
balance between revenge and law. The Elizabethan Protestant Christian
state was keen to root out of society the impulse towards personal vengeance in favour of the official system of justice, and almost every
'revenge' play written at the time is a cautionary tale about the perils of
taking the law into your own hands. The Church and the State were as
one in proclaiming loudly and clearly the Bible's injunction, 'Vengeance
is mine: I will repay, saith the Lord' (Romans 12, 19). But *Titus* is a play
that seems to breathe empathy for the honour code of killing beyond
the law when the law itself is corrupt. Our own minds still wrestle with
a paradoxical attitude towards justice and revenge, and any modern
production needs to decide to what degree it wishes to lead the audience towards taking satisfaction in the act of revenge – especially when

Titus cuts the throats of his daughters' rapists and she catches their blood in a bowl. How do you want the audience to feel as Tamora takes the first mouthful of the pie made from their bodies?

These choices are interwoven with decisions about how the actor plays the shading of grief into madness and reason into action, pinpointing precisely the moments at which the audience become clear about the true state of Titus's mind. As we shall see below, King Lear's descent into madness is charted reasonably clearly in the text, and with Hamlet we are let in on his feigned lunacy early in the plot. But in this play the junction points and boundaries are less clear, and the situations more enigmatic. This may be connected to the fact that, although both Lear and Hamlet experience grief, it is not the overwhelming tsunami of horror that makes Titus compare himself to the earth and the sea. What hits him is more primitive, more bloody and far more extreme than anything that happens to the young Prince or the old King. He is drowning in so much misery that he himself becomes the element of his own destruction:

> When heaven doth weep, doth not the earth o'erflow?
> If the winds rage, doth not the sea wax mad,
> Threatening the welkin with his big-swollen face?
> And wilt thou have a reason for this coil?
> I am the sea. Hark how her sighs doth blow.
> She is the weeping welkin, I the earth.
> Then must my sea be moved with her sighs,
> Then must my earth with her continual tears
> Become a deluge overflowed and drowned.

Titus himself does not fit the classic definition of a tragic hero, a great man who falls because of an inherent weakness. But he does fit the pattern of the revenger who brings about his own death; and the play is very much a *revenge* tragedy. Yet despite this, we constantly feel that the message is not that 'revenge is bad' but, rather, that 'revenge is sweet'. I think one of the reasons this play is not done that much is the odour of amorality that hangs around it. No one really wants to leave a theatre thinking *I'm glad those little bastards got their throats cut*. Some productions have attempted to get around this by sending the whole play up, by treating it as satire or a kind of Grand Guignol Gothic melodrama that is good for a laugh. But although, like all Shakespeare's plays, it contains a lot of humour if handled right, it is basically a deeply serious play exploring an issue which was profoundly important to Elizabethan society – and still is to our own.

The politics of *Titus Andronicus* is just as confusing as its morality. In the weirdly constructed first act, even the basic political structure of Rome is not clear. The 'election' of Saturninus is anarchic and chaotic, although it may reflect what sometimes actually happened in the transitions between emperors. In the course of the action we see a man totally unsuitable for leadership replaced by a potentially good leader, but the play is not interested in the politics of that change. It is a family affair and is only political insofar as politics in the ancient world was always dynastic at some level. In the Elizabethan world, political debate revolved mainly around monarchy and religion – what made a good monarch and what constituted good religion – with the two coming together in the concept of 'Divine Right', the idea that monarchs were ordained by God. In this play none of these subjects gets anything like the detailed treatment they receive in *Richard II*, *Henry IV* or *Henry V*, but there is a wild energy that directs the audience to think about the calamitous chaos that may be caused by emotionally insecure and narcissistic rulers.

Just as it's necessary for actor and director to immerse themselves in Elizabethan ways of thinking as a route to modern relevance, so with the Roman plays it helps a lot to know about the religious and social practices of that world. Understanding the mental landscape that underpins a person's thinking from childhood to adulthood is just as important as creating an individual personality; they are part of the same process because cultural influences help shape individual minds. What is going on in the heads of Lucius and his brothers when they demand the right to sacrifice Alarbus? 'Give us the proudest prisoner of the Goths,' says Lucius to his father in front of the family tomb, 'That we may hew his limbs and on a pile... sacrifice his flesh',

> Before this earthly prison of their bones,
> That so the shadows be not unappeased,
> Nor we disturbed with prodigies on earth.

The actor playing Lucius must embrace the fact that the character believes in Roman religion and its pantheon of gods as a literal truth, and in particular the cult of ancestor worship. The Romans believed that the Underworld was beneath their feet and that special access points, such as certain caves, lakes and even marshes, led to it. Whatever Lucius's character, the actor can't speak these lines with integrity unless they know this, any more than Lavinia can willingly let her father take her life unless she believes in, understands and agrees with the set of social and moral beliefs surrounding family honour, and which she learnt in her nursery from the story of Virginius, the Roman centurion whose only recourse to avenge the rape of his daughter was to kill her and bring her case to trial. Given this, you might ask why did I not simply set the play in Ancient Rome. The answer is that, for me, it was important to realise that the language is the rhetorical, imagistic poetry of Elizabethan theatre invented by Marlowe, Shakespeare and others – people who also understood the belief systems of the Romans, as they were the foundation of their own education and their own art. They knew that, for these Romans, ancestor worship was the defining principle of this patriarchal family, in which the tomb literally unites the living and the dead. Herein lies the dramatic intensity of the sacrifice of Alarbus and the centrality of that action to the energy of the whole play. The stakes are high in the moment of Titus's decision to allow the sacrifice to go ahead, but what was revelatory in rehearsal was discovering that if Titus was played as conflicted, confused, and very aware of how shocked the Goths were, but was himself also hesitant in his agreement, then the fever and drama of the moment were much greater.

The Classical curriculum of the Elizabethan grammar school was also underpinned by study of the Christian Bible, and my earlier point about Lucius's beliefs is actually challenged by a strange moment towards the end of the play, when there appears to be a place for a Christian presence. I have spoken so far only of the ancient world as pagan, but the Goth and Roman were overlapping around 400 AD, when Christianity was the Empire's official religion. Not only are the Renaissance and Classical worlds enmeshed in the play, but so too are the ancient pagan and early Christian worlds. Here is the dialogue as the captive Aaron pleads and bargains for the life of his baby son with the promise of revealing important information:

> LUCIUS. Tell on thy mind; I say thy child shall live.
> AARON. Swear that he shall and then I will begin.
> LUCIUS. Who should I swear by? Thou believest no god.
>   That granted, how canst thou believe an oath?
> AARON. What if I do not? – as indeed I do not –
>   Yet for I know thou art religious
>   And hast a thing within thee called conscience,
>   With twenty popish tricks and ceremonies
>   Which I have seen thee careful to observe,
>   Therefore I urge thy oath; for that I know

> An idiot holds his bauble for a god,
> And keeps the oath which by that god he swears,
> To that I'll urge him, therefore thou shalt vow
> By that same god, what god so'er it be
> That thou adorest and hast in reverence,
> To save my boy, to nurse and bring him up,
> Or else I will discover nought to thee.
> LUCIUS. Even by my god I swear to thee I will.

He refers to a singular 'god' – not 'gods'. What has happened to the pagan Lucius, the dedicated ancestor worshipper who demanded human sacrifice to appease the spirits of his dead brothers? At the beginning of the fifth century AD, many Goths converted to Christianity: so what's the internal backstory here? Has Lucius become a convert during the time he has spent in exile among them? As a group, they display no outward signs, despite displaying a restrained dignity. In any case, the only time Aaron could have seen him at prayer is far further back in the action – but how should it affect the playing of Lucius at the beginning and end of the story? This is exactly the kind of questioning that academics find completely irrelevant, taking the view that all the plays are littered with this kind of narrative inconsistency, and that this is merely a sign of an inexperienced dramatist making a minor slip that an audience would never notice. So what! You can't act that explanation, and besides, this moment of challenge by Aaron to Lucius is fascinating, and too rich in its implications not to be explored and used.

Has Lucius emerged as more sophisticated than his father? Are we seeing a man more in control of his emotions and now of sounder judgement than before? Is Shakespeare interested in the idea that by embracing Christianity (Catholic Christianity by the look of it, if 'popish tricks' means anything), Lucius has grown beyond the emotional impulsiveness of paganism: the impulse that led him to request, and his father to accede to, the ritual murder of a captive? In part this relates to how you portray Titus's early behaviour. If you retain that part of the script that includes the killing of Mutius, then you begin with a massively unsympathetic and violent act by the central character, an act compounded by his serious misjudgement concerning Saturninus's suitability as a leader and his weakness or cruelty in sanctioning the slaughter of Alarbus. But if you remove Mutius and his death from the action, then you won't feel that Titus deserves all he gets, because at root he's a brutal pagan, and like Lear we will come to pity him and feel sympathy despite his foolishness. But maybe Shakespeare (or Peele) placed the killing of Mutius there precisely to weigh things heavily against sympathy from the word go? And maybe this is what the strange exchange about Lucius's 'god' is there for: to imply a historical moral corner has been turned to the betterment of humanity. So the removal or retention of the killing of Mutius is a decision between improving the play's dramatic flow while increasing sympathy for the main character, or else possibly damaging the play's overall moral structure.

The playing of Tamora and her two repulsive sons brings a challenge to the actors' abilities to avoid stereotyping. Shakespeare knew his Classical authors and may have had a volume of Tacitus on the table beside him as he wrote *Titus Andronicus*. Tacitus tells us that the Goths listened to prophetesses and willingly and eagerly followed the advice of women who seemed to them to possess a knowledge of the world and its mysteries that was way beyond the comprehension of male warriors. This lies right at the heart of the mother and her sons who dominate this play. Tacitus wrote: 'They go so far as to believe that there is something divine about this sex. They listen to women's advice with docility and regard them as oracles. But as warriors they were filled with a wild, magic frenzy. They were young men to whom tumult, violence and the wild desire to murder were natural.' This is great rehearsal fodder. Tamora encourages their rape of Lavinia, admires and, to a degree, turns it into poetry:

> But when ye have the honey ye desire,
> Let not this wasp outlive us both to sting.

The evil thing they do is wrapped up in their love and respect, verging on awe, for their mother. To capture this on stage is to draw a picture of something more interesting than simple evil.

Aaron is an early version of Iago. He claims to be pure evil, but it's better not to take his claim too seriously. His actions are better understood as springing from his passionate love for Tamora, and a desire to revenge her humiliation and pain resulting from the murder of her son.

Shakespeare's ability to make characters who appear to have a life beyond the boundaries of their play begins with *Titus Andronicus*. Saturninus is a good example. His sudden decision to marry Tamora is an outlandish and highly theatrical gesture, and he is full of this random quixotic behaviour. '*Conbium*' – the right to marry a Roman citizen – was not awarded to the Goths till very late in the Empire's history. Flying in the face of convention, Saturninus is wilful, but clearly likes to think of himself as a spontaneous romantic. Like Nero, he probably loves the theatre. To pick an exotic, grief-stricken, savage woman up from the dust, when he has just been offered the beautiful, young, virginal Lavinia, has about it a rather magnificent sensuality. Perhaps it gives him a sexual kick, perhaps he is a bit of an actor: he certainly seems to see the performer in the Queen of the Goths. To control her rage and grief, and channel it into the performance that lays the groundwork for avenging her son's murder, requires huge acting skills. This is a talent that seems at times to take her over, as when she impersonates Revenge, the better to enjoy the spectacle of Titus's grief at close quarters.

And as for Titus himself, what is the key to his character? His gullibility, a childish innocence that blinds him to the dark side of human nature, an inability to see the effects of his actions on others, and his stubborn pride all spring to mind. But the characteristic that emerges most as the play progresses is his stoicism. He perfectly embodies the Stoic faith of Seneca and Marcus Aurelius, and the need to bear with fortitude the worst that life can throw at you. That character exists only through the poetry he speaks: it is the purest example of *language* becoming *character*.

The Taming of the Shrew

THE TRAINING OF KATE MINOLA

The Taming of the Shrew is a problem. It can be seen, very easily, as a sexist male propaganda manifesto. An instruction manual for repressing woman in marriage. A celebration of male, macho cunning that concludes with a once feisty and furiously independent girl being paraded in front of a wedding party to give a speech praising the domination of strong men over weak women. At the play's end, three couples have just got married. When the wives are out of the room and the three husbands are discussing marriage, Petruchio makes a wager that if each of them sent a message to his own wife to return immediately, only his wife, Kate, would obey. This is what happens: she returns bringing the other two wives, who have refused to obey, with her, and he doubles down on the bet by instructing her to speak about the duty wives owe their husbands. Here is part of what she says:

> Thy husband is thy lord, thy life, thy keeper,
> Thy head, thy sovereign: one that cares for thee
> And for thy maintenance; commits his body
> To painful labour both by sea and land,
> To watch the night in storms, the day in cold,
> Whilst thou liest warm at home, secure and safe,
> And craves no other tribute at thy hands
> But love, fair looks and true obedience –
> Too little payment for so great a debt.

OK, that's enough. It goes on. For quite a while longer. In similar vein. The men listening to this, having known Kate's old self, are astonished and purr their approval as she concludes:

> And place your hands below your husband's foot:
> In token of which duty, if he please,
> My hand is ready, may it do him ease.

As Petruchio leads his new tame wife off to bed, the remaining men mutter words of heartfelt admiration, and the last two lines of the play are:

HORTENSIO. Now, go thy ways, thou hast tamed a curst shrew.
LUCENTIO. 'Tis a wonder, by your leave, she will be tamed so.

All quiet and respectful, quite downbeat and sober after the rage and passion of the play: a strange, slightly flat ending. The struggle over the last century has been to find production ideas that recreate the play in ways twentieth- and twenty-first-century folk find acceptable, or at least bearable. There are of course many interpretations just of those last two lines – ways of playing them that avoid making them feel like a celebration of a man's victory over a difficult woman, but, rather, the sheepish, slightly ashamed tone of men who've just witnessed something rather terrible: the shocking change that can come over someone when their identity has been shredded and their spirit broken. Or indeed the very last line could be played as if there was something vaguely fishy about the whole business, things maybe being not quite what they seem. But this brings us to the second problem. I don't think it's the ending Shakespeare intended.

There is another text for *The Taming of the Shrew* which, rather like the Bad Quarto of *Hamlet*, has had academics intrigued for many years. It's called *The Taming of a Shrew* ('*a* Shrew', not '*the* Shrew') and, just like the *Hamlet* text, no one is sure whether it preceded or followed the version we have in the First Folio. It is clearly either some kind of earlier attempt, or something like a later memorial reconstruction of its performed script. Apart from Kate and Petruchio (here called Ferando), most of the other characters have Classical-sounding names, although all serve the same dramatic functions. It stands in an odd relation to the play we are used to. But by far the most intriguing thing about it is the Christopher Sly storyline. Those who know the play only from the Folio version will remember it begins with a man being chucked out of a pub. He falls into a drunken sleep and is discovered by a Lord out hunting with a group of friends and servants. They decide to play a trick on him and take him back, still asleep, to the Lord's manor house. In the second scene he wakes up to find himself dressed in expensive clothes, surrounded by fine paintings and fine wines and attended by servants. He naturally asks them what the hell is going on: why is he, Christopher Sly, a poor man, here in this luxurious house? They tell him he is not called Christopher Sly. They tell him he is a great, powerful, rich lord who has been in a coma for many years and is married to a beautiful woman who has been missing him terribly. They bring her in and she confirms the story. But 'she' is a pageboy in drag. Nevertheless it doesn't take long for Sly to be persuaded that what they are saying is the truth.

A group of travelling actors have turned up at the grand house to give a performance that night. They are warned that there is an unexpected guest who might cause trouble. The Lord, his friends, Christopher Sly and his 'wife' then settle down to watch the play: the play we ourselves are about to watch. So the 'play' begins with a young man (Lucentio) arriving in Padua with his servant, and that – apart from one tiny exchange between Sly and the Lord's servants early on in Act One – is that. There is no further reference to the fact that the play we are watching is a play about people watching a play. But in the other text – *The Taming of a Shrew* – there is much more of the Sly story. At several key moments the watchers interrupt the action, and at the end Sly falls asleep once more, is returned to where he was found, and is woken up by the pub landlord who kicked him out at the beginning. This structure, I think, represents Shakespeare's original intention. In both texts we are dealing with a play-within-a-play, and for me, *The Shrew* only makes complete sense when it is played fully as exactly that. The reason it usually isn't is fairly obvious. The text that went into the First Folio probably accurately reflects the way the Lord Chamberlain's Men played it: they didn't have the numbers to stage a production in which about a dozen actors do nothing but watch their fellow actors acting! The main play grows characters as it progresses, and it must have been the case that the actors playing Sly, the Lord, the pageboy, the friends and the servants had to slip away to play them, so the framing action (a group of aristocrats watching a play) gradually faded from sight, and this is reflected in the Folio text that has come down to us. The same thing applies today. Only a major theatre company or a drama school could afford the number of actors needed to have the characters of the framing action constantly in view on stage watching the play within the play. It is just possible that Shakespeare's company never liked the idea of the Sly story constantly intruding into the Kate story and dropped it for artistic rather than financial reasons; even so, I believe it is a far better play with *A Shrew*'s rather than *The Shrew*'s structure – especially today.

In the Elizabethan period the subject of the balance of power between a husband and wife within their marriage was a hot social issue. The majority of the original audience would have left the play-house probably feeling that domestic justice had been done, Kate's personality had been changed for the better, and her husband had handled the whole tricky situation extremely well; about the same proportion as those who would have felt Shylock the Jew got everything that was coming to him. That of course is not remotely true today, when a production of the play has to reflect the profoundly different society we are now. It cannot be a celebration of masculine dominance as an essential feature of a happy marriage. The most common solution to the ending is to create an internal backstory in which Kate and Petruchio conspire to trick the other wedding guests into losing the wager by acting out a scene in which Kate pretends to be the devoted, subservient, little wife, while Petruchio plays the loving but strict master. In this interpretation Kate's final speech becomes a parody of, rather than a genuine expression of, wifely duty.

But why does Shakespeare set up the central narrative as a play being performed to an audience that has its own strange and disturbing story going on? What is happening to Christopher Sly is as shocking as what happens to Kate, but it is also more real; it is the primary reality of the evening. When we look at the whole stage picture at any given moment we are constantly being reminded that what is happening to Kate, Bianca, Lucentio, Petruchio and the rest is only a play. We have even met the actors who are to play these characters, seen them being warned to expect strange behaviour from one member of their audience, and in the text of A Shrew, they are told to supply a boy actor from their company to play the role of Sly's wife. Whatever goes on in the tale about taming a shrewish woman into a placid and obedient wife is distanced by the bizarre and brutal psychological game that is being played out by the Lord and his friends. As an audience we accept the pretence that we are watching a group of actors acting a play while 'real' people watch them doing so. The play being watched is an old play based on many medieval stories about men learning how to put shrewish women in their place – for their own good! Kate is unhappy as the person she is; she falls in love with Petruchio, and appears a happier person once married to him: these could be seen as mitigations that soften the apparent harshness of the inner play. But the outer play has no such softening elements, nothing in it that excuses the astonishing cruelty that a group of aristocrats randomly inflict on an innocent, poor and gullible working-class man.

When I have directed this play (which I've done three times) I have taken care to give the aristocrats individual identities rather than presenting them just as 'a Lord and his followers'. I've also set the framing action in modern dress, so that servants, actors and aristocrats are all our contemporaries, but when the actors play the play, they are costumed as Elizabethans. Finally, I have taken the text of the Sly scenes from *A Shrew* and modernised it: the first two scenes, the interventions during the playing of the play, and the final scenes when Sly is put back where he was found, along with his subsequent conversation with the publican, have all been played in contemporary speech.

In all three productions, the cast and I created an internal backstory in which the players become aware of what is being done to Sly. We even invented a name for their theatre company and, to our astonishment, then found out about a real theatre company specifically created to put on Shakespeare in posh houses to small audiences of private guests! In all three productions, a part of what 'the Lord' (he was called Bertie last time) has bought by hiring this particular theatre company is the promise of audience participation. As the action progressed, the 'actors' handed the 'audience' scripts, and the Lord's friends began to play minor characters such as the servants in Petruchio's house. To cut a long story short, Bertie and his friends receive worse treatment at the hands of the actors than Kate does from Petruchio.

Putting the focus of the play onto class rather than male sexism is, I believe, closer to what Shakespeare was trying to say. I'm convinced that all the Sly scenes in *A Shrew* are by Shakespeare, and that they reflect his unease with the situation in which he found himself early in his London career: a poor player slightly overawed by the attention and flattery of the aristocracy, and beguiled by the life of Southampton and his circle of theatre-obsessed friends. But inside him, struggling to find expression, is our contemporary – a man of egalitarian instincts and social conscience. So in all three of my productions the men and women who put Christopher Sly through the psychological torture of forcing him to doubt his sanity, fooling him into believing he's a rich man with a beautiful wife, and then throwing him back in the gutter where they found him, have been shown as cruel, overprivileged rich kids wallowing in a sense of entitlement and superiority.

Does this contextualising of Kate's story into a bigger narrative concerning class and inequality remove the sexism implicit in her 'taming?' No, not entirely, but it certainly presents it in a different light. The play becomes about the power of theatre; the way a group of actors can take control of their wealthy paymasters and, instead of merely dancing to their tune, force them to experience what it is like to be swept along by life, without control, without the power of money and privilege: what it's like, in other words, to be poor Sly – a plaything of Fate, as we all are.

But let's return to that notorious final speech of Katherine Minola, as I renamed her. There is no other speech in Shakespeare that is so controversial or, frankly, bewildering to a modern audience. I can see five main ways that it might be approached in production.

- In an off-stage scene (which could be improvised in rehearsal) Kate and Petruchio have come up with a plan to win the wager. In front of the wedding guests she shows what a great actor she is by giving a consummate performance of the male chauvinist's dream wife. In love and in league with Petruchio, she transforms herself into a docile, compliant, conventional, modest, grateful, subservient woman, and it is absolutely convincing. Many variations of this idea are possible, but none will work unless the audience can see what's going on, and the other characters on stage clearly can't. This is tricky because there is no text to explain it.

- Kate hasn't really changed at all; she's just given up in exhaustion: she's defeated, and all she has the energy to do is make the speech she knows is required of her but in a tone of bitter irony that makes clear everything she says is the exact opposite of what she believes. So her husband wins his bet, but the mood of the ending is sour and uncomfortable. This is obviously perfectly playable, but begs a lot of questions, especially how to negotiate the earlier moment when they kiss for the first time – a moment, as I argue below, that seems full of exquisite and genuine tenderness. You would have to play the kiss Kate gives there as likewise the product of mental and physical exhaustion.

- She speaks almost robotically: deadpan, drained of feeling, like someone who has just received electric shock treatment for their 'madness', and is now possessed by a lobotomised 'sanity'. Again, this would need to be emerging before they begin the journey back to Padua, and sustained and developed through the meeting with Vincentio on the road, and through the kiss on the street and during the conversation at the feast before the wager has been agreed on. It's a long time for the actor to sustain a single, catatonic note, but it could have a chilling dramatic effect and be received as a powerful rebuttal of patriarchal manipulation of female identity.

- She really has totally changed, and she means every single word of it from the bottom of her heart. The actor need not imply that it is the sleep deprivation, the exposure to hunger, the denial of a desired dress or hat, or the remorseless driving will of her mad husband that have changed her; it is just that she has fallen in love. She loves Petruchio. This was what her father demanded of him, whereas he was prepared to let his youngest daughter go to the highest bidder. Her love makes her want to see marriage the way she describes it in her infamous speech, a speech she is happy, even joyful, to make. There's no textual problem with this interpretation: what's wrong with presenting Kate as a profoundly changed person? Nothing. Except that it's almost more than a modern sensibility can bear. We simply don't like to accept that a woman can say those things and mean them – mean them without a trace of irony. Maybe if the production was fully Elizabethan, in both its strands, and viewed within its historical context, an audience today would find Kate's speech tolerable; but it would certainly be interesting to see a modern-dress production, without the framing action, and experience the effect of the last speech if played by a happy Kate.

- Kate, the actor playing Katherine Minola, is working through the speech; a modern actor in Renaissance costume playing to a small group of rich men and women in a grand private house somewhere in Britain today. It has been a strange evening in which she and her company have experienced the play in an entirely new way. Inadvertently they have become part of a grotesque con in which a poor working-class man has been kidnapped and abused. He has been persuaded he is not who he thought he was. She doesn't know what will happen to him when he discovers the truth. Is anything possible? What, after all, is identity? How changed can we become when we live in a world that tells us we can be anything we want to be, and everyone tries to believe it, even though everyone really knows that it isn't true at all? Tonight the actor playing Kate explores her final speech in a new way. She speaks it exclusively to the poor man in the rich clothes and his 'wife', the woman he expects to sleep with tonight but who will laugh in his face if he tries to lay a finger on her. And she tries to find in Shakespeare's words some message from another time about respect and love. After the show her fellow actors will gather round her and say, 'What happened there?' And I think she'd reply, 'I don't know. Those were the only words I had.'

KISS ME, KATE

Usually it's instant. Love at first sight. So it is when Romeo first sees Juliet at the Capulet ball, and when Miranda first sets eyes on Ferdinand shipwrecked on the magic island. Viola has no sooner disguised herself as a young man than she realises she is in love with Orsino and yet cannot tell him. Rosalind loses her heart to Orlando within minutes of their first encounter. These blows of Fate are the norm for Shakespeare's young lovers: except for Petruchio and Kate. *The Taming of the Shrew* is the only play where we see two people going through the process of falling in love with each other. In their final private scene on stage together, before the weddings and the public banquet that end the play-within-the-play, having witnessed a piece of street theatre resembling the culmination of an old farce, they turn to face each other and share a delicate and brief dialogue that could have been written yesterday.

> KATE. Husband, let's follow to see the end of this ado.
> PETRUCHIO. First kiss me, Kate, and we will.
> KATE. What, in the midst of the street?
> PETRUCHIO. What, art thou ashamed of me?
> KATE. No sir, God forbid – but ashamed to kiss.
> PETRUCHIO. Why then, let's home again. – Come, sirrah, let's
>   away.
> KATE. Nay, I will give thee a kiss. Now pray thee love, stay.
> PETRUCHIO. Is not this well? Come, my sweet Kate.
>   Better once than never, for never too late.

I can't conceive of this tender moment being played ironically, or as a cruel and possessive man bullying a cowed and repressed woman. It feels gentle, playful and completely sincere. It feels like the shared language of two people deeply in love; and the kiss when it happens – surely halfway through Kate's last line – is one of the most honestly sensual in the whole of Shakespeare. How do we get here?

Back at the beginning of the action, when Petruchio, newly arrived in Padua, and looking for a rich wife, approaches Baptista, Kate's father, there is a significant and surprisingly neglected moment. No one wants to marry Kate; everyone wants to marry Bianca, his younger daughter, whom he will 'give' to whichever suitor can prove he has the most money. There is no mention of love, or indeed any consideration of how Bianca might feel about it. Yet he says to Petruchio, the only man ever to show an interest in Kate, that he can marry her:

> Ay, when the special thing is well obtained –
> That is, her love, for that is all in all.

This is incredibly important because of what it implies. It's all too easy to assume that Bianca – sweet, quiet, biddable – is her father's favourite, and that Kate is simply a nightmare he wants to be rid of, but I prefer to think that in fact she, his firstborn, is the one he loves the most. He knows that she needs love, whereas Bianca will be satisfied with possessions: he knows she is complicated, perceptive, creative, and possessed of the imagination to see the hypocrisy of the world in valuing wealth over feelings, a distinction that his philistine younger daughter would not bother to make.

I believe the actor playing Kate should focus on the root of her anger against the world, which lies in the fact she knows what makes her sister tick. She sees through the performance. She understands that Bianca's innocent docility masks a determination to achieve high marital and social status at low emotional cost – and in the last scene this is revealed to be nothing but the simple truth. Kate has become difficult probably because she has a father without the ability to show her the way he really feels about her; she probably believes Bianca is his favourite, and this is compounded by every other man who comes into their orbit lavishing their praise on her and her alone. On another level the rivalry between siblings for parental affection, which begins the minute the new baby absorbs the attention previously bestowed solely on the firstborn child, is a classic explanation for the displaced child feeling the resentment and incomprehension that can curdle into anger. This alone would suffice as backstory to Kate's troubled and aggressive personality; but add it to a sharp awareness of her sister's phoney niceness that surfs the waves of her own stormy discontent, and you have the perfect stage for a strange and complex man to step onto with an outrageous performance of his own.

Petruchio is attracted to Kate from the moment they set eyes on each other because he sees instantly that she is just like him, and his financial motives fade into the background; at least, this has always been my starting point when working with actors on the part. Petruchio's non-textual backstory has always gone something like this: like her, he is damaged by lack of childhood love. He was brought up by a father whom he worshipped and was always trying to impress, but who never showed him any real affection in return. This father was himself damaged by the loss of his wife in childbirth, and could never forgive the baby (Petruchio) surviving while she died. He got through all his money and left his son with virtually nothing. Petruchio was torn between, on the one hand, admiration for his reckless dad, partly wanting to be like him, and, on the other hand, a realisation that that kind of behaviour had bad consequences. Buried deep within him is a longing for some kind of peace and security. His father never married again; he gambled, drank, womanised, while neglecting this little boy, his only child, who as a result grew up selfish, unloved and angry. He became the kind of man who would cynically march into town demanding to know the way to the richest unmarried daughter:

> Be she as foul as was Florentius' love,
> As old as Sibyl and as curst and shrewd
> As Socrates' Xanthippe, or a worse,
> She moves me not – or not removes at least
> Affection's edge in me – were she as rough
> As are the swelling Adriatic seas.
> I come to wive it wealthily in Padua;
> If wealthily, then happily in Padua.

Brash, sarcastic and utterly devoid of any sentiment, this is not a happy man. Love is nowhere on his agenda, he has never learnt what love is or feels like: but this all begins to change the moment he sets eyes on Kate. During the short time he's been in Padua he has already heard plenty of bad things about the woman he is about to meet, but immediately before her entrance comes the news that she just tried to seriously injure her music teacher by smashing him over the head with a brand-new lute. Although he's made it quite clear he doesn't care what she's like provided she's rich, this latest insight into her temperament must intrigue him. As he waits for her arrival alone on stage, Shakespeare gives him one of the play's rare soliloquies.

For an audience, the effect of being spoken to directly by a character can be strange, as it always involves an assumption of complicity between speaker and listener. In the case of the *Shrew*, the director has to decide how best to use this intimacy: does the actor speak to the on-stage or off-stage audience? In either case, the first rule of soliloquy applies: the speaker is thinking on their feet.

The news about the lute assault sharpens the quality of the moment and concentrates Petruchio's mind. He begins to work out the broad outlines of a little play of his own, in which his role will be a generous-spirited soul who translates whatever aggression comes his way into the polar opposite of what it seems. In effect he'll be interpreting text as subtext from his co-actor. In this play-within-a-play-within-a-play, Kate's shouting will be singing, her scowling will be smiling, her silence will be eloquence, and when she tells him to get lost, it will really be an invitation to stay. As he tells us this plan, we should feel not only his developing curiosity about her, but also his relish for an encounter with someone who will take him out of himself into a mental space that is new, challenging and incredibly exciting. He begins to feel charged with an energy that is taking him beyond the grieving son, the cynical adventurer, the swaggering new dude in town. Curiosity about another is what lifts every one of us out of the clogged and overfamiliar sponge of self-reflection.

Here is Petruchio's first soliloquy, from Act 2 Scene 1:

> I'll attend her here,
> And woo her with some spirit when she comes.
> Say that she rail, why then I'll tell her plain
> She sings as sweetly as a nightingale;
> Say that she frown, I'll say she looks as clear
> As morning roses newly washed with dew;
> Say she be mute and will not speak a word,
> Then I'll commend her volubility
> And say she uttereth piercing eloquence.
> If she do bid me pack, I'll give her thanks
> As though she bid me stay by her a week;
> If she deny to wed, I'll crave the day
> When I shall ask the banns and when be married.
> But here she comes, and now, Petruchio, speak.

Each crystal-clear antithesis beats out the excited development of his thought: 'rail'/'sings', 'frown'/'clear', 'mute'/'volubility', 'pack'/'stay'. These contrasting words are placed effortlessly as the actor's friends, guiding him towards the moment of meeting and engagement, priming the atmosphere and whetting the audience's appetite for what is to come.

He sees her just before she enters, and she enters seeing him. That essential staging is apparent from the text. But despite his last word, 'speak', I like the idea that they remain silent, simply staring at each other, for as long as director and actors feel the moment will hold. What happens to them in that silence is open to multiple interpretations. I think there is recognition, suspicion, profound curiosity, apprehension and perhaps the seeds of love. It is not, I think, a *coup de foudre*, not Romeo and Juliet lost in each other's eyes, but something stranger and more interesting. Maybe one could describe it as an intense desire to be known by the other, a perilous moment of possibility before the egos take over and discovery begins? Whatever it is, it must be highly charged, poised before the danger of speech. Words spoken can never be retrieved, and, once they begin to talk, each choice of word is latent with meaning.

Petruchio is the first to speak. He bids her good morning and calls her Kate, 'for that's your name, I hear'. This admission that he has been talking about her to others is an interesting opening gambit, as it implies she is an issue, someone worth talking about, a problem to be solved. It's bound to make her curious: who exactly has he been talking to, what did they say? The fact is that when she replies –

> Well have you heard, but something hard of hearing:
> They call me Katharina that do talk of me.

– she is speaking nothing but the truth. She has been referred to eight times by that name: four times by her father and four times by Hortensio. The only person to call her Kate up to this point has been her sister Bianca (once). Petruchio refers to her as Katharina when introducing himself to her father. Other than this, no one else uses a name, instead referring to her obliquely as 'daughter', 'devil' or 'shrew'. So Petruchio's decision to call her Kate, against the evidence of his own ears, can either be played as petty macho cussedness and a form of taking possession of her by assuming the right to use a more familiar version of her name; or as something we know to be a straightforward lie and that she knows to be a lie: in other words, to establish an alternative reality in which he knows her better than she knows herself. The names he invents that others call her could be the titles of novels about her – Plain Kate, Bonny Kate, Kate the Curst, The Prettiest Kate in Christendom, Kate of Kate Hall – and they suggest a wide range of choice as to the story. It's an invitation to invent, to play, to choose, with him, her own storyline.

Or maybe he's just being deliberately irritating.

Or maybe he's trying to make her laugh.

Or maybe he's being a dominating male chauvinist pig, effectively saying, *I'll call you what I bloody well like!*

The point I'm making is that we can't really watch a play about a male chauvinist pig taming a disturbed young woman into submission – even if that was Shakespeare's intention, or the way it would have been received and celebrated at the time. That simply isn't interesting any more. That would be some kind of psychological porn. Every bit of our brain would resist giving serious time and thought to witness such a spectacle. Kate is unhappy because her father seems to love her younger sister more, even though she's a fraud; Petruchio is unhappy because he's just lost his father and doesn't believe in love. This is surely a play about two people falling in love – and that should be a much more interesting process to watch.

In their first fraught and edgy conversation (in fact the only conversation they have alone together in the entire play) the tension between them is marked partly by the choices they make with the most innocent-seeming of words: Petruchio claiming the right to address her with the affectionate, yet vaguely patronising 'thee', 'thy' or 'thou', while she sticks doggedly and pointedly to the formal (or cold) 'you'. Petruchio first uses 'your' with his obscene joke about her leaving the room 'with my tongue in your tail' for which effort she hits him (I imagine very hard!). He responds to the blow with the line: 'I swear I'll cuff you if you strike again.' It's a strange and powerful moment: it's taken a blow to the head (I imagine the head) to make him speak to her with the respectful 'you', the term he should, socially speaking, have been using all the time, given their lack of acquaintance – yet the respectful wording lies within a sentence threatening violence. So these few seconds between the joke, the blow and the threat must change and charge the entire atmosphere of the scene. Something has happened to them that is both frightening and intimate, the stakes have risen and, though the wordplay continues, the battle of wits is now electrified with a new level of breathless curiosity: how far would each of them go? Why do they remain in each other's company?

They do so because they are both fascinated that they seem to be effortlessly creating between them a very funny scene in which they both have very good parts; they are both scriptwriters and actors in full creative flow. Here are some of the lines – guess the speaker:

> You must not look so sour –
> It is my fashion when I see a crab –
> Why here's no crab, and therefore look not sour –
> There is, there is –
> Then show it me –

Had I a glass, I would –
What, you mean my face? –
Well aimed of such a young one –
I am too young for you –
Yet you are withered –
'Tis with cares –
I care not.

You can almost feel them trying not to smile. Kate could never have this kind of repartee with Baptista or Bianca or any of the useless bunch of men who hang around their house drooling over her sister. And Petruchio seems to have no one except the coarse and predictable Grumio to exercise his sense of humour, and that relationship, as we see from their first appearance on the streets of Padua, is little better than old-stage knockabout.

Interestingly, after the blow, Petruchio begins to alternate between 'you' and 'thou' in the way he addresses her. In rehearsals actor and director should explore why this is, even if the production is set in modern times: it's the nearest you'll get to subtext in Shakespeare. The only time Kate slips into the affectionate 'thou' (which, remember, could also be mocking or downright insulting) is after Petruchio's outrageous invention that everyone in the world talks of Kate as someone who walks with a limp. By plucking this idea out of thin air, he is brilliantly parodying the fact that everyone does indeed speak badly of her, but that he sees the person no one else does. In response, Kate says: 'Go, fool, and whom thou keep'st command.' That usage can't be accidental. It must indicate that she is warming to him and for a split second lets it show. And it cannot go unnoticed by him either, as it is the trigger for the scene's final speech in which he states baldly: 'I will marry you.' As soon as all the other interested men reappear, any softening on her part is instantly put back in its place beneath the hard and bitter carapace that is her manufactured protection from the world of stupid men. But the two have found a language – private, complex, and at this moment barely explored, barely understood, but a language that will lead to mutual, true love.

I realise that a lot of this might look like wishful thinking; an attempt to dress up plain Elizabethan male sexism as something subtle, modern and even 'woke'. Or even worse, the pathetic male fantasy expressed as *She wants to be dominated because she fancies me*. It's true, some of what Petruchio says is hard to either rationalise or stomach:

> For I am he am born to tame you, Kate,
> And bring you from a wild Kate to a Kate
> Conformable as other household Kates.

I can see this as ironic (but I also often question if there is such a thing in Shakespeare). I can see it as containing the subtext that they both regard this notion of 'taming' as bourgeois and laughable (but I always question the existence of subtext in Shakespeare). But maybe, as with *The Merchant of Venice*, we have no choice but to find the ways in which our modern sensibilities redress the balance of the unacceptable assumptions (whether sexist or racist) that thrived in Shakespeare's world. But at the same time we can celebrate the fact that his plays survive for the very reason that they contain within them a guidebook out of his world and into ours, because he recognised human complexity as something living beyond any one moment of social history.

The Merchant of Venice

THE GOLDEN GIRL

At the beginning of *The Merchant of Venice* Portia's situation is bizarre. It would have seemed bizarre when the play was written (about 1596 or 1597), but now it seems bizarre verging on incomprehensible. The Elizabethan world, fast-changing and unpredictable though it was, nevertheless retained class and family structures which were profoundly patriarchal and restrictive to women, despite the way in which visitors from the continent thought of England as a 'paradise for wives'. Even in this male-dominated society Portia's predicament would be seen by the play's first audiences as something from the realm of fantasy. So how to approach this part of the plot and endow it with believability is a real challenge for the director.

Her father has recently died and left behind a document that states she may only marry a man who makes the correct choice between three caskets; one of gold, one of silver and one of lead. The winning casket contains a portrait of her – this much she knows, but not which one it is. So she is shackled to the outcome with no agency of her own; as she puts it to her waiting-woman, Nerissa, in one of her first speeches: 'I may neither choose who I would, nor refuse who I dislike, so is the will of a living daughter curbed by the will of a dead father. Is it not hard, Nerissa, that I cannot choose one, nor refuse none?'

It does seem hard – ludicrous, even – but Nerissa's reply contains the first thought that begins to bring any sense or purpose to Portia's unique situation. 'Your father was ever virtuous,' she says, 'and holy men at their death have good inspirations. Therefore the lottery that he hath devised in these three chests of gold, silver and lead, whereof who chooses his meaning chooses you, will no doubt never be chosen by any rightly but one who you shall rightly love.' Portia does not contradict this, and the thought should be allowed to hover in the air between the two women for a vital and pregnant moment on stage. The pause is essential because it's not as if Portia is not articulate enough to respond, and in the next moment Nerissa is allowed to change the subject. The beat allows us a momentary speculation about the past relationship between Portia and her father. Here a carefully worked out backstory is useful. I would suggest to the actor that it helps everything about playing the part if she decides that Portia loved her father very deeply indeed. She is made to remember that love by effectively being challenged to think about his reasoning, to remember what a good man he was, and not a monster of control trying to play pointless games with her emotional life from beyond the grave. An extremely rich young woman in her position is vulnerable to predatory men who would want to marry her not out of love but because of her wealth. This is a timeless truth about the relationship between men and women, where sex and money cloud the mind, and love is confused with desire, fame, power, even in the most honest soul. But the director needs to note something more specific than that generality, and it peeps out of the text at the very end of the scene; to me it proves her father knew exactly what he was doing and did it because he loved her.

In rehearsals it's often debated why Nerissa prompts Portia to talk about all the ghastly men who have already turned up at Belmont to try their luck, and why she then reveals that they all went, once confronted with the lottery whose terms state that a wrong choice means they must swear to a life of celibacy. She asks her: 'Do you not remember, lady, in your father's time, a Venetian, a scholar and a soldier, that came hither...?' She does: it was Bassanio, and she clearly liked him; in fact, as we later discover, loved him at first sight. The crucial phrase is 'in your father's time' – so her father met Bassanio; he witnessed the spark of love between them, the exchange of looks that Bassanio later describes to Antonio. He saw his daughter fall in love and invented the challenge of the caskets as the only way he could think of to bring them together after his death. In other words, he believed he saw in Bassanio a man who would make the right choice: someone who would understand his meaning and recognise the symbolism of lead over silver or gold, in fact might even actually learn in the course of the ordeal that if it was her gold he wanted he did not deserve her love. This interpretation needs to be threaded into the development of Bassanio, too, throughout the play, because initially he may be a little confused about his motives as he seems to want, at least in part, to make Antonio believe it's all about the money.

It is vital to the dramatic development of the sequence of 'casket scenes' that it should be clear to an audience that Portia does not know initially which is the right choice, but that it is revealed to her through the wrong choices made by Morocco and Arragon. That way the audience move through the ordeal with Portia and learn with her the wisdom that underpins the seemingly fantastical idea. By the time it comes to the turn of the man she loves, the temptation to simply tell him has to be resisted because now she needs to know that Bassanio is indeed a good choice of husband for her. That's why she can't help him; she now gets her father's point – maybe he will prove to be no more than a gold digger, and her father will have saved her from a marriage to a man simply bedazzled by her wealth and beauty while ignorant of her true worth. The father we never see must be a character as vivid in the mind of the actor playing Portia as any of the characters that we actually meet. The caskets are not a silly game: they are the way in which revelation occurs, that spirit of revelation that animates, through narrative, so many of Shakespeare's characters. She learns at the same time both about the depth of her father's love and the worthiness of the man she marries. Bassanio learns that he is capable of seeing past glitter to the humble truth of love. These learning curves advance the story by showing two young people growing in emotional intelligence and, albeit inadvertently, preparing themselves for the way they can approach the challenges of the later, darker parts of the play. In choosing lead, Bassanio has to think about the nature of what matters in life in a way that was previously impossible for him, and he discovers the right sensibility in making his choice. The director must find ways to help the actors express this perfect example of how narrative is character in development through their discovery of the right language and what, when spoken aloud, it reveals to the speaker; language fractionally ahead of thought.

Portia's comments on her male suitors, who she thinks at the beginning of the scene are still in her house waiting to try their luck in the lottery of her destiny, have several dramatic purposes. Firstly, they can be used to build up the relationship between her and Nerissa, who is clearly used to being entertained by her. Why else would Nerissa ask? It transpires they've all gone anyway, yet she doesn't want to miss the chance to encourage Portia to exercise her wit tearing them to pieces. Secondly, it provides a way of leading up to reminding Portia about Bassanio, teasing out the contrast between this handsome Venetian and the shower of idiots who seem to represent every type of hopeless male that a girl might come across. But a third reason, and for me the most important one to fix on in rehearsal, is the opportunity to highlight the fact that Portia is an extremely good actor. If one can show how much she relishes nailing these characters' idiosyncrasies, how subtly and realistically she brings them to life, then you prepare the audience for the sight of her dressed as a man striding into a court of law pretending to be a lawyer. Instead of having to suspend disbelief or shrug it off as a Shakespearean convention that you just have to swallow, the audience should think, *Well of course that's what she'd do! She's a born actor.*

That's important, but there is a little more to it. What really motivates her to assume the character of Balthazar and risk the humiliation of exposure in a highly fraught legal situation has its root in the way she responds to Bassanio's reaction to Antonio's letter, the substance of which is: *If you love me, let me see you one last time before I die.* Every atom of joy at winning Portia has disappeared from Bassanio after reading that letter from Antonio; he is utterly devastated. This clearly means something, and it means something deep. What is her future husband's relationship to this man, Antonio? Who is he? What's he like? She simply has to know whether he is a threat. And, whether he is or not, she has to contrive to save his life because otherwise his death will sour her own future. Married to a man in deep mourning at what should be the happiest time of his life? She's not having that! That would be no fun at all.

There are, of course, alternative backstories. Perhaps Portia's father never met Bassanio; he was ill in bed at the time of the visit… So much for the intuitive man who spotted the spark of love. (Hard to play, though!) Or else Portia hated her father. He was a control freak and a bully. After all, Nerissa doesn't say 'your father loved you', she just says he was 'virtuous' and 'holy'. Maybe he was a puritanical prig who thought of himself as a saint who had to restrain his hot-blooded, impulsive and theatrical daughter from having too much fun. Then again, maybe Portia both loved and feared him, hated and respected him, and all those emotions are muddled up in her mind.

Interpretations in Shakespeare are, literally, infinite. Backstories can be written in almost any way you want, but when they stray too far from the hints in the text they must remain the actor's private property, unsharable with an audience. The person you, the actor, are will be what dictates the backstory you choose in order to make Portia the character you want her to be. But, ultimately, what she *says* is who she is; that's the objective side. What the director and actor create in the rehearsal room is purely subjective, but is better if welded to the written words and the clues they reveal.

THE GOLDEN FLEECE

The two other characters – Morocco and Arragon – that we see taking the plunge in the Belmont Lottery Show, and making the choice between the gold, silver and lead caskets, dismiss lead with disdain, revealing their lack of insight. Or at least they show their lack of insight into how the mind of Portia's father worked. Anyway, bold and over-confident they may be, but they are fully briefed. It had clearly occurred to Portia's father that there needed to be conditions attached to making the choice in the first place, otherwise the queue of men would have stretched halfway down the Adriatic coast, and sooner rather than later some lucky guy would have hit on the right answer. So Morocco, Arragon and Bassanio all know before choosing that if they get it wrong they must (a) leave at once; (b) never tell another living soul which casket they chose; and (c), because neither of those two things was much of an imposition, never get married. That last one is clearly what sent the Frenchman, the Englishman, the Scotsman and the German on their way. So the Moor and the Spaniard are not lacking in boldness. How does the young Venetian come to get it right?

Bassanio, like most people, has two sides to him, and like most people these sides are brought out according to who he is with. Given the infinity of interpretation in Shakespeare, let's just look at the contrasting ways he speaks to the two people in the play that he says he loves – Antonio and Portia. In his first scene with his friend Antonio, after taking a long time to get to the point about wanting to borrow yet more money, he describes the Portia Project as, more or less, a money-making expedition: he will sail to Belmont, win the lady's hand, and come back rich, able to pay off all his debts to his friend. He needs money up front, of course, to launch this enterprise, which he makes sound as much as possible like a merchant venturer sending his ships to faraway places to return laden with valuable merchandise: the world that Antonio himself is involved in. He wants to seem responsible and fiscally mature while at the same time talking about love. Many hours will be spent in rehearsal talking about this triangle of relationships in which love and money are so inextricably entangled. When he finally gets to the point, Bassanio tells Antonio:

> In Belmont is a lady richly left,
> And she is fair and, fairer than that word,
> Of wondrous virtues.

It's impossible to know how to say these lines until director and actors have worked out exactly what the relationship between Antonio and Bassanio is – or rather, what they want to make it. This opens up a can of worms almost too large to fit in the rehearsal room, and one we'll address below when discussing the 'bond' made with Shylock, but for the time being, note the description of the lady from Belmont: first, she's rich; second, she's beautiful; third, she's, well, a really lovely person in all sorts of ways, full of 'wondrous virtues'. He needs Antonio to know all this about her, but 'rich' comes first, and he says nothing about loving her; he's already said earlier, 'To you, Antonio, / I owe the most in money and in love.' Having established she's a great catch financially, he now has to indicate that Antonio's investment is unlikely to be wasted because, he says, 'Sometimes from her eyes / I did receive fair speechless messages.' She 'gave him the eye', in other words. How hard is this for Bassanio to say? Might it discomfort his friend? Or reassure him? He now throws in a Classical reference to highlight his scholarly side:

> Her name is Portia, nothing undervalued
> To Cato's daughter, Brutus' Portia.

And then the delicate point that there is no time to lose, so the sooner he gets on with it the better for both of them:

> Nor is the wide world ignorant of her worth,
> For the four winds blow in from every coast
> Renowned suitors, and her sunny locks
> Hang from her temples like a Golden Fleece,
> Which makes her seat of Belmont Colchis' strand,
> And many Jasons come in quest of her.

Note that everyone in the world knows about 'her worth'. Does he mean her wealth or her virtue? Depending on the way the actor says this, the audience will receive a message about both his character and the nature of his relationship with his friend. He could mean either – but, of course, he could mean both. (More of that later.) He finishes his pitch for sponsorship with a promise for them both; he is doing this for the pair of them:

> O my Antonio, had I but the means
> To hold a rival place with one of them,

> I have a mind presages me such thrift
> That I should questionless be fortunate.

But apparently Antonio has already invested all his existing capital in his latest enterprise, sending out ships to the four corners of the globe so that:

> Thou knowst that all my fortunes are at sea;
> Neither have I money, nor commodity
> To raise a present sum; therefore go forth:
> Try what my credit can in Venice do,
> That shall be racked even to the uttermost
> To furnish thee to Belmont to fair Portia.

Well, *did* Bassanio know that? If he did, he seems to have forgotten, because he never brought it up when explaining his plan. But leaving that to one side, he's just said he has no money, that it's all wrapped up in the ships at sea, yet, only a few minutes ago, he had told Salanio and Salarino (two colleagues with whom he doesn't seem to have the depth of relationship that he has with Bassanio) that:

> My ventures are not in one bottom trusted,
> Nor to one place; nor is my whole estate
> Upon the fortune of this present year.

The first part of this makes sense, as we later learn that he's sent out several ships (at least six) and all in different directions – a kind of spread bet. But the second part is a contradiction; he's either lied to them or he's lying now. This contradiction should be marked in performance. It's very rare for a character to lie without Shakespeare making it very clear to the audience that that is what they are doing, Iago being the perfect example. The decision to play the line to Salanio and Salarino as an evasive white lie would be the simplest: as someone not wanting to lose face or create an occasion for gossip and rumour. But a decision to make the lie to his friend Bassanio will have enormous psychological significance for the production. Here are just a few of the implications. Antonio has had enough of being fleeced by this young man; he feels he's being made a fool of; people are beginning to talk disparagingly about the relationship; he needs to hold on to a little of his money, if only for the sake of his pride. And for the latter end of the play the implications would be emotionally seismic. Antonio could have paid Shylock the three thousand ducats before the expiry date of the bond, *but chose not to.* He embraces the idea of martyrdom for love, the idea of *literally* losing his heart for his love. Now, in any case, he has lost Bassanio to marriage. At the same time it's a public religious opportunity, the chance to demonstrate, in an almost Christlike way, the evilness of the hated Jew... Or not. This would be an extreme interpretation, admittedly, but I think a valid one, depending on the period setting and the exact nature of the Antonio/Bassanio relationship.

Whatever the truth of that relationship, Jason/Bassanio arrives at Colchis ready to claim the Golden Fleece, as it were, and is confronted with the Casket Choice. Portia pleads for him to delay so she can enjoy his company a little longer. Thanks to the failures of her previous suitors, she now knows for sure which is the right casket, so why does she not tell him? Perhaps she doesn't trust him to make the right choice? Wouldn't that be a good reason to give him a big hint? Or perhaps she doesn't trust herself and her feelings? Remember that Antonio said that his credit in Venice would be 'racked' to find the money, using the image of that most popular form of Elizabethan torture, the stretching of a naked suspect under interrogation on a rack of wood, steel, rope and wheels until the pain was so unbearable they would confess to anything. When Antonio used the image, it was as a reminder to Bassanio of how much he loved him, a metaphor of commitment and sacrifice, essentially saying, *I would do anything for you!*

Now listen to the would-be lovers of Belmont:

> BASSANIO.   Let me choose,
>   For, as I am, I live upon the rack.
> PORTIA. Upon the rack, Bassanio? Then confess
>   What treason there is mingled with your love.
> BASSANIO. None but that ugly treason of mistrust,
>   Which makes me fear th'enjoying of my love.
>   There may as well be amity and life
>   'Tween snow and fire, as treason and my love.
> PORTIA. Ay, but I fear you speak upon the rack,
>   Where men enforced do speak anything.
> BASSANIO. Promise me life and I'll confess the truth.
> PORTIA. Well then, confess and live.
> BASSANIO.   Confess and love
>   Had been the very sum of my confession.
>   O happy torment, when my torturer
>   Doth teach me answers for deliverance!

If the word 'racked' in the earlier scene has been uttered by Antonio with the passion that I think it indicates he feels, then the audience will not only have registered it at the time but will be reminded of it here where the exact same metaphor is being used with an intensity of erotic energy that creates a metaphorical loop between the three people involved in this love triangle. This is how Shakespeare uses words. They are never casual, seldom subconscious or ironic, but always electrically charged with emotional intent. There is a rawness and often a violence about Elizabethan expressiveness that we tend to shy away from now. It is intended to reveal, whereas we often use language to conceal. How Antonio says that word 'racked' needs to grip the audience by the throat, so that when they hear the term again in erotic interplay between two potential lovers, a circuit of sensual meaning is complete and the audience should gasp with the recognition of what is going on.

So our man finally gets to choose. He's lucky: he gets a song to listen to while doing the choosing, which is more than the lady laid on for poor Morocco and Arragon, now on their way home, each contemplating a life of chastity. As a prelude to their shared erotic fantasy casting of the Lady of Belmont as the torturer and her potential husband as the victim, Portia has made a lengthy speech urging Bassanio to delay his choice, at one point saying that she could tell him the right answer were it not for breaking the oath she had sworn – a swearing that we have to take on trust as we never actually see it. Then, finally, she implores him to get on with it, comparing herself to Hesione, the virgin daughter of a legendary Trojan king due to be sacrificed to a sea monster before being rescued by Hercules. (She certainly has a view of herself!) To complete the theatricality of the event, she orders music to be played: 'Then, if he lose, he makes a swan-like end, / Fading in music.' The nature of that piece of music, a song called 'Tell me where is fancy bred', gives the director an interesting two-pronged dilemma. The first three lines of the song go:

> Tell me where is fancy bred,
> Or in the heart, or in the head,
> How begot, how nourished?

The last word would have been pronounced with a strong stress on the final syllable – 'nourishèd'. It hasn't escaped notice over the last four hundred years that all three rhymed words themselves rhyme with... 'lead'. Is she giving him a clue? Well, I don't know what Shakespeare's intention was and no one ever will; but what the director does have to do is decide how to play it. The other dilemma is whether to have Bassanio listen to the whole song while examining the caskets and reading *to himself* (since the audience already know) what's written on them; or else to have the song playing while he makes his speech. The first option makes more logical sense because it gives him time to read what is written on the outsides of the caskets, so most directors naturally go for that, especially because the Folio text, with rare detail, specifies as much. But that way, he also can't avoid hearing the 'clue', if clue it is. The problem with playing him getting the rhyme as a hint, and choosing the lead casket because of it, is that none of the soliloquy in which he ponders the meaning of the choice remotely refers to it; Portia would be breaking her oath in helping him, which she has sworn she will never do; and the revelation of Bassanio's capacity for intelligent moral deduction would be fatally undermined. The point is that the caskets themselves have a point: a point about human value, about the complex relationship between money and love; a moral point about marrying someone for the wrong reasons; and a point about thinking very hard when making crucial decisions, and the importance of examining your own best and worst instincts, and recognising the difference. The idea of this kind of choice may have its origins in fable, fairy tale and fantasy, but that doesn't mean that in its essence it is not very, very real. For the director to be embarrassed by it and treat it as some kind of comedic and ridiculous game show is to totally give up on the text and its message that love is far greater than gold. Bassanio's choice is worked through in a beautiful speech, one in which he grows up from feckless boy to decent man. That's what is exciting about the scene, and – strangely enough – what can be funny about it too.

HEARTS AND BONDS

'I will have the heart of him if he forfeit,' says Shylock at the end of Act 3 Scene 1 of *The Merchant of Venice*. How did we arrive at this moment of savage intent; a man determined to literally take the heart out of another man? And who is this man, so hated by the Jew? When we first meet Antonio (whose heart is at stake) at the very beginning of the story, he is in the company of two people who seem to know him well, although we don't know how deeply or how much he trusts them: they are the aforementioned Salanio and Salarino. His first line to them (and the first line of the play) implies they have been questioning his mood, his state of mind, and that he is giving them the best answer he can:

In sooth I know not why I am so sad.

He goes on to say that he finds his sadness as wearisome as they do, but he doesn't know how he 'caught it, found it or came by it', that his melancholy makes a 'want-wit' of him, and that because of it, 'I have much ado to know myself.' They offer an explanation: he is a merchant venturer, with ships at sea loaded with valuable merchandise, and is worrying, quite naturally, about their safety, the possibility of them being wrecked in storms, broken up on rocks with their precious cargoes scattered on the waves. As we've seen, he tells them this is not so:

> My ventures are not in one bottom trusted,
> Nor to one place; nor is my whole estate
> Upon the fortune of this present year.

A statement one might examine the truth of. But true or not, it has an immediate and surprising effect. It prompts Salanio to offer another suggestion:

> Why then, you are in love.

The precise nature of Antonio's relationship with these two men is open to multiple interpretations: they can be anything from casual acquaintances with a fascination for gossip (possibly fellow merchants), to close friends who genuinely care about him and his state of mind. His reply to the idea that he may be in love tells us little about it: he says simply: 'Fie, fie.'

How he says it will tell us much more. Muttered almost inaudibly under his breath? With a chuckle and a shake of the head? With a tired and irritable sigh? With palpable astonishment? With a look of incredulity? With an explosion of anger, as if to say, *How dare you say that to me?* It feels that they have spoken out of turn and gone beyond the allowed boundaries of their relationship; broken some kind of unspoken understanding, and stepped into emotionally forbidden territory; or that they have assumed an intimacy between them that he does not share. Whichever choice you make, it should be clear that they have trespassed, touched a raw nerve and been rebuked, and Shakespeare manipulates the tension brilliantly, for – within a mere ten lines of muddled, embarrassed, barely comprehensible backtracking from Salanio – Bassanio (along with Gratiano and Lorenzo) enters, and by the timing of this narrative moment, this loaded entrance, we know Antonio and he are profoundly connected and, potentially, dramatically and dangerously so.

Throughout the Middle Ages and into the Tudor and Elizabethan eras we come across a great deal of literature that implies or even directly asserts that true, deep and unselfish love is only possible between two men. To put it crudely, this school of thought is based on the assumption that men are superior to women – physically, intellectually and emotionally! It asserts that two men may feel for each other a common identity, unqualified trust, and sense of loyalty that expresses itself in a love that is pure because free of any element of sensuality or erotic desire. This pure love was deemed impossible with a woman because (a) women didn't have the depth of soul, and (b) sex would always get in the way. This rubbish was around for many centuries, and it is an aspect of Shakespeare's genius that he had the skill to refute it by creating plays of such genuine insight into the reality of the relations between men and women that he helped shift forever the worst and most misguided notions about the nature of love. Is *The Merchant of Venice* part of this quantum shift? If so, how does that play out in the relationship between Antonio and Bassanio, and what did he conceive that relationship to be? Let's look at a few of the alternatives.

First, it's important to say that the two characters may not view their friendship in the same way; but one possibility is that they do, and that their terms of reference are explicitly drawn from the cultural tradition described above. This could be what Shakespeare intended, and, in a production set in a medieval or Renaissance world, to explore that option in rehearsal, while researching the literature surrounding the male friendship tradition, might lead to a very comfortable relationship between actor and text. It would mean that Antonio and Bassanio felt the situation in the same way, completely understood each other's feelings on every step of the emotional journey from Venice to Belmont to courtroom in pursuit of the objective they both shared: the successful marriage of Bassanio to Portia, resulting in a loving union and a freedom from debt. Love and Money in happy-ever-after harmony.

So that's one end of a spectrum of infinite options. A starting point. A thesis. What might the antithesis be? Would the above interpretation work in a modern-dress production? If not, why not? But the answer to that depends on many other factors.

For the antithesis, let's focus our imagination on a production set very much in the now: a modern Venice, perhaps even with mobile phones, but without the tourists. (That's the beauty of theatre: you can do anything!) In this treatment, Bassanio and Antonio are lovers. Apart from the body language between them, which might be explored during rehearsals, there are plenty of lines in the text that can be played making sense of that: the Elizabethan language of friendship used between men was intimate and deeply affectionate. So what we would be seeing in their first scene together, as Bassanio asks his partner for yet another loan, is a kind of break-up.

When they are finally alone, having got rid of Gratiano and Lorenzo at last, the first thing Antonio says is:

> Well, tell me now, what lady is the same
> To whom you swore a secret pilgrimage,
> That you today promised to tell me of?

Can you hear nervousness in that question? A slight irritation? A tightness of vocal tone? The audience learn from it an important fact: this is a meeting Antonio has been preparing for, perhaps even dreading. He knows there is a girl involved, a 'lady', that his lover wants to talk to him about. What could this mean? Exactly what has been said between them, and when, should be clearly established by the actors, maybe using improvisation, if that's part of the director's rehearsal method. Even more significant is to start the discussion about whether the line holds the clue to Antonio's state of mind as revealed in his first speech: 'In sooth I know not why I am so sad.' Is his 'sadness' directly the result of his boyfriend saying something like *Next Tuesday I need to talk to you about this girl I've met*? Or is he describing a persistent melancholic state of mind that he truly doesn't understand? Whichever it is, if director and actors play these two men as lovers on the verge of a radical change to their relationship that may mean either a total split or a reorganised social and sexual schedule, there is a lot they leave unsaid in the dialogue Shakespeare has written. But that's all right. In our modern lives important things are often left unsaid, sometimes for better, sometimes for worse. Although I'm always keen to stress that subtext is absent from Shakespeare, that doesn't mean that in certain circumstances it can't be invented if the dramatic pay-off is big enough.

If as a director you are looking beyond the two polarities of best friends or gay lovers, the most obvious interpretation of the Antonio and Bassanio relationship (and the one perhaps closest to Shakespeare's own thinking) is to see Antonio as an older man in denial about the sexual attraction he feels for his younger friend: is he a repressed homosexual, a classic victim of 'the love that dare not speak its name'? (Mind you, I don't know why he is often perceived to be older; there is nothing in the text to suggest this.) Bassanio becomes in this reading a heterosexual man who cannot see, or does not want to see, the emotional turmoil of his supposedly older friend.

On top of this (or indeed any other) way of seeing the two men is the complicating issue of class. The younger man is clearly significantly above his friend in the social hierarchy. He is from the upper classes, perhaps even minor aristocracy, and often referred to as 'Lord', although in the context of seventeenth-century Venice this is a slippery term referring more to an English than a Venetian reality. Antonio is the eponymous hero – the merchant of Venice – and merchants were from middle-class backgrounds. It's important to remember that Shakespeare's imaginary city is really a palimpsest of English and Italian social structures. In Elizabethan England successful merchants were some of the wealthiest men in the country, often far wealthier than the aristocracy, a fact that was the cause of confusion, tension and social unease. The text seems to suggest that Bassanio is a young man from a 'noble' family who has squandered his inheritance and gone on to spend a large slice of his 'friend's' money as well. If the director suggests something like this as the backstory of the two characters (whether in period or modern dress), then the main issue in rehearsal would be to explore how much Antonio tries to reveal or conceal the truth of his feelings, and to what degree Bassanio is either genuinely blind to them, or artfully pretending not to notice. If the latter, then his behaviour is cruel on some level. To ask for yet more money in order to pursue an objective that he knows will be painful to his friend is either callousness or wilful blindness. To say that he is doing it for both of them for their financial gain is pure hypocrisy. If you don't want him to be devious, then you have to play him as genuinely unaware of his friend's feelings for him, once you've decided those feelings exist. In exploring this particular version of the relationship you can begin to unearth a rich complexity. Antonio both does and doesn't want to be known: after all, as he has said at the very top of the play, 'I have much ado to know myself.' And Bassanio both does and doesn't fully understand what he has got into with this melancholic rich man from a lower stratum of society whose friendship he desperately needs. Sometimes it's as if the truth is actually changing moment by moment, and the challenge of playing is to let the audience see and fully understand exactly what is going on between them as they struggle to understand each other. But you need to be cautious – it's possible to get too clever, too complex, so that in their conversation about the lady of Belmont all the audience experience is confusion, a vague sense of bewilderment and a sensation of being excluded from some private game they don't know the rules of. The fact is that the scene in which they discuss Portia, the money and the plan (with no mention of love, by the way) is the only scene they have together in the whole play, apart from an exchange of four lines after Shylock's exit when the 'bond' has been agreed. (All these decisions about this central relationship, which actually takes up a very small percentage of the text, would be the same, however the parts are cast. The characters could both be female, but the same choices would apply.)

Antonio ends his conversation with Bassanio like this:

> Thou knowst that all my fortunes are at sea;
> Neither have I money, nor commodity
> To raise a present sum; therefore go forth:
> Try what my credit can in Venice do,
> That shall be racked even to the uppermost
> To furnish thee to Belmont to fair Portia.
> Go presently enquire, and so will I,
> Where money is, and I no question make
> To have it of my trust, or for my sake.

Assuming he is telling the truth – and the way the narrative unfolds suggests he is – this is quite an admission. Here is one implication: Bassanio has more or less cleaned him out, and to get back on an even keel financially Antonio has invested literally every penny he has left in a few ships that are all at sea on trading missions to places as diverse as England, Mexico and the West Indies (details we later learn from Shylock). So if Bassanio wants money, he will have to go and borrow it from someone else using Antonio's name as collateral. Antonio is clearly imagining that fellow merchants within the Christian community will oblige, but, equally clearly, he is wrong, because they both end up at the mercy of his worst enemy, Shylock the Jewish moneylender. If improvisation is part of the director's process, useful time might be spent imagining scenes between various Christian merchants comparing notes on their conversations with Bassanio. As they have all refused loans, they must all take a very negative view of the relationship between their fellow merchant and this young spendthrift aristocrat who seems to have such a hold over his heart and mind. The humiliation Antonio feels when he finds out who Bassanio has finally approached to borrow money is the fuel for the anger and hatred that pours out of him in Act 1 Scene 3.

Anger often springs from fear, and for someone like Antonio, the greatest fear may be the fear of ridicule. He and his friend have been going around Venice trying to borrow money and have ended up in the company of a man whom Antonio has abused, mocked and railed against in public and even spat upon in front of other traders on the Rialto, while delivering impromptu sermons to anyone who will listen on the evils of moneylending for profit. Usury was the greatest Christian complaint against the Jews apart from the crucifixion itself. I think Antonio is beside himself with fury when he finds Bassanio and Shylock discussing the loan of three thousand ducats. As he enters, Shylock turns and speaks to the audience (one of the few soliloquies in the play).

This speech generates several key motivational questions, but the most basic is purely practical: what do the two Christians actually do during Shylock's lengthy aside? Do they converse silently, and if so what are they 'saying'? Or do they just stare at each other? Has Bassanio hoped to get away with meeting Shylock without Antonio finding out about it, or have they pre-arranged to meet here? If he hoped to secure the loan and get out before Antonio discovered where he was, how has Antonio found out? Does Bassanio know the extent of Antonio's public attitude to Shylock in particular and usury in general?

The most important questions of all are: what is the full meaning of Shylock's soliloquy? And what are its consequences for the rest of the play?

> How like a fawning publican he looks.
> I hate him for he is a Christian;
> But more, for that in low simplicity
> He lends out money gratis, and brings down
> The rate of usance here with us in Venice.
> If I can catch him once upon the hip,
> I will feed fat the ancient grudge I bear him.
> He hates our sacred nation, and he rails,
> Even there where merchants most do congregate,
> On me, my bargains and my well-won thrift,
> Which he calls 'interest'. Cursed be my tribe
> If I forgive him.

On the surface, the meaning, sentiment and intention are plain enough. Shylock hates this man for the abuse he's suffered from him; and here he sees a perfect, almost God-sent, opportunity for revenge. For him, the situation is almost too good to be true, and Shakespeare, by giving Shylock this speech to the audience, has signposted how to interpret the scene. Shylock's intention is the entrapment of his old enemy. He cleverly wrong-foots him by saying he will not take any interest on the loan – an offer that astonishes Antonio. Instead Shylock makes a black joke about their mutual hatred which he wants to turn into a friendship: if Antonio defaults, Shylock will have a pound of his flesh. He says he's only joking: what good would a pound of human flesh be to him? No, it's purely to 'buy his favour I extend this friendship'. But he's a lying, devious Jew, and sure enough, when Antonio eventually fails to repay the money, Shylock does demand the pound of flesh, which by now has been specifically documented in the bond as 'nearest to his heart'. The payment will inevitably result in his enemy's death, the outcome he had hoped for all along. Simple. No problem with motivation: Shylock is evil, Antonio is a brave, loyal friend prepared to sacrifice himself for love.

I don't think so!

There are many problems with this easy equation. Some of them are connected with the radical difference between our modern sensibilities and those of our Elizabethan ancestors. Some of them are to do with a post-Holocaust revulsion at all expressions of anti-Semitism and a moral repugnance against the idea of caricaturing a man as 'a lying, devious Jew'. Some of the problems are rooted in the text. But the possibility of a very different interpretation indeed does exist. Sometimes I feel that Shakespeare wrote for three audiences simultaneously, and *The Merchant of Venice* is one of the best examples of this. The first audience is the majority: people of all classes – tradesmen, merchants, courtiers, secret Catholics, Protestants, city folk, country folk, etc. – all of whom would share the basic, never discussed assumptions of the time; that God existed, the sun went round the earth, the monarch was God's representative on that earth, hanging people publicly was necessary for the rule of law… and Jews were devious liars. The second audience was a minority: intelligent and sensitive people of all classes and walks of life who didn't necessarily believe in any of those things and who could hear in Shakespeare a gentler and wiser voice than the mass of common thought usually expressed. And finally, perhaps without even realising it, he was speaking to a future audience. To us. As Ben Jonson put it in his dedicatory poem in the First Folio, 'He was not of an age, but for all time.'

So let's explore another version of what might be going on in this scene, beyond the lying Jew entrapping the honest Christian. Just before Antonio arrives, Shylock has asked if it would be possible to speak to him about the loan, and Bassanio has suggested they have a meal together, just the three of them. This suggests that Antonio did know of Bassanio's intention to visit the moneylender and so his arrival doesn't come as too big a surprise, uncomfortable as it might be. Rather, it will be Shylock who is amazed to see Antonio walk into the scene, and Shylock's aside to the audience is in part a response to the shock of it, utterly instinctive, based on his present state of mind and utterly in the moment. The next thing that happens is that Shylock pretends not to have noticed Antonio come in and continues talking to Bassanio as if they were still alone together for six and a half lines, finally addressing his rival with the faux-astonished 'Rest you fair, good signior, / Your worship was the last man in our mouths.' It's a great line for showing that Portia isn't the only natural actor in the play, although Antonio is not having any of it, going straight on the attack with:

> Shylock, albeit I neither lend nor borrow
> By taking nor by giving of excess,
> Yet, to supply the ripe wants of my friend,
> I'll break a custom.

It's as if Antonio feels he instantly has to address the irony of their situation by stating awkwardly and pointlessly his attitude to usury, an attitude Shylock knows only too well. But it's the reason he gives that can change things when he says he will contradict the beliefs of a lifetime for the sake of his 'friend'. Listen to the sound of that line: 'Yet, to supply the ripe wants of my friend…' What does Shylock *see* when he hears this rather lush explanation? An awkward young man blushing and staring at the ground with a tense, prickly, agitated older man by his side, taking over the meeting with an unconvincing and uncomfortable briskness? Does Shylock see a man hopelessly in love? A man far from his Rialto Bridge comfort zone where he can rail against usury to an audience of merchant admirers, while a humiliated Jew shrinks back against the parapet? Does the seed of something take root here? Does Shylock perhaps sense Antonio's own burden of 'otherness', of a different nature but of equal weight to his own?

It may be fanciful to try to create a moment of identification or even empathy, but one thing is certain: Shylock has never seen Antonio like this before, and the scene takes a very strange turn when they begin to discuss the issue of usury. 'Methought you said you neither lend nor borrow / Upon advantage,' Shylock says, to which Antonio brusquely replies: 'I do never use it.' What follows is a passage of dialogue about a story from the Old Testament that both men (Christian and Jew) would have been familiar with since childhood. This tale of Jacob, Laban and

the sheep – from a book sacred in both their religions and which Shylock brings up in defence of the practice of usury – means that for a
brief few minutes they are actually having a theological discussion
about a shared text. Their interpretations differ, but the material is
equally well known to both of them. It feels like Shylock is seeking out
common ground, quoting a piece of scripture to make Antonio feel
better about the situation they are in and to ease his conscience about
paying interest. It is possible for the actor playing Shylock to colour the
two Jacob speeches as an attempt at friendliness rather than deceit: in
fact it's very hard to see how telling the story of Laban's sheep could
serve any deceptive purpose at all. It doesn't work, of course. Antonio
ends the discussion with the sarcastic and scathing:

> The devil can cite Scripture for his purpose.
> An evil soul producing holy witness
> Is like a villain with a smiling cheek,
> A goodly apple, rotten at the heart.
> O, what a goodly outside falsehood hath!

Shylock ignores this and returns to talking about money and the rate
of interest, and, after one more burst of sarcasm from the merchant,
once again something seems to change – one of those subtle psychological shifts in the interpersonal atmosphere. Shylock seems to sigh,
to become clear-headed and calm, to take his time; and he makes one
of the great speeches of the play. There are many ways of navigating this
speech, which begins:

> Signior Antonio, many a time and oft
> In the Rialto you have rated me
> About my moneys…

But in the course of it, the speaker moves from naming the amount of
interest to be paid on the loan, which he is about to do, to making the
extraordinary offer that there should be no interest paid at all. In the
speech Shylock is basically, with great wit, pointing out the absurdity
of the situation: *You call me a dog, kick me and spit on me, and then
come round here asking me to lend you money. That's crazy!*

I think it is during this speech that Shylock begins to form the idea
of the pound of flesh. As he delivers the offer he uses the words 'kind'
and 'friendship' to describe it. He calls it a 'merry bond', and at one
point he says: 'I would be friends with you and have your love.' What if
he is telling the truth? What if he means it – that he would prefer

friendship to hatred, to be respected rather than spat on? What if the idea of taking a piece of his enemy's flesh is no more than a bitter black joke? He knows how humiliated in front of his peers Antonio will feel if word gets round, as it will, that he is paying interest to a Jew to raise money to finance his friend's marriage project. Shylock is giving Antonio a way of saving face and at the same time letting him know that he understands him, understands his feelings for this beautiful young man. And I think for a brief moment Antonio realises that he is understood and is grateful for it:

> Content, in faith: I'll seal to such a bond
> And say there is much kindness in the Jew.

How can Shylock possibly imagine anyway that the merchant adventurer's entire fleet of huge and majestically seaworthy ships, all in different parts of the world, would every single one be wrecked, when a fraction of the goods on only one of them would bring in enough to repay the three thousand ducats? I believe if you play the 'pound of flesh' bond as a knowing joke containing a plea for friendship, or at least acceptance, the play is deepened and enriched. What is more, the subplot, involving the elopement of Jessica with Lorenzo, a friend of Antonio, in pursuit of a Christian lifestyle, creates a perfect dramatic fulcrum for the plot. It was a joke until his daughter was stolen from him, and then it became deadly serious: 'I will have the heart of him, if he forfeit.' A bitter pledge to vengefully slaughter the Jew-hater has taken the place of the timid offer of friendship and acceptance.

Hamlet

HAMLET'S ACT

One of the most fascinating aspects of Shakespeare's writing is the way in which he transformed his source material. Part of the key to creating good productions out of the scripts is for director and actors to reach a common understanding as to why he made the changes he did and what lay behind those choices. The single most significant change to the medieval story of Amleth the Viking prince was the addition of a group of travelling actors. Much of the play is about acting and the different meanings of that word. It is about acting in the sense of doing, committing an act, making a decision and turning it into an action; in this case, Hamlet avenging his father's death by murdering his murderer. It's also about acting in the sense of dissimulation – acting in life by pretending to be something other than you really are. Hamlet acts being mad, Claudius acts being a loving stepfather and an honest man, but as his nephew observes, 'a man may smile and smile and be a villain'. And then at the very centre and heart of the play, exactly halfway through, it becomes about the art of theatre acting, the imitation of life on a stage, telling a dramatic story to shock, entertain, inform or, sometimes, to reveal the truth.

The character, Hamlet, spends much of the play, *Hamlet*, pretending to be mad – acting. So the actor playing Hamlet has to figure out the best way to act Hamlet acting. It's a similar challenge when playing Viola or Rosalind – how to 'act' the male character they each assume. Sane Hamlet's performance as mad Hamlet is in itself a lesson in acting, which is one of the reasons it's such a satisfying play to work on with actors: it deals with the subject of acting in a wholly original way. Playing Hamlet makes the actor think precisely about how to mould their own spirit and personality into an imaginary character who both is and is not them. His purpose is to survive, discover the truth and then act upon it: the situation is deadly serious and his capacity to act convincingly is tested to the limit, causing him to verge on becoming the person he is pretending to be. Taken seriously, acting can be a dark, difficult and even dangerous art form, especially when undertaken with a subjective rather than an objective purpose. To overindulge in it as personal therapy, to take one's own inner workings too self-importantly, can easily lead to the actor getting in the way of the play, of the author's purpose. But at the other extreme, to over-objectify, to behave as if the actor's job is simply to learn the lines, speak clearly and let the play do the rest, is damagingly to minimise the way in which an individual's spirit and personality, if sharply focused, can animate a written character into active life. *Hamlet* can make us more alert to the nature, purpose and potential of acting than any treatise ever written on the subject, while at the same time being a ghost story, a revenge tragedy, a love story, a religious debate, a philosophic exploration of appearance and reality, madness and sanity, and the meaning of life and death. Quite a hefty checklist! Acting, as a problematic idea, is present from early in the play, not only in Gertrude's implication that her son may be *overplaying* his grief, or the Prince's reference to his uncle's false smiles, but in the very fabric of its central question: what is the ghost? To understand the importance of this question, the director needs to be clear about one of the central issues that dominated the intellectual and theological debates of the Elizabethan age.

The Catholic–Protestant divide had created a national schizophrenia of belief in many ways and in many minds, and one of the profoundest and most contentious was the difference between the Catholic and Protestant visions of the afterlife, of Heaven and Hell. For the devout Catholic there were three possibilities for the human soul after death. For those who had led a blameless and God-fearing life, full of good deeds and regular worship combined with deep faith, the prize was Heaven, salvation and eternal bliss. For those who had led a life of sin, selfishness and indulgence with little thought of God or consequences, the price was Hell, eternal damnation. But the Catholic Church had to face up to an obvious fact: for the vast majority of people, the life they'd lived had not been quite so cut and dried. Most people did good things and bad things. Sometimes they behaved well, and other times not so well. People would go through periods of religiosity and times when they didn't think much about religion at all. Sometimes they would pray, sometimes they would sin, and their lives passed by in a messy mixture of aspiring to the angelic, then sinking to the bestial, bouncing around in the human section of the great chain of being: a 'mingled yarn' woven of the good, the bad and the indifferent. So the Catholic Church invented the idea of Purgatory. Here was the third afterlife option, a sort of halfway house between Hell and Heaven, a supernatural prison term in which accounts could be settled for sins committed and a balance worked out between punishment and redemption. Souls were cleansed and purged to prepare them for Heaven. This was a clever idea and led to a huge trade between men and monks, who, having plenty of time on their hands, were paid to pray for the dead to shorten the time spent in Purgatory. Those who believed in the Catholic way – and there were still plenty of them in 1600 when *Hamlet* was written – heard the voices of the souls of their dead relatives (mothers, fathers, grandmothers, grandfathers, sons and daughters) crying out to them from this theatre of suffering and paid the prayer-mongers what they could.

Almost everyone in Christian Europe at the time of Shakespeare believed in a life after death, but their spiritual leaders disagreed about its nature. The Catholic idea of a clearing house for different degrees of sinners was anathema to the religious reformers of the Lutheran revolution. Protestants had no time for the concept of Purgatory. They believed that you were either damned or saved. They believed God knew what lay in your heart with an instant and infallible judgement and had no need for flexible periods of post-life torture as a prelude to Paradise. Nor (and most significantly for our play) did the Protestants believe in ghosts, and theirs was the official state religion. At least, they didn't believe in ghosts in the Catholic sense, that it might be the spirit of a dead person who had returned to earth to give warnings, or offer advice, or make requests. To them, a ghost was a demonic spirit, come from Hell to lure you into error or sin on behalf of their master, Satan. A ghost was a special kind of demon performing the part of a particular dead soul. A ghost was always acting.

Or was it? The old and new beliefs snaked and threaded their way through the consciences of Shakespeare's audience. Confusing, contradictory and terrifying, a restless uncertainty must have shrouded the thinking of a huge proportion of the population. In the most famous speech of all, when he asks 'in that sleep of death what dreams may come', Hamlet was speaking for an awful lot of people. Whatever else might be said about the afterlife, whatever it consisted of, it was there waiting for you, one way or the other. Most people accepted that judgement was inevitable in the end, and on the whole they probably tended to go along with the messages that issued from Protestant pulpits every compulsory church-attending Sunday of the year. So what were they, and what are we, to make of the ghost of Hamlet's father?

> I am thy father's spirit
> Doomed for a certain term to walk the night,
> And for the day confined to fast in fires,
> Till the foul crimes done in my days of nature
> Are burnt and purged away.

The description is pure Catholic theology. Either the ghost is speaking the truth and bearing witness to an afterlife that is just as Catholic theology would describe it, or he is lying and is therefore the kind of demon actor that Protestant authority would caution against. So right at the beginning of the play we have the main character placed in a dilemma that is all about acting. Is it really his father returned, or a dissembling spirit?

Hamlet recognises the problem, but he loathes his uncle and wants to believe the ghost, and his immediate instinct is to act on the demand for revenge. Acting these initial reactions to this first encounter with the ghost is about capturing the agonisingly paradoxical nature of the character's situation. He seems to know himself well enough to be aware that he's a man who tends to wear his heart on his sleeve and finds it difficult to conceal strong emotion. His problem is how to control that emotion and contain it, so he doesn't reveal what he has learnt and risk becoming another victim of his murderous uncle. On the other hand, how can he be sure that the ghost is telling the truth? His solution is to act. Not act on the ghost's request, but to act the part of a lunatic. By seeming to have gone mad, he can channel the turmoil of his feelings into a performance that will make him appear harmless. The grief for his father's death, the anger towards his uncle, the revulsion and jealousy he feels towards his mother, can all be poured into an 'antic disposition' that will keep him safe. It should work because it was a commonplace of Elizabethan thinking that grief was a primary cause of madness.

Assuming that actor and director broadly agree on this, the question will be how to make Hamlet's thinking clear to an audience. The whole theme of 'acting' needs to be set up from the text's earliest references to it, and emphasis placed on these moments will generate awareness. The question of acting has come up well before Hamlet meets his father's ghost or the demon player. In only the second scene of the play he makes it clear he thinks his uncle/stepfather's manner towards him is fake or acted. Claudius's friendliness is a 'seeming' that makes Hamlet extremely prickly. When his mother asks him about his signs of grief without choosing her words carefully enough – 'Why seems it so particular with thee?' – he rounds on her with a caustic diatribe about acting and emotion:

> 'Seems', madam – nay it is, I know not 'seems'.
> 'Tis not alone my inky cloak, good mother,
> Nor customary suits of solemn black,
> Nor windy suspiration of forced breath,
> No, nor the fruitful river in the eye,
> Nor the dejected saviour of the visage,
> Together with all forms, moods, shows of grief,
> That can denote me truly. These indeed 'seem',
> For they are actions that a man might play.

Interestingly, the word 'actions' in the last line has become a term today for describing the intentions, or motivation, of a character in many rehearsal rooms all over the world.

Acting and religion are linked in Hamlet's state of uncertainty. He doesn't know what to believe about Claudius and doesn't know what to believe about the afterlife. He wants to believe the ghost, but he was educated at Wittenberg University, a rock-solid intellectual bastion of Lutheran and hence Protestant teaching, an education that leads him clearly to the thought that has to be at the centre of any actor's interpretation of the part:

> The spirit that I have seen
> May be the devil; and the devil hath power
> T'assume a pleasing shape. Yea, and perhaps
> Out of my weakness and my melancholy,
> As he is very potent with such spirits,
> Abuses me to damn me.

You can't forget just how alert he must be to that possibility. Rehearsals have to focus on it as a key thought which both colours and sets up much of what follows. It's a good example of character and narrative coming together at a moment in the play crucial to the clarity of the action. Hamlet is exceptionally self-aware, the exact opposite of Lear who 'hath ever but slenderly known himself'. He is honest, knows that he is prone to melancholy and that the devil can work with great effectiveness on 'spirits' such as his. If he is not shown as being acutely aware that he could be tricked into damnation by a demonic actor impersonating his dead father, then there is no reason for the introduction of the players into the play, the single most significant addition that Shakespeare made to his source material other than the ghost itself. The speech concludes:

> I'll have grounds
> More relative than this. The play's the thing
> Wherein I'll catch the conscience of the King.

His theological education cannot give him a definitive answer; only theatre can show him the truth. He develops his idea by telling us something remarkable, something that might have had a real story behind it, possibly many stories.

> I have heard
> That guilty creatures sitting at a play
> Have by the very cunning of the scene
> Been struck so to the soul that presently
> They have proclaimed their malefactions.
> For murder, though it have no tongue, will speak
> With most miraculous organ. I'll have these players
> Play something like the murder of my father
> Before mine uncle. I'll observe his looks;
> I'll tent him to the quick. If he but blench,
> I know my course.

The whole idea is, of course, triggered by the arrival of a company of travelling actors that he appears to know well, greeting them as old friends and sharing the latest theatrical gossip with them. They've barely got there before he is imploring them to act something for him, instantly becoming immersed in the leading actor's performance – a speech about the grief of Queen Hecuba during the fall of Troy. It's while he listens to this speech that director and actor need to locate the exact moment the idea, of establishing Claudius's guilt or innocence by monitoring his reactions to a play, comes to him. Normally ideas should strike characters in the moment of speech; but in this case it seems to me that the audience need to register something earlier, something that is then developed in the soliloquy just quoted. The audience will then feel complicit in the idea rather than it appearing arbitrary. It should almost be as if the audience have put the idea into Hamlet's head.

As the actors are shown to their lodgings, Hamlet takes the leader of the troupe aside, asking him if he remembers an old play, *The Murder of Gonzago*, and would he mind the addition of a few extra lines of his own composition? This is agreed, then alone on stage he tells us the plan.

This play-within-a-play is a major new element to the old tale of Amleth. It's remarkable not only for its theatricality but for what it indicates about the place and importance of theatre in England at the time. Apparently there is good evidence that on at least one occasion 'guilty creatures sitting at a play' had indeed 'proclaimed their malefactions'. A woman who had paid two professional hit men to murder her husband, watching a performance at the theatre of what may have been *Arden of Faversham* (a play about precisely that), broke down in hysterics and screamed out her confession to the amazement of audience and actors. This was the mirror of theatre held up to nature in a shockingly dramatic way. Exposure to the kind of passionate yet realistic acting that the new drama demanded could be a kind of shock therapy to ordinary people never before exposed to anything like it. For most people it was completely novel to be confronted with truths about themselves and their private thoughts. In a sense, actors began to have more psychological power than priests, and more moral authority than the royal court, and probably more than the law courts, as well. This capacity to tell the truth in an emotional and often disturbing way might sometimes have been too much for some people to take. At the end of the 'Hecuba' speech, Polonius reacts to what he's just heard in words that seem genuinely shocked and slightly disgusted, as if something faintly improper had just taken place: 'Look whe'er he has not turned his colour and has tears in's eyes. Prithee no more!' It's as if he responds to that degree of emotion in acting as tasteless because it's hard to tell where artifice ends and reality begins – and maybe also because it has created an unwanted emotional response in himself. Hamlet knows the power of acting to get to the truth:

> Good my lord, will you see the players well bestowed? Do
> you hear, let them be well used, for they are the abstract and
> brief chronicles of the time. After your death you were better
> have a bad epitaph than their ill report while you live.

His plan works perfectly. The performance the players give has exactly the effect on Claudius he was hoping for, although strangely it is never clear which lines were the ones he added. The King's reaction clearly reveals his guilt, so nothing now stands in the way of the revenge demanded by (what he now knows to be) his father's spirit. So the ghost was telling the truth: he is an 'honest' ghost. The narrative of the play therefore seems to uphold a Catholic point of view. It seems to underline what Hamlet has said to his fellow student at the Protestant Wittenberg University:

> There are more things in heaven and earth, Horatio,
> Than are dreamt of in our philosophy.

The clear implication is that the Catholic version of the afterlife is the correct one. But if that's true, then his father is leading his soul to eternal damnation by inciting him to an act of murderous revenge. You would be confused, wouldn't you – and a little hesitant? But that's another story.

HAMLET'S PROOF

The sudden ending of *The Murder of Gonzago* and the King's frantic exit would seem to give Hamlet all the proof he needs that the ghost was speaking the truth. This would imply a bigger truth vindicating Catholic beliefs about life after death. There is a delicate choice to be made in the way an actor interprets Hamlet's reaction to Claudius's exit. Some questions for both character and player: is the nature of the exit ('Give me some light, away') really definitive proof of guilt? Could it not also be interpreted as the blind fury of a deeply insulted man responding to an appalling public accusation; anger despite innocence? Hamlet's weird chanting of childlike jingles could be played ambivalently, as if confusedly trying to convince himself he'd got to the truth, rather than the hysteria of triumph. In any case, at this point in the play Claudius's act of good-natured well-meaning to his nephew has finally broken down, and although there's another possible explanation for his dramatic exit, it's very understandable why Hamlet gets so excited. But is the moment as revelatory for the audience as it is for him? No. We have not actually been in the same state of uncertainty as he has. He still only had the ghost's word for it, who, up until this moment may still be a devil seeking to lead a soul to damnation. But we, on the other hand, have been privy to the King's private thoughts in the form of an aside in Act 3 Scene 1. Polonius says:

> 'Tis too much proved, that with devotion's visage
> And pious action we do sugar o'er
> The devil himself.

And then Claudius turns to us and says:

> O, 'tis true.
> How smart a lash that speech doth give my conscience.
> The harlot's cheek, beautied with plastering art,
> Is not more ugly to the thing that helps it
> Than is my deed to my most painted word.
> O heavy burden!

So we, the audience, arrive at the play-within-a-play knowing that every word Old Hamlet's ghost said was true. His son does not. Our position of knowing more than the hero is why we accept his post-play behaviour as the reactions of a man freed from doubt; we would find low-key ambivalence puzzling and unconvincing. This is how directors and actors narrow choices – by forensic examination of the evidence in the text. So the text is the only true guide, but where does that leave background historical information? Is it really helpful in rehearsal to think about whether or not Catholic beliefs are being upheld, while Protestant ones are thrown into doubt? And if so, how could you play that? How could an actor ever hope to communicate, to a modern audience, points of Elizabethan theology that most people these days know nothing about and care even less? And what difference does it make that to the Globe audience in 1600 it would have been a massive issue of interest and perhaps even the entire point of the play? I don't know; perhaps it's useless even to try to imagine the furious rows that may have erupted between friends and among families on the way home from the theatre. But I do know that, for the actor playing Hamlet, every single line and thought that touches on the question has to feel like ice and fire fighting in their veins. The audience will only receive its significance through the intensity of the performance.

Meanwhile, what of the murderer? When we see Claudius alone, on his knees attempting to pray, we have double confirmation of his guilt. What should his situation evoke in us? We are the only witnesses to the agony of his conscience in this moment, and it is a deeply unsettling experience:

> O, my offence is rank: it smells to heaven;
> It hath the primal eldest curse upon't –
> A brother's murder. Pray can I not,
> Though inclination be as sharp as will.

In the same way as Shakespeare, throughout his work, shades comedy into tragedy, and tragedy into comedy, so here he bleeds the proof of villainy into an aching pity. Playing Claudius truthfully in this soliloquy is to show him as lost, frightened and made utterly vulnerable by the thought that he has passed beyond redemption. At the start of the play he should appear so plausible that the ghost's story seems unlikely. Directors and actors are battling against a huge weight of knowledge with a play as well known as *Hamlet*, which carries with it an extra amount of hard work, the purpose of which is to make every member of the audience doubt what they think they know and to see the play for the first time, even if they have seen it several times before.

It's true that a man or woman might smile a lot yet have a cruel, even criminal nature. People in general are seldom exactly what they seem, and every one of us, to a certain extent, acts the part of ourselves. We are our own creation that we play to the world. The way we 'act' in life illuminates for the actor how to play Hamlet, who spends so much of his story acting. I've always found it so strange that the question 'Is Hamlet really mad or only pretending to be?' never quite goes away when the text makes it crystal clear. He tells his best friend, Horatio, perfectly plainly, shortly after his first meeting with the ghost, that from that moment he will put on 'an antic disposition'. It's an idea taken directly from the original story of Amleth. There the hero poses as insane in order to appear harmless and thereby stay safe. Like Claudius he's pretending to be someone he isn't to gain advantage. What he produces is a performance good enough, 'real' enough, to convince his mother, his sister and the crafty and suspicious Polonius, who seems to know a thing or two about duplicity, that he really has gone mad. Possibly at times he is so deeply into this act that it begins to feel real even to himself, and he wonders if he might actually be going mad, but at any moment he's able to flick the switch to become himself again. Only Claudius seems to have doubts, which is a richly ironic and beautifully balanced dramatic situation as he is the only other character also giving a major performance. The two 'actors' instinctively doubt one another.

As both men try to prepare themselves for action a moral confusion begins to emerge which needs to be confronted and dealt with in the rehearsal room as it has a bearing on Hamlet's motivation and evolving state of mind. It is a dilemma that Shakespeare appears not to have worried about or tried to solve, as Hamlet himself never addresses it, despite being highly sensitive and deeply intellectual. It's the kind of lapse in psychological consistency that simply didn't bother the Elizabethans, but that modern actors have to find a way of resolving.

In the profoundly Christian world of early modern England, revenge
was seen as solely the prerogative of God. Old Hamlet's plea from
beyond the grave that his son should avenge his death is therefore
deeply un-Christian. This paradox may explain the way in which, after
the proof provided during the play-within-the-play, Hamlet speaks a
soliloquy of an untypically crude and bloodthirsty tone, as if trying to
conjure up the killer in himself. Convinced beyond further doubt that
his uncle killed his father, he says:

> 'Tis now the very witching time of night
> When churchyards yawn and hell itself breathes out
> Contagion to this world. Now could I drink hot blood
> And do such bitter business as the day
> Would quake to look on.

These are the first 'sane' words he has spoken for some time. So long as
he was acting madness, the performance came easily to him. He was so
mentally churned up that the pretence of lunacy acted as a safety valve,
or a way of expressing his real emotions without giving away what he
knew. As with any actor, the drawing on real feelings about his mother,
uncle, father and girlfriend, fed directly into the authenticity of his performance. Now the time for acting is past and the time for action has
arrived. Now he needs to find the assassin within him and lose, if only
temporarily, the University Intellectual. His new part, the Revenger, was
a contemporary favourite.

However, the actor playing Hamlet has to figure out why the character doesn't express, and so presumably doesn't feel, the dilemma
mentioned earlier. The ghost has seemed to be a repentant spirit, so
how can it ask him to take on God's role and become a murderer putting his own immortal soul in danger? The clever student from
Wittenberg must know the Bible with its clear statement: 'Vengeance is
mine: I will repay, saith the Lord.' That piece of spiritual instruction is
strangely ignored by the same man who elsewhere speaks so eloquently
on the Christian prohibition of suicide wishing that 'the Everlasting had
not fixed / His canon 'gainst self-slaughter'. Even Laertes, who is no
one's idea of a deep thinker, has to admit to himself that to avenge his
own father's murder is to 'dare damnation'. The shade of Old Hamlet
has told us that his purgatorial punishment is to last until the sins he
committed on earth are 'burnt and purged away'. Are we expected to
believe that revenge on his brother is worth another thousand odd years
on his tariff, which is probably the going rate in Purgatory for ordering

a murder? Even if we can accept that that's what a couple of months in hell can do to a spirit, how can we possibly believe that young Hamlet never considers the consequences for himself? I can hear the reader beginning to silently scream that none of us these days takes any of that kind of stuff remotely seriously! But that's just the point. If as a director you are asking the actor to truly get inside the language rather than float on top of it, never quite meaning what he's saying, and allowing a modern patina of irony to cover the cracks in those crazy old Elizabethans' primitive ways of thinking, then you have to confront the fact that the actor has no choice but to accept that his character believes in an afterlife of the kind described in the play. If that isn't the case, then there is no logic to the tortuous dilemma he finds himself in. There is no way round it. The actor's imagination has to be flooded with this reality. Although the past is another country and we can never know it utterly, I am certain that in 1600 most brains were awash with an awareness of and apprehension about a vast 'undiscovered country from whose bourn / No traveller returns'. Unless, perhaps, as a ghost.

At the beginning of Laurence Olivier's film of the play, a voiceover intones that we are about to see a story concerning 'a man who could not make up his mind'. I don't think that's a good summing-up of the play at all. After the 'hot blood' speech, Hamlet has the perfect opportunity to kill Claudius when he comes across him unguarded, alone, unaware of his presence, on his knees and at prayer. At least, Hamlet thinks he is at prayer, and the misconception temporarily saves the man's life. Hamlet's strong sense of the justice of his cause and the horrible nature of his father's fate, as well the depth of his criminal betrayal, makes him hesitate. Claudius appears to be praying, and to kill him now in a state of grace, sending him to Paradise while his father remains suffering torture in Purgatory, seems little short of an insane idea, something only a madman would contemplate! The fires of Hell are real to him, and a place in this eternal inferno is what his uncle deserves. If at this moment the actor plays Hamlet as putting off something he hasn't the stomach to do – that the argument about his uncle going to Heaven is just an excuse by a man incapable of making up his mind – then the spirit of the text is betrayed, the energy of the scene dissipated, the passion, intensity and sheer magnitude of the situation diminished. A wholly false relationship between thought and speech is created instead. In other words, it is to make a subtext where none exists. Characters in Shakespeare speak what they are thinking – their speaking *is* their thinking. The actor's job is to make thought and action one; speech as revelation to the speaker – speech that is located right in the moment of thought, not speech *about* thought, and certainly not saying one thing while thinking another. So what the actor needs to create is the feeling of passion and fear that comes from a mind that believes in Heaven and Hell, not as metaphors, but as realities, and is expressing the alive, unmediated thought of the moment. This is different from the modern mind, which loves the idea that language is often used to conceal thought rather than reveal it. But this doesn't put it beyond our reach – we can access this immediate relationship between thought and language.

Prevarication is a very modern mental state. It's also very easy for a modern actor to play, especially as irony can have a pleasingly endearing and comic effect on an audience. On the other hand, expressing revelation is hard, because today our default sensibility is ironic, downbeat, knowing, and on the back foot. The Elizabethans were just discovering layers of sensibility that have become commonplace to us. Just as their mariner adventurers were discovering new countries, so their artists and intellectuals were discovering new mental landscapes full of new associations and possibilities of motive, action and self-awareness. In the second in which he might bring down the sword on Claudius's neck, Hamlet has a starkly vivid picture of this man in Paradise, the same man that heaved and sweated drunkenly in his mother's bed, and poured poison in his father's ear. For an incredulous moment he has a vision of what he might inadvertently cause to happen, something so absurd and inappropriate that it shocks him into restraint, causes him to pull up just in time. This is absolutely not prevarication. The energy trapped by this aborted action is then carried through into the next sequence of events. A state of indecision would be far too limp to work as motivation for the electric confrontation with his mother and recklessness of the accidental murder of the man behind the arras.

In most Elizabethan revenge drama, both before and after *Hamlet*, there is sympathy for the avenger until they actually kill someone, at which point they become contaminated and are condemned, usually suffering death as a consequence of their actions. Whatever revenge God might take was His business, but when it came to the Elizabethan State, the position, in law, was clear: private revenge was strictly forbidden. There was a strong system of justice in place and any action outside that framework was illegal. No one in authority wanted a return to medieval notions of honour codes and the taking of personal retribution. And here is a remarkable thing about *Hamlet*: there is no sense in the play of Shakespeare presenting, or even hinting at, an authorial point of view; no indication of what he thinks his hero ought to do. This was revolutionary, for it implied that the audiences were expected to decide for themselves. There is no moral message. In the texts he drew on, not only are there no players, there's no ghost either; it's just a straightforward morality tale. The principal source for *Romeo and Juliet*, a long poem by Arthur Brooke, based on the Italian novella by Matteo Bandello, is a cautionary story about the perils of falling in love too young and not taking parental advice. Under Shakespearean transformation, both narratives become complex webs of conflicting imperatives and contradictory passions. This is where Shakespeare speaks to us, this is where we feel part of the same complicated world as him and where outmoded ideas about Hell and damnation cease to matter. But it doesn't mean they can be ignored, because what we find familiar and what we find alien are wrapped up in each other; you cannot extract one strand and leave the other intact without fatally enfeebling the whole play.

Consider Hamlet's state of mind after the accidental murder of Polonius, and after the trip to England that was meant to end in his death, when we meet him again in the graveyard. I have always found it puzzling and hard to describe. I think it is hard to play, too, because it feels like a kind of moral limbo. Whether reflecting on mortality by the side of an open grave, or responding to the unexpected challenge of a fencing match, his mood seems passive and fatalistic. The complexities of life appear to have stripped him bare of motivation, of any 'cue for passion'. Is he now simply waiting for God, or Providence, to deliver an answer? The emotion and anger that drove the task of revenge has seeped away, leaving him apparently calm and philosophical. Is this how he was before the start of the play, before we meet him? How he was before the chaotic moral confusion that the crisis of his father's death and mother's marriage overwhelmed him with? When he innocently loved Ophelia? There seems something deeply and quietly Christian about his thoughts, as in:

> There is special providence in the fall of a sparrow. If it be
> now, 'tis not to come; if it be not to come, it will be now; if it
> be not now, yet it will come: the readiness is all.

Is that what he was like before? Is that question worth asking? How many children had Lady Macbeth? Academics sometimes express the view that Shakespeare's characters spring into view fully formed, ready to go, without a past, and to ask questions such as 'What was Hamlet like before his father died and his mother married his uncle?' are irrelevant. What they mean, I think, is that they are not part of the writer's purpose and that such speculation would have meant nothing to him; that such a way of thinking was unhelpful to the effects he wished to create. Maybe. But a modern actor needs a backstory, needs to know the character as deeply as possible – as if they were real. But this pre-Freudian writing seems to have no need of it, so the director and the actor have to invent it by working backwards from the information in the script. You can't play Lady Macbeth without knowing how many children you've had. And you can't play Hamlet without having some idea of what you were like before your father died, and even assuming that his death hasn't changed you much, you need to know what your relationship was to him when he was alive.

Here Elizabethan and modern sensibilities part again, and the rehearsal room is where you build the bridges.

UNDERSTANDING OPHELIA

Hamlet pretends to be mad, but Ophelia, whom he might have married, does actually go mad. Her story is the most convincing and disturbing depiction of mental breakdown in the Shakespearean world, and it makes me feel he must have witnessed psychosis in a teenage girl. Where is the starting point for the actor faced with the responsibility of showing this mind breaking apart, without using tricks, sensationalism or audience attention-seeking, but with truth and tenderness?

In Act 2 Scene 2 Polonius seeks out Gertrude and Claudius, convinced that he has understood the reason for Hamlet's apparent madness. He may be chief counsellor to the King, but clearly doubles as the court psychiatrist as well. He has with him a poem and letter written by Hamlet to his daughter, Ophelia, that clearly pre-dates the action of the play. He reads it out:

> 'Doubt thou the stars are fire,
> Doubt that the sun doth move,
> Doubt truth to be a liar,
> But never doubt I love.
> O dear Ophelia, I am ill at these numbers. I have not art to reckon my groans, but that I love thee best, O most best, believe it. Adieu.
> Thine evermore, most dear lady, whilst this machine is to him.
> Hamlet.'

Ophelia confirms it came from Hamlet and that it was one of many. It's a genuine love letter: nothing exists in the text to make us doubt that or to suspect any phoniness or ulterior motive or game-playing on the part of the Prince. He reveals himself to be totally in love, showing a sweetly innocent side that is a million miles from the traumatised intellectual on display for the majority of the play. This was the man that Ophelia knew during the events leading up to the appearance of the ghost of Hamlet's father, throughout the time of mourning, and the time of the re-marriage of his mother a mere few weeks later. In rehearsal, you could argue, in creating the backstory, that the simple fact of his mother's second marriage was enough to turn him against all women, including Ophelia, the one he loves; but if we are trying to understand Ophelia, his rejection of her seems dramatically linked to what his dead father tells him. So let's go back to the beginning of her story as Shakespeare reveals it.

In her first scene Ophelia is being berated by her brother; perhaps 'bullied' would be a better word. Shakespeare is very rarely explicit about the age of any of his characters, but Ophelia seems to fit into a group of girls in their mid-teens, all of whom are dominated by an older male authority figure – a father, elder brother or uncle. Loved, but tightly controlled, they are not expected either to have agency or to express any desire for it. This group would include Juliet, Miranda, Hero and Ophelia. The boys that played them originally would have been between fourteen and sixteen years old, and my guess is that Shakespeare conceived of all four characters as that age (and in the case of the first two, we don't have to guess), so that the actors would have been exactly the right age, even if not the right sex. However, the category of 'teenager' didn't exist in Elizabethan England – not as we understand it – so behavioural comparisons are difficult. The social expectation that a teenage girl would obey her father in matters of marital destiny is nowadays low in Western culture, although surviving in other ethnic groups. In Shakespeare's day it was a cornerstone of family relationships. So today's realities challenge the ones implicit in the text of Ophelia's scenes. Furthermore, in the professional theatre, casting these 'teenage' parts isn't straightforward, as the actor is likely to be in their mid-twenties, and rehearsals would, amongst other things, be about digging back a decade to access the emotions and expectations colouring an earlier stage of life, as well as an earlier period of history.

From the moment we meet Ophelia she is being overwhelmed by a barrage of advice, instruction and moral lecturing from her elder brother and her father. They have heard – we never know how, but Renaissance courts were claustrophobic echo chambers of gossip – that Hamlet is wooing her, so they are basically ordering her to have nothing more to do with him. They tell her to stop encouraging him and to refuse any more letters or visits. Laertes, at some length, makes the point that Hamlet just wants to get her into bed and will then dump her, or at least that could be the case, while her father follows up with the view that Hamlet is far too grand for her, and anyway that the choice of marriage partner doesn't lie only in his hands but is a matter of state. Though hard for a modern audience to swallow, she humbly acquiesces to both of them, saying she will follow their instructions.

What I would work at in rehearsals is giving an audience the sense that she is not just innocently biddable, but also confused and exceedingly fragile. I would also spend time finding ways of underlining the point that Hamlet's poem and short letter have touched her because she feels they come from genuine and deep love, not that they are insincere contrivances. She knows they would have been written under the influence of his disgust at his mother's sudden re-marriage to his uncle and his own grief at his father's death. She would experience them as an expression of his need for innocent love while separating himself from the emotional betrayals of a messy adult love triangle.

Hamlet is revolted by his mother's continuing sexuality and worships the teenage Ophelia's unpolluted virginity. This is his state before his father's ghost tells him that he was murdered and that his mother has married the murderer. After this, the way he sees the world is transformed by the challenge to revenge. He acts madness, as we have seen, both as a disguise and as a way of channelling his rage, but the plot tells us that Ophelia is the first audience he tries his mad act out on, and she overwhelmingly falls for it, blaming herself for following her brother's and father's advice to reject him. She is infected by his 'madness', and her already fragile sense of herself, her immaturity and lack of experience are now joined by oppressive feelings of guilt in her volatile teenage mind. She is treated like a whore by the man she thought loved her, sneered at as someone fit only for the convent or the brothel, and then this man murders her father while her brother, who should protect her, is sowing his wild oats in Paris, a choice condoned by his father. The man she would marry has rejected her, the man who raised her is dead, and the man closest to her has left. All these men she loved, yet they have made her mad. But in madness she finds the ability to act the very thing that had always been denied her – the ability to make people listen to her. In her final scenes, the court is a stage on which she can become the goddess Flora distributing healing herbs and flowers to a silent, awe-struck audience. She can become a female Orpheus plucking on a lute (as the Q1 stage direction uniquely specifies) and singing songs to bewitched spectators engrossed in her performance. For the first time in her life she is being heard. Like Lear, in madness she discovers herself, or at least what she might have been. Lear finds out too late the meaning and responsibility of leadership, and Ophelia never has the chance to express the wisdom, kindness and creativity that were, perhaps, inside her: latent qualities squeezed out by jealous men.

Laertes describes Hamlet's interest in his sister as 'a toy in blood'. As one of the four categories in the Elizabethan theory of humours, blood represented the seat of emotion and passion, especially sexual desire. 'Toy', in this context, suggests something frivolous, a lightness of intent. He is warning her to protect her 'honour', and maybe the actor could play this as an urgency driven by his imminent departure for France, but here is the whole of Laertes's speech:

> For Hamlet and the trifling of his favour,
> Hold it a fashion and a toy in blood,
> A violet in the youth of primy nature,
> Forward, not permanent, sweet, not lasting,
> The perfume and suppliance of a minute,
> No more.

So what is motivating this? Laertes is leaving his sister and may feel guilty about it, but as to the substance – well, I suppose he would know, wouldn't he, being a young healthy male himself? Where else does he get his ideas from? Why does he feel it necessary to hammer it home? What has he witnessed? Does he feel Ophelia is about to 'fall', bringing disgrace to the family and ruin to herself? This straining for poetic language to emphasise a danger implies he thinks that things have progressed quite a long way between Hamlet and Ophelia, that she is being pressurised and is encouraging the pressure. We learn at the end of the play that the love was real: Hamlet says so as he leaps into her grave. Her sad reply to the speech quoted above is: 'No more but so?'– which expresses her yearning to disbelieve what her brother is saying and provokes an even longer and more elaborate lecture from him, focusing on a different argument. But the point here for understanding Ophelia is that Laertes is wrong and that's where her tragedy lies. She lacks the inner resolution to contest what her brother is arguing and to defend Hamlet's integrity. Perhaps in the moment of her question Laertes senses how much she wants to believe in Hamlet's love, which is why he replies, 'Perhaps he loves you now,' and goes on to change the argument, focusing instead on the politics of the situation, effectively saying that even if Hamlet does love her, he won't be allowed to marry her:

> Then weigh what loss your honour may sustain
> If with too credent ear you list his songs,
> Or lose your heart, or your chaste treasure open
> To his unmastered importunity,
> Fear it, Ophelia, fear it my dear sister.

Fear is the key to the preserving of honour: fear of Hamlet's possible deceit and of her own sexuality. This fear is the seed of psychosis, and the audience should feel how deeply it has bitten into her mind and how much it will dictate her future actions when she says:

> I shall the effect of this good lesson keep
> As watchman to my heart.

Her own fear then immediately transfers itself into a fearfulness for her brother. *Don't give in to your own sexual desires*, she says, *and while showing me the way to heaven, yourself end up in hell*. Laertes has succeeded in making a fragile person very frightened. Frightened of herself. Frightened of the man she hoped to marry. And frightened for the brother she loves. This overwhelming fear is the gateway to her breakdown, and the actor playing Ophelia needs to take the audience through that portal of change into the person she is becoming while leaving behind the person she was. This is Shakespeare's art – charting change, pinpointing the turning points of human lives as they happen before our eyes. For an audience, the experience of watching should be one of constantly feeling the need to intervene, the impulse to caution, almost the burden of knowing more than the characters, yet unable to warn them of the dangers they are in. I understand the impulse to not take things this seriously, to employ irony, placing the tongue in the cheek, and playing this scene as banter, siblings teasing each other affectionately. I understand the desire not to get too 'heavy' with it. But making any drama work is ultimately about getting convincingly from A to B using the available stepping stones (otherwise known as the text). This scene leads to the horror of a mind broken in fragments, and that breakdown begins right here.

When Laertes leaves to catch the boat to France, Polonius instantly begins to question his daughter:

> POLONIUS. What is't, Ophelia, he hath said to you?
> OPHELIA. So please you, something touching the Lord
>   Hamlet.

Polonius then lays into the subject along very much the same lines as his son, ending with the order to neither see Hamlet nor speak to him any more. Ophelia isn't given the opportunity to say much, but what she does say when she can get a word in is worth examining without the intervening pontifications of her loquacious and irritable father.

> He hath, my lord, of late made many tenders
> Of his affection to me…
> I do not know, my lord, what I should think…
> My lord, he hath importuned me with love
> In honourable fashion…
> And hath given countenance to his speech,
> My lord, with all the vows of heaven…

And finally, at the end of Polonius's lengthy harangue instructing her to end the relationship:

> I shall obey, my lord.

Understanding Ophelia entails understanding that Hamlet loves her and that she is forced to doubt it, despite the words of his poem to her. In these lines you can feel her trying to hang on to a belief in what he has said. These are the great unseen scenes in the play – the scenes of Hamlet in love; in love with Ophelia, and telling her so. This is one of the most vital internal backstories. Where can we find this character in the text that we have? If we don't see him, we need to feel his real presence through the actor playing Ophelia. Listen to her beautiful speech in Act 3 Scene 1 when overwhelmed by his 'madness'. It is her only soliloquy.

> O, what a noble mind is here o'erthrown!
> The courtier's, soldier's, scholar's eye, tongue, sword,
> The expectancy and rose of the fair state,
> The glass of fashion and the mould of form,
> Th'observed of all observers, quite, quite, down.
> And I, of ladies most deject and wretched,
> That sucked the honey of his music vows,
> Now see that noble and most sovereign reason

Like sweet bells jangled out of tune and harsh –
That unmatched form and feature of blown youth
Blasted with ecstasy. O, woe is me
T'have seen what I have seen, see what I see.

This is the man she knew – a man who enters the play only through her memory and estimation of him. No one else talks about him like this, no one else so wonderfully evokes the horror of a fine man reduced to seeming madness. Through him she believes in madness enough to make the journey there herself – and the tragic, pitiful irony that we the audience must feel the full force of is: that HE IS ONLY ACTING! Acting on the stage is reasonably safe; it is a tiger caged. But in real life it is as dangerous as a tiger in the wild; and the world can sometimes seem just as Titus describes Rome: 'a wilderness of tigers'.

Twelfth Night

FINDING ILLYRIA

The very title *Twelfth Night* sometimes influences the style of production that the play receives. Some directors decide to begin the action as if it were just after Christmas, the melancholic end of the party season with a snow-bound landscape, half-dead Christmas trees that have shed their needles, and over-indulgence (emotional and physical) hanging like a sickly-sweet scented mist in the air. This type of production will then perhaps proceed to a springtime ending suitable for weddings and happy outcomes lined up for everyone except poor Antonio and Olivia's hapless steward, Malvolio. Time is an elusive concept in this play. A winter-to-spring time frame can be justified by a line in the final act which states Viola has been with the Duke for three months. But the play with its double time scheme has a shape and impetus that feels more like three days. And then there are lines like 'this is very midsummer madness' and 'Away before me to sweet beds of flowers', which suggest the heat and passions of high summer and would require ironic inflection if spoken in the snow. Both three months and three days are useful in different ways in rehearsals, but to assume both are true is hard to reconcile with the work of creating naturalistic backstories for the characters. Three days gives a sense of reckless speed and things happening with a momentum that is out of control; it sits nicely with the idea of events being driven by 'midsummer madness'. On the other hand, when Orsino says of Viola in Act Five, 'Three months this youth hath tended upon me,' you believe it because emotionally so much has happened to so many. The action certainly becomes more believable if that amount of time has passed, but then a suspension of disbelief has been required on quite a grand scale and in a variety of ways right from the start. The realism of time and the way Shakespeare manipulates it to dramatic ends is constantly at odds with modern naturalistic tendencies, but the truth is that a double time scheme allows him to have it both ways, creating a feeling of pace and excitement alongside a maturing sense of credibility. Part of preparing to rehearse a play like *Twelfth Night* is having a strategy for balancing an actor's need for a believable and useful backstory with the non-naturalistic stage conventions of the time, which Shakespeare, for all his radical departures, fully embraced.

Before beginning to create an Illyria, it's worth asking where it is, or was, because it's remarkable how many people still think of it as an imaginary, invented place. In fact it's actually the old name for the country we now know as Croatia. As a director, this is worth thinking through because the fundamental question about creating a world for *Twelfth Night* is: should that world be fantastical and purely imaginary or should it feel real? An imaginary world I would define as one composed of different elements that would never normally co-exist and would only be found together on a stage, perhaps involving design concepts chosen to highlight the different themes within the text. A realistic approach would be based on creating a world that has a recognisable social ambience located at some broadly identifiable point in history, with a set of social practices and ethical codes against which behaviour can be measured or explained. Most actors prefer the second of these broad options because real worlds are easier to play than fantastical or 'themed' worlds.

Of course, it's not quite as neat as that: even an invented world has to be grounded in some realities because all Shakespeare's plays are, on some level, masterpieces of realistic drama. Besides, a real-seeming world need not be an exact copy of any known world, which by definition would make it in some sense imaginary. The meaning of these choices is particularly relevant to *Twelfth Night* because the play seems to exist in some strange space between fantasy and normality, and the decision about the nature of that world will inevitably affect the kind of questions asked in the rehearsal room. You can argue that, in a made-up world, basic points of backstory have little or no relevance beyond the narrative specifics actually mentioned in the text. For example, Olivia's father and brother have both recently died, and Viola and Sebastian's father had a 'mole upon his brow'. We must think about these things because they help give shape and texture to the story being told. But if the director was to decide that what was realistic about the play outweighs its fantastical elements and therefore that the best way of serving the text was to root the action in a specific time and place, a whole new category of backstory could be seen as important to inform character and motivation. So what becomes important in playing Olivia is not just the fact of her father's and brother's deaths, but also what she thought of them, how much she loved them or how little. The degree to which she is bereft or liberated plainly affects her state of mind and so shapes her attitude to Orsino, 'Cesario' and Malvolio. Sebastian and Viola were clearly on a voyage from somewhere to somewhere else when their ship was wrecked. Where were they going and why? Does it matter? How much time should be spent in the rehearsal room discussing it? The extent to which speculating over backstory can be valuable or a waste of time is central to a director's approach. Is it possible to identify categories of backstory in this play, some of which may be more useful than others? Shakespeare didn't feel the need to tell us either about Olivia's feelings towards her father and brother or the nature of Viola and Sebastian's boat trip: why not? Probably because he realised his audience wouldn't care and certainly didn't need to know in order to enjoy the unfolding plot, but we've already established that maybe Olivia's feeling for her father might be germane to her character and therefore helpful to the actor playing her. On the other hand, does anything helpful emerge from speculating why Viola was on a ship off the Croatian coast?

The text tells us the twins come from Messaline, which is the old name for the port of Marseilles. So they set off on their voyage from the south of France. There is no indication of any strong purpose to their voyage (unlike those shipwrecked in *The Tempest*, who are returning from a wedding). The most likely thing we can imagine is that the two young people were on an educational trip, a kind of upper-class Grand Tour of the Mediterranean and Adriatic taking in cultural hotspots, probably mainly in Italy, probably intended to climax in Venice, which would explain why they were close to Illyria/Croatia, having sailed round the boot of Italy. Illyria certainly wouldn't have been on the schedule, as it was regarded as a wild and uncultured place with nothing to offer the young and curious mind reared on the history and language of Greece and Rome. A ship making its way up the Adriatic Sea towards Venice is caught in a sudden storm and breaks up on the dangerous coastline known to the Elizabethans as Illyria. Viola has no idea where she is: 'What country, friends, is this?' She gets the answer: 'This is Illyria, lady.' Does she shudder at that reply? Possibly her reaction is one of absolute terror, given its reputation as a wild and lawless place, but whatever the degree of her reaction, the bottom line is that the audience needs to believe in the necessity of her decision to disguise herself as a man wherever in time the director locates the play. In 1600 there's no problem with her decision, but what about a production set now? If the survivors of the wreck look like they are in a world we recognise as our own, then surely there's no point in becoming male? How to fix Illyria in time and place? It's worth remembering that, at the time of the Balkan wars of the 1990s, it may have been even more dangerous than in 1600. In the tourist boom of the 1970s and 1980s, when it was part of the former Yugoslavia, the shipwreck might merely have disturbed a few sunbathers, and only a serious blow to the head might justify Viola's desperation to disguise herself as a man. But the progress of the play demands we believe in her sanity and rationality, her doing her best in a frightening situation. If we simply feel her disguise as a comic stage device rather than a logical inevitability, the scenes of mistaken identity will never be truly funny. Real comedy is only possible if we believe in the danger of alternatives. It's also true that steeping this play in an over-detailed 'real' world – Orsino as a nationalist Croatian warlord; Malvolio as a communist party apparatchik – could clog up the veins of the text and stifle its intended meanings, offering the audience a constant alternative to the play Shakespeare wrote. So are the reasons for Viola's disguise important? Would a director's decision to make time and place real have a straitjacket effect on the imagination? Everything that is so truthful about human behaviour in the play cries out against creating a fantastical dream world, and we have to think of Viola's disguise as a reasonable precaution in a precarious situation, yet all the time the plot's farcical contrivances pull in an opposite direction.

It may well be that the whole Croatian notion is a complete red herring. Shakespeare probably knew where Illyria was but, almost certainly, had never been there and is unlikely to have known much, if anything, about it. Maybe all he knew was that it was a lot hotter than England. He writes mainly about the manners and behaviour of the race he knew best, the English, whether he sets his story in Windsor or Padua. The name Sir Toby Belch hardly sounds foreign, after all, and everything that happens in the play is suffused with the spirit of Englishness. So why is it, like all his romantic comedies, set abroad? Apart from one play, his friend Ben Jonson set all his comedies in a very realistic and contemporary London. As only mad dogs and Englishmen go out in the midday sun, as Noël Coward sang, perhaps Shakespeare was creating a kind of pressure-chamber environment in which human interactions are intensified under unfamiliar heat, and a set of broadly familiar English types succumb to a form of midsummer madness? At the heart of the fantastical aspect of *Twelfth Night* is the notion that opposite-sex twins, if dressed in the same clothes, can be so identical in body and voice as to be completely indistinguishable from each other. However, for the comedy to work, the audience have to be easily able to tell which is which or they would be totally confused. So the paradox of the suspension of disbelief demands that what must be obvious to the audience is unknowable to the characters. This is not a very 'real' proposition, yet the emotional life of the play is deeply realistic, perceptive and truthful. Rehearsals will focus on these qualities and on finding ways to articulate, in performance, the relationship between love and madness. Everyone struggling with extreme heat may work for this as the characters sweatily stumble towards the fulfilment of their desires, simultaneously becoming the victims of those desires. Orsino, tortured by his unreturned love for Olivia, says it: 'my desires, like fell and cruel hounds... pursue me.' So finding Illyria too hot to happily handle their greed, passion, deceit, love or ambition, and living in a condition of permanent sunstroke, may be a way for director and actors to bring realism to an unreal and highly contrived narrative. On the other hand, that could be to entirely miss the point that love, and especially the act of falling in love, is one of the few completely inexplicable facts of life; that it is without logic, and so to create an Illyria that is magical and outside the realm of the ordinary, beyond pedantic explanations, may lead an audience closer to the mystery and confusion of what love is.

Some directors (and a lot of academics) caution against falling into what they call 'the naturalistic fallacy'. What they mean is the failure to recognise and embrace Shakespeare's habit of shifting styles – his movement from naturalism to high poetic fantasy, often within the same scene, depending on what he felt appropriate to the dramatic moment – and that this is part of the richness of his work. Those who hold this view would also maintain that a director who is concerned only with making their production as 'real' and naturalistic as possible is putting shackles on the writer's multi-dimensional imagination: that to be concerned in rehearsal with geographic literalism (such that the twins are French because they set sail from Marseilles, that they were on their way to Venice and were wrecked on the coast of Croatia falling prey to the passions of a group of sun-addled Croatians) is all a total imposition on the way the Elizabethans would think. Very few of the comedies of the period show the remotest interest in either geography or anthropological accuracy. This is obviously true, but it doesn't invalidate creative discussion about background details that lie outside the scope of the play. The key in the rehearsal room is to extract from the text the background provided and enrich it with the selective imagination of the actors. It is about finding backstory that is playable and useful in developing character. This will vary from actor to actor, but sometimes, such as in this example from Act Five, it can add depth and richness to vital dramatic moments:

VIOLA. My father had a mole upon his brow.
SEBASTIAN. And so had mine.
VIOLA. And died that day when Viola from her birth
    Had numbered thirteen years.
SEBASTIAN. O, that record is lively in my soul!

They knew that little birthmark on their father's forehead so well. One can readily imagine how a small child upon a parent's knee will examine every detail of their face, touching, laughing, enquiring – and, when their father died at the very moment they were making the awkward transition from childhood to the beginnings of adulthood, how profoundly they were thrown upon each other's love and how much this present moment means, when for three months they had believed each other dead. The mole and the death are in the text, but the meaning for them both needs to be embroidered and made real in the rehearsal room. Emotional details like this have little to do with being Elizabethan and everything to do with being human. So where does worrying about a specific historical mindset come into it?

Imagine a modern-dress production, and focus on the things in the text that are totally bound in to the period in which it was written. Is the dissonance destructive, creative or irrelevant? Take Fabian's reference to bear-baiting. He says Malvolio 'brought me out o' favour with my lady about a bear-baiting here'. What would the backstory to this be and how should the actor be thinking about the incident when saying the line? If there's no answer to that then you must simply cut it, but what about Elizabethan attitudes to madness? They were radically different to ours: we don't live in a world where someone thought to be mad can quite legitimately be locked in a dark room and chained to the wall. Our societies are not run by dukes with the absolute power of a despot in matters of life and death. Ethical assumptions about virginity and marriage are profoundly different. A modern-day Viola would go to the consulate, not the palace, and wouldn't find it necessary to dress as a man in the first place. Duelling doesn't exist now, so what kind of challenge is Sir Andrew meant to be making to Cesario? Class, social etiquette, servants, fools and much else have all changed significance since 1600. Does any of this really matter? Do the themes and stories in the play emerge clearer and with less strain if it is set in or close to the period in which it was composed? Or, on the other hand, in a modern-dress production does the cultural disparity between the way people look and the way they behave and speak weaken the narrative? Can you solve this tension by bringing to the stage a world that is boldly eclectic, one that floats free of period and in which anything and everything – even bear-baiting – can happen? It matters because however you do it, the one thing you cannot change is the intensity of the actions. What they do to Malvolio is truly terrible. Orsino does possess absolute and intimidating power. Sex is shockingly unthinkable if it happens outside religiously sanctified marriage. Sir Andrew is utterly terrified he may be killed. To turn a blind eye to these things is to fatally weaken the emotional fabric of the play and undermine the essence of the comedy by ignoring the potential for tragedy. Comedy and tragedy are themselves twins; they are identical until the lens of perception alters them.

Maria tells Feste, who as a paid Fool in an aristocratic household has no modern equivalent, that he risks being hanged for being absent without leave. Now it's true that in Elizabethan society hanging your in-house comedian was thankfully rare, but there are many references to whippings and other exotic punishments. I would always encourage the actor playing Feste to have good reasons for risking such treatment. The world in which *Twelfth Night* was first performed was a place in which visits to the madhouse to laugh at the insane, trips to the bear pit to watch animals being tortured, feasting on meat pies during a public hanging, applauding the whipping of a prostitute tied to the back of a cart, or gaping while a thief had his ears cut off were normal pastimes competing with the theatre as forms of public entertainment. Whatever you do with the play you can't extract this brutal and bitter essence from the text and narrative. Make it modern but embrace the Elizabethan.

THE FOOD OF LOVE

Why does Shakespeare begin his play with music? Was he tempted to begin with the sound of a storm? Of the productions I've done, I began one by reversing the order of the first two scenes, as many other directors choose to do. As the auditorium lights faded, the sound of crashing waves introduced the image of the bedraggled and soaking survivors of the shipwreck huddled on a beach before Viola's first question to the sailors. But all my other *Twelfth Nights* have begun, as in the Folio text, with music. The Duke's first speech feels like a kind of key signature to the whole play: it establishes a tone, a mood to a story that will deal with the torment, confusion and ecstasy of love.

> If music be the food of love, play on,
> Give me excess of it, that surfeiting
> The appetite may sicken and so die.

So what we see is a group of musicians playing and one man listening. Now the questions begin. Why do they stop? This is the first beat of interpreting the text. How long have they been playing? Are they exhausted? Has their Duke been demanding a constant flow to feed his mood? Have they simply come to the end of that particular piece and now await further instruction? It's as if his words give an answer to a silent question, so does there need to be a look from the leader of the musicians to provoke that first line? And if that line is the answer to an enquiring look, isn't the answer strange? He appears to want them to continue playing till he becomes sick of the music and loses his appetite for it. Or is it love itself he wants to lose his appetite for? Or is he hoping that if he grows tired of the music, he will grow tired of love? The implication here is that the state of being in love is a torment from which he wants to escape. For the actor playing Duke Orsino, establishing this idea is to make the first move in the character's progress towards self-knowledge, towards making the transition from loving someone who doesn't love him to loving someone who does. It's a small subjective move in terms of character, but a massive objective one in terms of narrative. The director, in interpreting this moment, needs to be thinking of linking this beginning to the very end when the audience need to believe in Orsino's love for Viola – a love he wasn't even consciously aware of when he thought her to be a man. If, when we first see him, he seems to be wallowing masochistically in the torment of being in love, you create a mood of stasis where you need it to be dynamic. His active desire for release from his present state will have energy and create a sense of momentum. The narrative is then being driven by the character. Narrative is character in action.

> That strain again, it had a dying fall.

Does he mean *Play that bit again*, or *There's that bit again*? The clue perhaps lies in the word 'had'. If he said 'has', it would be an explanation for why he wants to hear it again, but 'had' implies it is there for a moment and then gone, an image that captures the brevity and elusiveness of experience; how you cannot hold on to a moment, however beautiful, without it passing and becoming something else. If the actor plays the line as an instruction to the musicians, then a pause is needed, either in the middle of the line or at the end. The more obvious choice would be the end of the line so that the instruction is immediately followed by the explanation for the instruction. Entangled with this is the decision as to when the music, that had stopped before he first spoke, actually starts up again. The problem is that the next sentence is in the past tense.

> O, it came o'er my ear like the sweet sound
> That breathes upon a bank of violets,
> Stealing and giving odour.

Now it appears as if both instruction and explanation are not completed until the end of this whole thought, and only then should the Duke pause to listen again to the phrase of music he's asked for. In fact no sooner has he begun to listen than he says:

> Enough, no more,
> 'Tis not so sweet now as it was before.

His asking for those few bars of music to be repeated is all part of his desire to be so sated with the sound that he is sickened by its sweetness and hence by the associated feelings. The repetition of the word 'sweet' allows the actor to express an awareness of this; that the self-imposed aversion therapy is working.

There is an oddity within these lines that has to be confronted and worked through. It is not 'sound' that makes you smell the scent of flowers, it is a breeze or sudden gust of wind. The image changes its nature halfway through as the 'sweet sound' behaves like the wind delivering the 'odour' of violets. Nor do you inhale a scent with your ears. Some editors have assumed a misprint in the Folio text here and changed the word 'sound' to 'south' (as in the south wind), but that doesn't really alter the paradox because it is still the ears that do the smelling. It may be that Shakespeare is deliberately mixing the metaphor to emphasise the indulgent sensuality of Orsino's state of mind in which music and the aroma of flowers both become one dual-faceted experience. Perhaps the Duke is experiencing synaesthesia, which is defined as 'the subjective sensation of a sense other than the one being stimulated; e.g. a sound may evoke a sensation of colour'. Somehow, director and actor need to find a way of embracing this imagistic illogicality to illuminate the character and his dilemma. His obsession with wallowing in the torture of unrequited love is itself illogical: it is damaging and reveals him as a patient needing a cure, one that only mutual, reciprocated love can provide. When the music stops his self-reflection becomes more complex:

> O spirit of love, how quick and fresh art thou
> That, notwithstanding thy capacity
> Receiveth like the sea, naught enters there
> Of what validity and pitch soe'er,
> But falls into abatement and low price
> Even in a minute. So full of shapes is fancy
> That it alone is high fantastical.

To get further into the head of this tormented man, the actor needs to understand how these two sentences are related to each other. Both are statements, but what's the connection? If love, or the 'spirit of love', has an infinite capacity to suck up every genuine and deeply felt sentiment that a lover has to offer and then quickly ignores or neglects them, what follows from that? The last sentence of this passage cannot just be further comment because, if so, the two thoughts will have only an arbitrary relation to one another, and Shakespeare is good at avoiding that kind of randomness. It must be a revelation. Orsino is seeing something for the first time, specifically that 'fancy' (a derogatory word for love) is like a fantasy or a hallucination. He is demonstrating a capacity to understand the state he has got himself into, is on the verge of thinking it through and lifting himself out of his sickly situation. Sadly, this moment of near insight doesn't survive his re-engagement with himself as the melancholy hero of his own story. When his courtier Curio offers an innocent distraction from his present mood by asking, 'Will you go hunt, my lord?' Orsino can't resist setting up a bitter and self-indulgent joke:

> ORSINO.   What, Curio?
> CURIO.   The hart.
> ORSINO. Why so I do, the noblest that I have.
>   O, when mine eyes did see Olivia first
>   Methought she purged the air of pestilence;
>   That instant was I turned into a hart,
>   And my desires, like fell and cruel hounds,
>   E'er since pursue me.

He can't keep away from this masochistic self-image, seeing himself as a hunted creature, but the thought is not entirely without an understanding of his condition. At least he doesn't present Olivia as a huntress wounding and tormenting him. His perception has moved on enough for him to recognise that his own desires are the hounds. In performance the actor could dwell long enough on the word 'desires' to let the audience feel the Duke has the intellectual muscle to be a combatant in his own inner struggle. To care about him we must do more than merely understand his pain, we need to glimpse his potential route out of it. Helping an audience to care about a character and to sense the possible actions open to them is one of the ways actors engage their listeners in both story and individual. The director needs to enable this process by always subtly bringing an awareness of that objective into the actor's subjective identification with their character, remembering the aim of performance in the comfort of rehearsal.

At this point in the first scene a piece of vital internal backstory arrives with the sudden appearance of a second courtier, Valentine, who is returning from a mission to Olivia's household.

> ORSINO.   How now, what news from her?
> VALENTINE. So please my lord, I might not be admitted,
> But from her handmaid do return this answer:
> The element itself till seven years' heat
> Shall not behold her face at ample view,
> But like a cloistress she will veiled walk
> And water once a day her chamber round
> With eye-offending brine: all this to season
> A brother's dead love, which she would keep fresh
> And lasting in her sad remembrance.

This flowery and stilted language has a purpose. The choices for the director and actor around Valentine's account of his visit and his own attitude to it depend on the particular backstory they want to give him in respect of his comings and goings to Olivia on behalf of Orsino; especially how many and over what period. I think the humour lies in conveying the sense that the messages coming back are increasingly loaded with a satirical, if not downright sarcastic, attitude to the situation, definitely from Olivia and possibly even Valentine as well. On this visit he didn't even get to see the lady herself but had to be content with a message via a servant. She's not going outside for seven years! Meanwhile she must be thought of as a weeping nun, a permanently

veiled recluse, intent only on mourning her dead brother! This moment
between the two men, courtier and Duke, is funny if we can see that
Valentine gets it (*The answer is NO! She's not interested!*), but Orsino
doesn't. If he ever had one, his sense of humour has now gone completely missing. The next beat of the scene is brilliant comedy as, in the
classic manner of those in love who can't take no for an answer, Orsino
simply re-interprets a message that is clear to anyone but himself, and
hears only what he wants to hear.

> O, she that hath a heart of that fine frame
> To pay this debt of love but to a brother,
> How will she love when the rich golden shaft
> Hath killed the flock of all affections else
> That live in her – when liver, brain and heart,
> These sovereign thrones, are all supplied and filled
> Her sweet perfections with one self king!
> Away before me to sweet beds of flowers:
> Love-thoughts lie rich when canopied with bowers.

It is fascinating how Shakespeare gives poetry with more than a flavour
of chocolate-box romanticism to his delusional would-be lovers. There
is no depth to the thoughts: only a kind of gaudy colour. Orsino argues
himself into a condition of hope. He persuades himself that she is demonstrating how powerful her capacity for love is if she can lavish this
amount of devotion on someone who is not only dead, but only a
brother. Showing how his mind is working and how both his status and
character combine to move the story forward gives the actor a dual
challenge in this speech: on the one hand to show Orsino's apparent
inability to read a situation correctly, and his insistence instead on taking information in entirely the wrong way, but also to convey that he
really means it when he implies that his chances have improved, that
he genuinely feels more optimistic as a result of the message.

For the audience, becoming engaged with a character is about being
allowed to follow the movement of their thought in detail, to understand
the way they think things through. Our empathy for them then fuses with
our own greater objective understanding as spectators of the whole narrative of which they are only a part. It is true, as I've said, that narrative is
character in action, but, as the characters' individual drives, personalities
and desires collide and entangle with the lives of others, it's also true that
only we the audience ever see the whole picture. By the end of the first
scene of *Twelfth Night* we should have understood Orsino's state of love-

sickness, but also gained a sense of his ability to understand and, perhaps, conquer it. We should also have seen how it changes in a moment into an emotional blindness that might make a cure impossible. This fluctuation of potential outcomes is what grips an audience while feeling the privilege of a heightened perspective, a sense of the unpredictability of events and hence the excitement of engagement. Good storytelling is linked to enabling your audience to understand enough to care about what happens next and having a view as to what that might be.

Should Curio and Valentine follow the Duke as he sweeps from the stage, or should they hang back slightly to exchange an exasperated look? Or would you, as an actor or director, worry they had disobeyed the command 'Away before me'? It depends on what relationship has already been established between the two of them, and between each of them and Orsino. (Perhaps there is a rivalry there?) But it also connects to the physicality of the scene – how it has been 'blocked'. There is a temptation to stage it with the love-sick aristocrat lounging on soft cushions or a luxurious sofa, which could be fine, but equally it might suck energy out of the situation. Orsino's mental state is restless, and I think his physical state should reflect that. If he is constantly on the move, what effect would that have on the two courtiers? To some extent this depends on the design, as the power relationships between the three men will differ according to the social structures of the chosen period. In a modern-dress production they may just all be friends, for instance, and capturing the vibrations of that will feed the absorption of the audience. Detail is everything. Good rehearsing is accumulating details without stopping the flow of energy.

The flow of energy between scenes is strongly affected by the amount of stuff on stage, by the elaborateness or simplicity of the design. This is a tricky moment as the story moves from ducal palace to seashore. I have always been drawn to simplicity because I love the sensation created by the last line of a scene being followed almost instantly by the first line of the next, and by the overlapping of bodies as one set of characters is replaced in the blink of an eye by another. Having said that, set changes can themselves be strikingly enjoyable. It's a difficult trade-off as you can't really have it both ways, although the compromise of the actors themselves moving whatever needs to be moved is always available.

Why do I feel so strongly about last and first lines being linked to each other? In this case it's to do with character. Both lines say a lot about the speaker. Orsino's 'Love-thoughts lie rich when canopied with bowers' is a line both indulgent and syrupy, that could only come from a man who is in love with the idea of being in love – a cliché, but a useful one. What he's actually saying is *Thinking about being in love is enriched by lying around surrounded by flowers*; he sees himself as the languid young man lounging on the grass in that painting by Hilliard of the reclining Northumberland, a self-image full of narcissism: cloying, self-obsessed and slightly ridiculous. He sees love in theatrical images that star himself as lead actor. Contrast this with Viola's first words: 'What country, friends, is this?' Direct, practical, polite and brave, her whole personality is announced in that line. This is the woman who will show Orsino what love really is and is not.

THE SEA CAPTAIN

'What country, friends, is this?' This famous line marks Viola's entrance into the story of *Twelfth Night*. Friends? Who are they? Survivors of the wreck presumably. Are they all sailors? Were Viola and Sebastian the only passengers? It's rare for most productions (outside of drama schools, the RSC and the National Theatre) to have the resources to put a big cast on stage in a Shakespeare production. You won't often see a performance of this play where a dozen or so courtiers and servants follow Orsino off stage at the end of Scene 1 to be replaced by a similar-size group entering as the crew and passengers of the wrecked ship. In fact you'd be lucky to see anyone else besides the Sea Captain, who is the only person to speak to Viola in the scene. With clever doubling you can do *Twelfth Night* with twelve actors, but even this doesn't really allow for a group of other survivors. I've never minded about this because in a strange way the presence of silent others would make it harder to stage. Apart from the obvious problem of visual distraction, it would be hard for a curious audience not to speculate about how many might have drowned besides Viola's brother. It means, of course, that the actor playing Viola will say 'friend', and the use of the singular actually intensifies the relationship right from the start. She is alone with this man in a place she doesn't know, having just experienced a terrifying ordeal and quite possibly lost her twin brother to the sea. The stress the actor lays on that word 'friend' will begin to colour their interpretation of the character. It might almost be a question within a question as if she is saying, *You are my friend, aren't you?* Or by endowing him with that title, she is prompting him cautiously into the role. Or maybe it is far more casual. Talking about backstory here in the early stages of rehearsing the scene must be helpful, as her whole attitude to the Captain will depend on how well she has got to know him on the voyage. The text doesn't help on that point, and the two actors need to agree: they might have barely spoken until this moment or they might already be quite at ease in each other's company, even have become friendly. Why does she ask this question at this precise moment? What motivates her, and what does it tell us about her? It can't be casual: we have to receive the sense that the answer is vitally important as a guide to how she will move forward. It implies the rational and thoughtful mind of a practical person who will plan carefully and make the best of her situation, but who first needs to know more about what exactly that situation is, how safe she is. That's just one way of looking at it. She might be seen as a messed-up, grief-traumatised drama queen who has become completely deranged as a result of being suddenly and violently separated from her twin brother and conceives the mad idea of dressing as a man and selling herself to the local aristocracy as a eunuch with a great voice. Honesty in acting Shakespeare requires an acknowledgement that two radically different options, such as the above, which could be multiplied hundreds of times, are best subjected to the evidence in the text before acting choices are made. What should always be resisted is to skim quickly through the text, write the character you'd like to play in your head, then go back and read the text again looking for supporting evidence.

Behind every line of Shakespeare there has to be an intention on the part of the speaker, which is sometimes called an 'action'. This intention, chosen by the actor and based on their interpretation of the textual evidence, is what gives both energy and clarity to the thought. Focusing on how and why a thought is forming itself into language is the only way to avoid generalisation and acquire specific intent. In rehearsals I always try to convince actors that it's more important for the audience to know what the characters are *thinking* than what they are *feeling*; that way they are engaged with the argument, so that their own emotional intelligence can breed a personal empathy for the character's situation.

'This is Illyria, lady.' Whatever inflection the actor gives to his reply, it turns out that the Captain is actually an Illyrian, born and bred only a short distance from the very place where his boat has just been wrecked. This turns out to be fortuitous! But before Viola finds this out, the name triggers a brief outburst of grief and hope.

And what should I do in Illyria?
My brother he is in Elysium.
Perchance he is not drowned. What think you, sailors?

Now, this simple line raises a very simple point about cutting. If there are other, silent, sailors on stage there's no problem, but if the Captain is on his own, you obviously have to make the word singular and have Viola address him as 'sailor'. This might seem very trivial, but it isn't. The line 'What think you, sailor?' sounds odd – even mildly comic. To replace with 'friend' is possible, but the repetition of that word doesn't seem natural. To substitute 'Captain' is a choice, but may weaken the power of the word when it appears a little later at a key moment of plot development. Assuming there are just the two of them on stage, I think it's best she says 'What think you?' I know this sounds petty, but it's merely to illustrate how every single word counts and every second matters. There is a huge difference in tone and meaning, depending on the scene being between just Viola and the Sea Captain or between Viola and a group of soaking sailors only one of whom speaks. Every page of Shakespeare will have at least one of these minor textual dilemmas for the director and actors to work through, and the tiny cuts are as important as the big ones.

> CAPTAIN. It is perchance that you yourself were saved.
> VIOLA. O my poor brother! And so perchance may he be.
> CAPTAIN. True, madam, and to comfort you with chance,
>   Assure yourself, after our ship did split,
>   When you and those poor number saved with you
>   Hung on our driving boat, I saw your brother,
>   Most provident in peril, bind himself –
>   Courage and hope both teaching him the practice –
>   To a strong mast that lived upon the sea,
>   Where, like Arion on the dolphin's back,
>   I saw him hold acquaintance with the waves
>   So long as I could see.

So there were other passengers, and a few survived, but not all. Sebastian may have been one of the lucky ones; at least he was last seen alive. It is never any good telling an actor that the reason a character is making a speech is to convey plot, even if that is part of the reason. In this case providing the Sea Captain with both a personality and a reason for speaking, other than to give hope to a distressed woman, is intimately tied up with the two distinct meanings of the word 'perchance'. It could mean either 'perhaps' or 'by chance'. When Viola first uses the word, it means the former; then the Captain uses it in its other sense; and finally Viola uses it in a way that could mean either or both. This shared wordplay indicates a shared sense of humour and therefore empathy between them. Even if the audience is unaware of the word's double meaning, they can be made aware of an emerging warmth between the two characters that is leading one to give comfort to the other. For the narrative it's important that we understand there's a chance that Viola's brother is still alive. More significantly from the character's point of view, she needs the vestige of hope being offered her in order to credibly draw on her reserves of courage and practicality. Without us knowing that she has the image in her head of her living brother battling to survive, it would be much harder to accept her subsequent actions. So in the above speech we need to see the Captain actively instilling hope in order to encourage qualities he has already seen in her. Consequently she finds in him a man she can trust to help her, not exploit her, and that together they can develop a plan. We are again witnessing narrative develop from characters in action.

Creating this scene in the rehearsal room as one where two people discover each other is much more dramatic and alive if the backstory is minimal – they were acquainted but no more. If the actors' minds are filled with an elaborate and detailed backstory, the text cannot then do the work. Unplayable backstory is useless; it undermines the excitement of watching people change each other, and create each other, moment by moment. In other relationships in other plays it can of course be a different story. Iago's background with his wife Emilia is worth creating in detail; even if it doesn't all find its way into full revelation in performance, it will feed the complexity of their marriage and give depth to everything that passes between them on stage. The actors playing Macbeth and his wife need to agree about their child. And the actor playing Sir Andrew must vividly recall being 'adored'. This encouraging or discouraging the imagining of the 'ghost world' outside the text is a directorial skill that is elusive – but vital.

Viola's next line always causes a lot of rehearsal-room debate:

> For saying so, there's gold.

Does she have a purse strapped to her waist, hidden under a skirt, tucked into the front of her dress, or lying on the ground nearby? Does she take it from an item of her luggage that has been washed ashore, remove a ring from her finger, or take a chain from around her neck? Why does she pay him in the first place simply for telling her something it would have been wrong to withhold? Is it patronising on her part to assume he would want payment for telling the truth? Should the Sea Captain accept the gold? If he doesn't, will he seem churlish? Will he appear unpleasantly mercenary if he keeps it? Whether he refuses or returns it, how is that moment to be physically negotiated, since there are no words to accompany any action? These and many other questions can be asked about this small but important interaction. The decision about how to play this moment will depend as much upon the design as on the characters, but whatever the period design, the Sea Captain is a character wide open to various interpretations. For instance, why assume he is a decent and good man? Could he be played as devious – an opportunist telling a traumatised young girl what she wants to hear to advantage himself? Such a man wouldn't hesitate to take the money. Perhaps he made up the story of Sebastian tying himself to a mast, or had heard something similar from another sailor. Her brother might have survived the storm anyway. Again, the issue might seem trivial, but it raises two important points about a strong characteristic of Shakespeare's writing. First, he is always internally consistent about characters speaking the truth. Everything the Captain says about Olivia and Orsino in the next section is proved to be true, so what he says about Sebastian and the 'strong mast' must also be true. Second, Viola makes a favourable character assessment of him, and the unfolding events prove her to be a good judge of character. Here is the dialogue in which she first hears about the two people whose lives become excruciatingly entwined with her own:

> VIOLA. Mine own escape unfoldeth to my hope –
>   Whereto thy speech serves for authority –
>   The like of him. Knowst thou this country?
> CAPTAIN. Ay, madam, well, for I was bred and born
>   Not three hours' travel from this very place.
> VIOLA. Who governs here?
> CAPTAIN.   A noble duke,
>   In nature as in name.
> VIOLA.   What is his name?
> CAPTAIN. Orsino.
> VIOLA. Orsino: I have heard my father name him.
>   He was a bachelor then.
> CAPTAIN. And so is now, or was so very late.
>   For but a month ago I went from hence,
>   And then 'twas fresh in murmur – as you know,

What great ones do, the less will prattle of –
That he did seek the love of fair Olivia.
VIOLA. What's she?
CAPTAIN. A virtuous maid, the daughter of a count
That died some twelvemonth since, then leaving her
In the protection of his son, her brother,
Who shortly also died; for whose dear love,
They say, she hath abjured the company
And sight of men.
VIOLA.   O that I served that lady,
And might not be delivered to the world –
Till I had made mine own occasion mellow –
What my estate is.
CAPTAIN.   That were hard to compass,
Because she will admit no kind of suit,
No, not the duke's.
VIOLA. There is a fair behaviour in thee, Captain;
And though that nature with a beauteous wall
Doth oft close in pollution, yet of thee
I will believe thou hast a mind that suits
With this thy fair and outward character.

When she delivers this assessment of the Sea Captain's character they have been in conversation for only a few minutes. Even if director and actors have created a little bit of a backstory between them, this is still a big, intimate jump for Viola to make. It shows an extremely confident person displaying either an astuteness of judgement or the canniness to flatter by endowment. The little we've seen of her so far indicates someone composed and insightful. Given the way Shakespearean psychology works, her estimation of this man is bound to be correct, even if as moderns it doesn't automatically satisfy us. But if Shakespeare was up to anything else – for example writing a scene in which a gullible, naive young girl is duped by a con artist – he would let us know. On this principle, which is consistent through all his plays, it would be misguided and confusing to play the Sea Captain as anything other than an honest and decent man. Viola's attitude may contain elements of the flatterer's art as well as composure and intelligence, and the Captain's text doesn't prevent the playing of an interest and attraction that grows the more he talks; and whatever the backstory, they are bonded by both having survived a catastrophic experience.

Returning to the subject of honesty, there is an interesting comparison here with Othello, where it would be dramatically meaningless to watch the way in which Iago works on his victim if it was unclear whether he was telling the truth or not about Cassio and Desdemona. There the liar works as a dramatic figure because he has told us, the audience, that's what he is, and we are therefore involved and complicit in a way we could never be with the good captain. In the second scene of *Twelfth Night*, being at ease with the Sea Captain as a truth-teller is also vital for narrative clarity, the pure storytelling of the scene. We need to take in very clearly and in a very short time the background information that is essential for our enjoyment of what is to come, so we shouldn't be worrying about whether the person supplying all this information is telling the truth or not. We learn that Orsino loves Olivia, who has no father or brother because both have recently died. This narrative emphasis on Olivia's vulnerability and the absence of a protective male family member is an important component of the chaotic situation around her which features three household males, Toby, Malvolio and Feste, and two hopeful suitors, Andrew and Orsino, all of whom are totally inadequate for the role of protector. Under these circumstances, for the actor playing Olivia, falling in love with Cesario becomes a great deal more understandable.

The conversation between the Captain and Viola, which sets up so much of the plot of the play, concludes with the most crucial element of all: Viola's disguise.

> VIOLA. I pray thee – and I'll pay thee bounteously –
> Conceal me what I am, and be my aid
> For such disguise as haply shall become
> The form of my intent. I'll serve this duke.
> Thou shalt present me as an eunuch to him.
> It may be worth thy pains, for I can sing
> And speak to him in many sorts of music,
> That will allow me very worth his service.
> What else may hap to time I will commit;
> Only shape thou thy silence to my wit.
> CAPTAIN. Be you his eunuch, and your mute I'll be.
> When my tongue blabs then let mine eyes not see.
> VIOLA. I thank thee. Lead me on.

The subject of payment has not been dropped, Viola continues to offer money on top of the earlier gold. Does this imply it was accepted or not? In any case, that offer was for a service already delivered, whereas this negotiation is an invitation to enter into a conspiracy of deception with her against the leader of the country for reward, and is therefore on a completely different level. She is suggesting that the Captain introduce and recommend her to the court while concealing her true identity. This verges on the criminal and is not without risk. Does the line 'It may be worth thy pains' imply a reaction that needs appeasing? A look of shock countered by the reminder of reward? Such moments are good to find because they help keep the silent listener active and help drive the speaker's need to speak. It would also force Viola to elaborate on her idea, and carries the implication that she'll be such a fine singing eunuch that her new friend will bathe in reflected glory – inviting him further to join her in an adventure from which he'll benefit, and will therefore be worth the risk. Whether you consider the plan utterly mad depends almost entirely on the period setting. It wouldn't have been a completely crazy idea in the context of Croatia circa 1600. Set in 2022, you have to ask yourself if you can ever apply realistic motivation and logic to this kind of material. But nothing alters the fact that actors need to know why their character is doing something. However you contextualise it socially or historically, Viola's choice has to be connected, through the acting, to a perceived threat that is dangerously real for that individual in that moment. And the Sea Captain's choice to do what she asks has to be connected, through the acting, to a warmth of feeling and an admiration for this young woman that would make you long to see their next scene together. He certainly needs a sense of humour – even if he does think her idea might be due to a blow to the head – and he shows it with his last line: 'Be you his eunuch, and your mute I'll be. / When my tongue blabs then let mine eyes not see.' As Viola never has to prove how good a singer she is, but operates for the rest of the play purely in the role of glorified pageboy, there is a temptation to change 'eunuch' to 'page'. The price to be paid would be to entirely lose the Captain's joke; his only joke! What he is saying is, *You be without balls, and I'll be without tongue.* It's a very black joke, and if you look it up in the notes of any edition of the play you will learn that the reference here is to the Turkish court at a time when eunuchs were employed as harem guards, and mutes were their subordinates: silent servants who had had their tongues removed lest they give away state secrets. This 'joke' of the Captain has of course passed beyond comprehension, but whether you cut it or not, it has a use. It's a reminder that under the comedy of this play (perhaps under all comedy) there is a darkness, a fear, that drives the actions of these two people, and, as I've said before, if you ignore it or skim over it, or say it doesn't matter, the acting will never be truthful – nor ever funny.

In the rehearsal room (and this can't be repeated too often) you have to engage with the contradictions between the world the text was born in and the world you are creating on stage with whatever level of modernity. Even if the dissonance is insoluble, confronting it pays off because it takes you deeper into the text, and playing solutions will be found, and interesting ideas will surface, that might not otherwise have been thought of. But if a director takes the view that none of this matters and the audience won't care anyway, you'll get a performance that, however good to look at, skips superficially over the surface of the language, producing only a generalised effect where the words lack roots, purpose and meaning. Pictures to look at, with no thoughts to hear.

LOVE TRIANGLE

Drama loves the moment when life hovers at a fine point of balance, when things might go one way or another, when a word or a gesture, a chance encounter, a closed door or a fleeting mood, changes things for ever. Many of Shakespeare's plays have a single key pivotal moment on which the action hinges and by which the drama is shaped. In *Twelfth Night* this is when Olivia falls in love with Viola while believing her to be a young man. When exactly is that moment? Who is present in the lead-up to it? Malvolio, Olivia's steward, who has brought the news of the newcomer at the gate, has been dismissed and Maria summoned, so Olivia has at least one other person with her to receive Orsino's latest emissary. In Shakespeare's day a common measure of your status if you were rich and powerful was the number of people you had following you around all day ready to take orders, give advice, entertain you, run errands and generally wait on your whims. In the (unique) Folio text Olivia enters Act Five with 'attendants'; whether the director sees these figures as servants, courtiers, ladies-in-waiting or a mixture will depend on the importance given to the cultural and dramatic significance ascribed to the human activity around a countess in mourning. A rich and interesting social ballet could be created with the movement, reactions and functions of virtually any number of nameless characters operating around the central figure with varying degrees of deference, each with their own imagined backstory. However, it's much more likely that the director, having a tight budget and a small cast, won't have any choice in the matter and that Maria will be the sole 'attendant' throughout. Whether set in a period or modern world the psychological rationale for Olivia not having a huge entourage hanging about is clear enough to establish anyway – she's in mourning, she wants to be alone, and this heightens the human importance of the few she does keep close – Malvolio, Feste and Maria. Anyway, let's work on the assumption that there are no attendants besides these three, and that Maria is the only other person present when Olivia first meets Cesario.

In RSC productions over the years, where extra actors are usually available, directors have become very keen on a particular visual gag. On Olivia's lines –

> Give me my veil; come throw it o'er my face.
> We'll once more hear Orsino's embassy

– she indicates to Maria, and however many other ladies-in-waiting are present, to also veil themselves (after all, the whole court is meant to be in mourning), so Viola makes her entrance to a room full of identical, faceless, black-clad females. The laugh is meant to come on Viola's first line:

> The honourable lady of the house, which is she?

It's not a bad gag, but if you think about it, it's not actually as funny as the situation in a 'poor theatre' production where she would be just addressing two women, neither of whom she has met. If she is looking at Olivia, veiled, and the servant, Maria, unveiled, it is perfectly obvious which of the two is the glamorous countess who has captured the heart of the man Viola has so recently fallen in love with. Her question therefore becomes a cheeky act of micro-aggression towards a female rival, and the 'Will she, won't she, lift the veil?' issue generates a force field of comic emotional tension. This energy is increased both by Viola's inability, while pretending to be lower status, to actually *feel* lower status, and her perfectly understandable curiosity to see Olivia's face. When she finally does, it is a huge gear change in the narrative momentum of the scene as she absorbs the face that has launched Orsino's mind onto the wild ocean of obsessive infatuation.

Viola's first line asks a very straightforward question: *Which one of you is the Countess Olivia?* The reply she gets is childish game-playing:

> Speak to me, I shall answer for her. Your will?

Viola, on edge and unhappy to be there, could be forgiven for thinking, *Is this the behaviour of a grief-stricken sister and daughter?* Does this skittish play-acting reveal a hypocrisy in Olivia's state of mind and put a question mark over her character? There is a moment here where power shifts: Viola may be pretending to be someone she isn't, but then Olivia too may have been posing, manufacturing a phoney emotional state for her own ends. The actor playing Viola might want to pause here and gaze at the veiled woman, who has already effectively declared herself to be the 'lady of the house', with an expression that says *You cannot be serious!* followed by a silent beat of *OK, if that's the way you want it,* and then the first line of her prepared speech: 'Most radiant, exquisite and unmatchable beauty –' a speech immediately aborted by the thought, *This is ridiculous,* and expressed with great wit in the words:

> I pray you, tell me if this be the lady of the house, for I never saw her. I would be loath to cast away my speech, for, besides that it is excellently well penned, I have taken great pains to con it. Good beauties, let me sustain no scorn: I am very comptible, even to the least sinister usage.

From Olivia's point of view, the arc of the whole scene is from curiosity (a state of mind that begins even before she meets 'Cesario' and is based on Malvolio's account of the conversation at the gate) to love. In the condensed energy of Shakespeare's writing, this massive emotional shift that the actor has to make, takes only about ten minutes of stage time in which a great deal has to happen. This is why the beat-by-beat evolution of the relationship has to be so carefully plotted in rehearsal. In the speech just quoted there are several small but significant changes of direction. There is the moment when Viola decides not to continue with the prepared speech in defiance of Olivia's question ('Your will?') until her own question has been answered. Then she speaks to Maria *about* Olivia, which could be construed as downright rude, or at least a refusal to be cowed and bossed about: 'I pray you, tell me if this be the lady of the house.' Then there is the display of confidence in making a joke about the danger of making her speech to the wrong person and so wasting it. She wittily dramatises the situation by begging her audience to be considerate, given that not only is it a good speech but one that she's gone to the trouble of learning by heart. Finally, she transgresses well above her presumed status by asking them not to be rude ('Good beauties, let me sustain no scorn'), and ends by suggesting they respect her nature by telling them she's highly sensitive to the merest hint of discourtesy. Basically: *Don't mess me about!*

Viola freely makes references to acting as if, perhaps for her own comfort, she can't resist hinting that she is playing a part. It's an interesting rehearsal-room question: how far does the actor want to take this thought? Although on the Elizabethan stage the convention of disguise was absolute – no one in any play ever sees through anyone's disguise –

it's possible to play Viola as almost wanting to be found out, so excruciating is the trap she has caught herself in. The image of an actor on a stage deepens as the dialogue continues with her refusal to answer the question: 'Whence came you, sir?' – a question about her background, not her mission from Orsino, something that Olivia knows about only too well. She says: 'I can say little more than I've studied, and that question's out of my part.' She's trying desperately hard to tell the truth even while living a lie; the 'part' she is playing is Cesario, a servant/courtier of Orsino, a young man born into the character only days ago. When Olivia asks ironically, 'Are you a comedian?' the actor needs to remember that the primary meaning of the word 'comedian' was a professional actor, and this delicate verbal dance between pretending and trying to be as honest as possible takes her to the edge of revelation on the line, 'I swear – I am not that I play.' This is such an extraordinary thing to say that, as the moment hangs in the air, it needs a huge distraction, which it gets with: 'Are you the lady of the house?' It's almost as if Viola is saying, *I'm not the person you think I am, but are YOU the person I think you are?!* By now Olivia is comprehensively intrigued, and from this moment on, the scene becomes progressively about falling in love. After she sends Maria away and is alone with Viola – who to her is a beautiful, strange, confident young man who treats her with a judgemental disdain – she becomes increasingly immersed in 'his' personality and opinions. Hearing that he can't understand her rejection of Orsino, she asks, 'Why, what would you?' and prompts Viola's famous speech beginning:

> Make me a willow cabin at your gate
> And call upon my soul within the house.

Its poetic intensity is generated within Viola because, deep down, she is speaking about her feelings for Orsino, accidentally catching Olivia in her verbal web.

'Even so quickly may one catch the plague?', as Olivia puts it when Viola has gone, and with that common Elizabethan metaphor, the love triangle is complete: Olivia loves Viola who loves Orsino who loves Olivia.

WHAT'S YOUR METAPHOR?

The twin masks of comedy and tragedy revolve, blend and fade into each other in plays like *Twelfth Night* and *Hamlet*. Two of Shakespeare's greatest plays, they were probably composed within the same year, 1600, almost exactly at the midway point of his career. We call one a

comedy and one a tragedy, but neither reveals their true nature in production if that is the only way director and cast treat them. It is part of
the definition of what makes great drama that an audience should not
only suspend their disbelief but are, at the same time, suspended
between laughter and tears.

It's said that humour doesn't translate well between cultures, and the
same can be said of periods of history, given that the past is another
country, and one with a different funny bone. Finding the balance
between sad and funny, tragic and comic, may be a vital part of
rehearsals for any play, but with Shakespeare there is the extra challenge
that you are often dealing with material that is clearly meant to be
funny and that the Elizabethans obviously found funny, but which to
us is bewilderingly unfunny. Act 1 Scene 3 of *Twelfth Night* is a classic
example of the problem, where obscurity of language and unfamiliar
references so combine that the director's choices are: leave, distract,
change, or cut!

The scene begins with an ill-tempered dialogue between Sir Toby
Belch, Olivia's ne'er-do-well uncle, and Maria, Olivia's waiting-gentle-
woman, who we gradually come to realise is Toby's girlfriend – sort of.

> SIR TOBY. What a plague means my niece to take the death of
> her brother thus? I am sure care's an enemy to life.
> MARIA. By my troth, Sir Toby, you must come in earlier
> o'nights. Your cousin, my lady, takes great exceptions to
> your ill hours.
> SIR TOBY. Why, let her except, before excepted.
> MARIA. Ay, but you must confine yourself within the modest
> limits of order.
> SIR TOBY. Confine? I'll confine myself no finer than I am.
> These clothes are good enough to drink in, and so be these
> boots too; an they be not, let them hang themselves in
> their own straps.

I have directed *Twelfth Night* five times and have always had to use the
notes to remind myself what these jokes mean. '*Exceptis excipiendis*' was
a common legal phrase, so that was one for the young trainee lawyers in
the Globe audience. Toby's 'confine' twists Maria's use of the word to
refer to getting himself dressed, which pun then sets up the mention of
'boots' and thereby the use of the then well-known proverb about
hanging yourself with your own bootlaces. Equipped with this
knowledge, director and actors can then get down to working out how
they want to play the scene, the relationship between Maria and Toby,

their relationship to the broader household, and what they will actually be doing while talking to each other. After a few rehearsals it's perfectly possible that everyone involved will have forgotten that to begin with none of them understood what they were saying. By the time the first performance arrives and the actors have confidence that they are making sense, it may well be, if the playing is beguiling enough and the audience are charmed and intrigued by these new characters, that they won't notice that they don't understand the text, or don't care if they do notice.

Another possibility is to create some hilariously comic physical 'business', probably involving either Toby being drunk or hungover and Maria helping him on (or off) with his boots, in the hope that the audience are laughing too much to hear the lines anyway. Another option might be to change the lines in some way to make them more comprehensible, if – jarringly – un-Shakespearean. Or perhaps they could simply be cut?

Any of these four solutions – leave, distract, change or cut – could be absolutely fine, but I'm interested in the more fundamental question: how much should you care about text not being understood by an audience? Actors can become deeply fond of lines they have worked hard to understand and are very good at persuading themselves that they can make them understood. There is, I suppose, the remote possibility that one may actually be able to make listeners understand the precise meaning of 'let her except, before excepted', but certainly the actor has to remember that they once themselves found it deeply obscure, and that the audience is hearing it for the first time with no opportunity to ponder its meaning. In rehearsal this dilemma needs to be thought through carefully, remembering too that if someone in the audience is thinking hard about what they've just heard they probably won't hear the next line at all. This is the framework in which you should make the decision about whether to leave, distract from, change, or cut an obscure line of text:

1. The actor must know what it means.

2. The character wants the person they're talking to to know what they mean.

3. There is a purpose behind them saying it.

However he says it, Sir Toby wants to communicate what he's thinking. If the actor energetically and with total commitment embraces this fact, there is a chance that, even if not understood exactly in terms of the original meaning, he may be understood in a different, but relevant way such as: *Let her accept me for the way I am without taking exception to everything I do.* It matters to Toby that he is treated with some respect; it must be hard for him to accept that his young niece has authority over him and is in the position to police his behaviour. He is a man denuded of any authority in a household coming to be dominated by the Puritan ethic of a servant, the steward Malvolio, whom he suspects of gross hypocrisy. The way Toby and Olivia clash in the play will never be funny unless the underlying tension created by the balance of power between them is understood and played to the hilt. No actor in Shakespeare should ever speak a line unless they believe it will be understood by the entire audience in a way that is constructive to the story being told.

But if audiences should always understand a character's lines, Shakespeare often creates wonderful comedy from another character's incomprehension – in this play the 'foolish knight' Sir Andrew Aguecheek. This is how he is introduced:

> MARIA. That quaffing and drinking will undo you. I heard my
> lady talk of it yesterday, and of a foolish knight that you
> brought in one night here to be her wooer.
> SIR TOBY. Who, Sir Andrew Aguecheek?
> MARIA. Ay, he.
> SIR TOBY. He's as tall a man as any's in Illyria.
> MARIA. What's that to th' purpose?
> SIR TOBY. Why, he has three thousand ducats a year.
> MARIA. Ay, but he'll have but a year in all these ducats. He's a
> very fool and a prodigal.
> SIR TOBY. Fie that you'll say so! He plays o'th' viol-de-
> gamboys, and speaks three or four languages word for
> word without book and hath all the good gifts of nature.
> MARIA. He hath indeed, almost natural, for, besides that he's a
> fool, he's a great quarreller, and but that he hath the gift of a
> coward to allay the gust he hath in quarrelling, 'tis thought
> among the prudent he would quickly have the gift of a grave.
> SIR TOBY. By this hand they are scoundrels and substractors
> that say so of him. Who are they?
> MARIA. They that add moreover, he's drunk nightly in your
> company.
> SIR TOBY. With drinking healths to my niece. I'll drink to her as
> long as there is a passage in my throat and drink in Illyria.
> He's a coward and a coistrel that will not drink to my niece
> till his brains turn o'th' toe, like a parish top. What, wench,
> Castiliano vulgo, for here comes Sir Andrew Agueface.

There is not too much obscurity in this passage until the reference to the 'parish top' and the bizarre pseudo-Spanish phrase that Toby comes out with on seeing Andrew approaching. The movement through the dialogue up to this point lets the audience begin to feel the shared sense of humour between the two of them as Maria's reprimand gradually changes to complicity with Sir Toby. It's classic role play: Toby's mock-defence of his guest is an attitude put on to encourage Maria's acid wit, and we should begin to see how much these two enjoy each other's company.

There is an important narrative point that can easily get missed at the start of this section: that Andrew is here notionally as a potential husband for Olivia, 'brought in… to be her wooer' – the first mention of the device being used to keep the man around long enough to milk him of his money. Toby has managed to persuade Andrew he's in with a realistic chance of marriage to his niece. This is backstory worth working on: how on earth did he do it? In the absence of her father or brother, Toby can validly claim to be the only senior male figure in the household with any authority over Olivia – he's her uncle. I should qualify that: 'authority' in a period setting; 'influence' in a modern one. That he is using his position for wholly selfish reasons and doesn't care about the annoyance this will cause Olivia, or the mental damage his certain rejection will do to Andrew, are important measures of his character, but the actors playing Andrew and Toby need to find ways of avoiding clichés and stereotyping. As there is no good comedy without tension and the possibility of sudden reversal, it is best to assume that Andrew is not a complete fool and that Toby is a superb actor, as most successful con men are. The dialogue above sets this up. Maria's description of Toby's supposed friend as a fool, coward, drunk and inveterate quarreller needs to be set against the assertion that he is tall (which also meant valiant), a talented linguist, and a competent musician. Even though these compliments are clearly tongue-in-cheek and designed to wind up Maria's wit rather than actually convince her, it is also the kind of flattery that must be working. Andrew is still there, still believing in his chances and still believing Toby is a friend who admires him deeply. If this is to be credible in performance it's better to assume there is a smattering of truth about it; the con man needs something to work on. Why shouldn't Andrew be able to speak a little bit of Spanish and Italian? Why shouldn't he be able to pluck a few chords on a lute? Many men of his class in the Elizabethan period had this kind of training in music and languages; he will become a caricature if all ability is denied him. He can't be played as a total idiot because that eliminates the possibility that he might, at any moment, realise he is being conned, and that will leave the relationship stuck in the realm of pantomime. An interesting exercise would be for Maria to be a little uncertain about what Toby says. Maybe he can play the bass viol a little bit; maybe he does speak another language, and even if she thinks he's cowardly, she's also heard he's always getting into quarrels… Uncertainty is richer territory than bland assumption for exploring one character's view of another. Later in the play Sir Andrew has one of my favourite lines in the whole of Shakespeare: when his 'friend' Toby boasts of being adored by Maria, Andrew replies, 'I was adored once too.' I would rather believe that was true; it's both funny and sad, like so much of life.

Let's go back to where he enters the action.

SIR ANDREW. Sir Toby Belch! How now, Sir Toby Belch?
SIR TOBY. Sweet Sir Andrew.
SIR ANDREW. Bless you, fair shrew.
MARIA. And you too, sir.
SIR TOBY. Accost, Sir Andrew, accost.
SIR ANDREW. What's that?
SIR TOBY. My niece's chambermaid.
SIR ANDREW. Good Mistress Accost, I desire better acquaintance.
MARIA. My name is Mary, sir.
SIR ANDREW. Good Mistress Mary Accost.
SIR TOBY. You mistake, knight. 'Accost' is front her, board her, woo her, assail her.
SIR ANDREW. By my troth I would not undertake her in this company. Is that the meaning of 'accost'?
MARIA. Fare you well gentlemen.

It's easy to forget that Maria has never met Sir Andrew before, only heard about him. Her opinions about him earlier when talking to Toby were second-hand. So what should her attitude to him be in this brief encounter? She must be curious; and I think that would dictate her behaviour. It always makes good theatre to see two people forming a view of each other on a first meeting, especially someone we've heard about. We tend to be curious not only about others but also about our own reactions to others. It's as if, in feeling out where we can go with someone, we are also finding out something about ourselves, often measuring our capacities for admiration or scorn. In this particular moment it seems Maria satisfies her curiosity fairly quickly, but Toby is

determined to prolong the situation savouring the collision between
Andrew's clumsy hopelessness with women and Maria's sharp wit.

> SIR TOBY. An thou let part so, Sir Andrew, would thou
> mightst never draw sword again.
> SIR ANDREW. An you part so, mistress, I would I might never
> draw sword again. Fair lady, do you think you have fools
> in hand?
> MARIA. Sir, I have not you by th' hand.
> SIR ANDREW. Marry, but you shall have, and here's my hand.
> MARIA. Now, sir, thought is free. I pray you, bring your hand
> to th' buttery-bar, and let it drink.
> SIR ANDREW. Wherefore, sweetheart? What's your metaphor?
> MARIA. It's dry, sir.
> SIR ANDREW. Why, I think so. I am not such an ass but I can
> keep my hand dry. But what's your jest?
> MARIA. A dry jest, sir.
> SIR ANDREW. Are you full of them?
> MARIA. Ay, sir, I have them at my fingers' ends. Marry, now I
> let go your hand, I am barren. [*Exit.*]

The first question is how to make the meanings clear concerning the
Elizabethan belief that dry hands indicated sexual inadequacy; and
even if you can convince yourselves that this is possible, there remains
the issue of exactly what physical activity is implied by the text. Clearly
at some point Andrew and Maria need to make hand contact, probably
immediately after 'here's my hand' – but how does he actually offer his
hand? A modern handshake? Offering it to be kissed in reverse of convention? How he offers it conditions how she takes it, but essentially
she must really feel it as dry and play the sense of wanting to help his
sexual problem by giving the hand a drink. He, of course, doesn't get
the joke, but the joke isn't for him, it's for Toby. What we need to understand from the moment is that it's not about cruelty to Sir Andrew: it's
a step along the path of seducing Sir Toby. Maria is every bit as much a
social climber as Malvolio, and she has Toby in her sights. At the end
of the play they marry, underlining the very real possibility of class
mobility in this society – and, incidentally, that Malvolio is not so crazy
after all. But we will come to him below.

For the rest of the scene the two men are alone together; in performance we should suddenly feel an enormous change in the atmosphere.
Andrew no longer has to think of impressing his friend with his chat-
up technique, and Toby has lost his audience. While Maria was there he

had someone to play to while enjoying the secret complicity of shared mockery. By making a quick exit, Maria has made clear her disapproval of the scam that he's engaged in. To be alone with someone you despise while pretending to admire them is not much fun, and, for Toby, keeping up the act of being Andrew's best friend must feel like hard work. The effort should show through; not enough for Andrew to be aware of it, but just enough for the audience to sense it. Toby Belch is treating his guest appallingly in pretending to like him, but there is a weird kind of poetic justice about the situation. In forcing himself to spend time with a person he can't stand, he suffers stress, boredom and irritation, and he deserves whatever discomfort this brings. The effect would probably be to make him permanently angry, which he would have to work hard to conceal, and that effort would make him even angrier. He has to be on his guard not to give himself away – he is his own punishment. So here is the source of tension the director needs to create. Toby needs the money, and the deeper he lures Andrew into thinking of him as a dear friend the more dangerous the situation becomes for him. On top of this, Andrew's lack of confidence means he might give up on the Olivia project at any moment, so Toby has to pile on the encouragement, but it is tiring work. Andrew, thinking his friend has faith in him, is in constant need of personal therapy and reassurance.

> SIR TOBY. O knight, thou lack'st a cup of canary: when did I
> see thee so put down?
> SIR ANDREW. Never in your life, I think, unless you see canary
> put me down. Methinks sometimes I have no more wit
> than a Christian or an ordinary man has; but I am a great
> eater of beef, and I believe that does harm to my wit.
> SIR TOBY. No question.
> SIR ANDREW. An I thought that, I'd forswear it. I'll ride home
> tomorrow, Sir Toby.
> SIR TOBY. *Pourquoi*, my dear knight?
> SIR ANDREW. What is 'pourquoi'? Do, or not do? I would I
> had bestowed that time in the tongues that I have in
> fencing, dancing and bear-baiting. O, had I but followed
> the arts.

So maybe Sir Andrew's linguistic skills are not so great after all, but with his nervy butterfly mind it's hard to know where his true personality lies. He is being indulged by his friend to think of himself as the heroic centre of his own fascinating story in a way he is not used to. I think it is interesting in rehearsal to find the most detailed ways of building the notion of Andrew's dependency on Toby; the feeling that he is the best, maybe the one true, friend that he has ever had. By the time of their final joint exit in the fifth act, nursing the wounds inflicted by Sebastian, Andrew says tenderly, 'I'll help you, Sir Toby, because we'll be dressed together,' and it is that assumption of closeness and comradeship in adversity that finally unleashes in Toby the anger I was speaking of that must be growing inside him throughout the play. As the rosecoloured spectacles of their 'friendship' are brutally ripped from Andrew's eyes we should experience one of those moments where comedy and tragedy are indivisible: one thing, one complex emotion, typical of Shakespeare and typical of this play.

> SIR TOBY. Will you help? An ass-head and a coxcomb and a
> knave, a thin-faced knave, a gull?

Sir Andrew has no reply, but he knows that someone, somewhere, adored him once. Who that was we will never know.

WHO IS MALVOLIO?

What is Malvolio's place in the social world of the play? Can it be easily identified and is it recognisable? I think it, is and we have several clues to go on. Researching for my RSC production, I spent some time exploring the structure of an Elizabethan household and finding out what a 'steward' was in that context. I was interested to discover that he was a far more important figure than I had thought, far more than just a glorified butler. He was a highly trained, highly educated person, responsible for aspects of the house, gardens and land. He was often a very erudite man and probably an expert huntsman and archer. He had to have a strong sense of economics, as he kept the books and controlled the finances, making him a key figure in the successful running of the house and staff. It's the importance of the steward's role that makes the character both ambivalent and intriguing, not only in this play but in all dramatic literature of the period. When Malvolio muses that 'The Lady of the Strachy married the yeoman of the wardrobe,' he may be referring to a slightly ridiculous topical example of upward social mobility, but unless you take his aspiration as genuinely realisable you undermine the realistic, satirical comedy of the play and make it purely fantastical and farcical. It's not particularly important that Sir Toby finds it genuinely outrageous that the hated steward should contemplate marriage to his niece Olivia; all that tells us is something about

Toby, and nothing about the reality of what Malvolio wants and believes in for himself.

If director and actor don't accept that such a union is possible, as indeed it was in a period of emerging social mobility, then you simply have to conclude that Malvolio is effectively mad, in which case the project to drive him mad, or at least lead him to the edge of madness, loses its complexity, and that part of the play becomes thinner and too obvious. *The Duchess of Malfi*, written only a decade later by Shakespeare's younger contemporary John Webster, is a play about a steward marrying a duchess. It is a bitter tragedy where the author's sympathy is clearly with the two lovers whose brutal treatment at the hands of an outraged aristocrat sharply reflects the sensitivity to social changes of the time. Malvolio's dreams were dreams shared by many.

We know other things about Malvolio. He is without a sense of humour but called upon to express his opinion all the time. We have to remember that he is invited by Olivia to offer advice: 'What think you... Malvolio?' She has recently lost her father and her brother, and she appears to need his guidance. Why would he not be encouraged by that need to feel his importance to her growing by the day; to see himself as the only stable male in a world of men who are either drunkards (Toby), wimps (Andrew), or infuriatingly oblique comedians (Feste)? She is well aware of his weaknesses, but one of Olivia's challenges is to keep the discordant elements of her household in some sort of equilibrium. *Ignore him too much*, you can hear her thinking, *and he will only get worse and more isolated*. She wants to bring him in, but the audience needs to understand that, as he sees it, she wants to make him special. He is an unforgiving man and judges people harshly. Also, the male competition is not great: he can be forgiven for thinking he stands out. He can be forgiven for misreading the signals. It is crucial to set this up very clearly in the audience's mind before the 'letter' scene if he is not to seem merely a caricature of a narcissistic fantasist. He is often played as a straight-backed Puritan in the narrow religious sense, the polar opposite of a free-wheeling, life-loving Sir Toby, but I think he is indeed 'a kind of Puritan', as Maria says, and when she goes on to elaborate ('The devil a Puritan that he is, or anything constantly but a time-pleaser, an affectioned ass'), the implication is that he will be anything that he thinks will advance him. His pose is the pose of a Puritan because that's what gives him a sense of authority, dignity and purpose within the household.

All the time in rehearsals the director has to keep reminding the cast what an absolutely crucial body of people the real, on-the-ground, active Puritans were in Shakespeare's England. Another forty years and they were running the country. The theatres were all closed, and party-time Belch-style was well and truly over. Malvolio offers a foretaste of this. If the Countess's house is seen as a microcosm of the country as a whole, then Head Steward to the Countess Olivia is the equivalent of the Lord Chamberlain to Queen Elizabeth; more or less the same as being Prime Minister today. He regards himself as important because he *is* important. If it wasn't for Malvolio, the place would be in total chaos. If it was left to Sir Toby, filling the house with his drinking pals and carrying on an affair with his niece's maidservant, things would fall apart completely and Olivia would be overwhelmed by the spirit of anarchy. Like him or not – and most people in the play do not – without the humourless steward the place would be a shambles. And as prime gatekeeper of his mistress's privacy, which is currently under siege from the amorous Duke down the road, he is second to none.

In rehearsing his scenes you also have to look at the obverse side of that situation – how he uses his position, how he is keeping Olivia to himself, how he is relishing, and probably encouraging, the extended period of mourning that the household is under. He might even have come up with the seven-year-long cloister-haunting himself. So what I would always stress to the actor playing Malvolio is not only that he thinks he's important because he is important, but that this is the very thing that is pulling his personality out of balance and filling his head with false notions of what is achievable emotionally and what isn't.

IN THE DARK ROOM

Malvolio is a tragic portrait of the kind of delusional man who certainly should not go out in the midday sun. The things that he believes about himself and is persuaded to believe about his situation are quite extra-ordinary. He is a picture of a particular kind of human vanity that can truly lead to madness; actually, already is a kind of madness. Olivia calls his behaviour, as he struts and beams in his yellow stockings, 'mid-summer madness'. As with Sir Andrew, acting such a lack of self-awareness in a character demands great self-awareness in the actor in order to avoid falling into caricature. Malvolio is a man who has blin-kered himself to the reality of his situation and the viable aspirations he can expect to have within it. He is (sober soul that he is) drunk on the spirit of his imagination, and, as a result, incapable of seeing things clearly. After his display of stockings and smiles to a woman whose reaction most would read as unmistakably negative, he is astonishingly capable of interpreting the encounter in a wholly positive way. So sucked into his own illusion is he, that he is deaf to the satirical tone of mock-concern from Toby, Maria and Fabian. Everything that has just happened is seen only through his own distorted vision of himself, a classic case of a man hearing only what he wants to hear despite all the evidence pointing in another direction. Why should the Lady Olivia not marry her steward ? How can this man be taken seriously when his self-delusion is on such a scale? How can he not be a caricature?

As I mentioned above, a decade after *Twelfth Night* went before the public, Shakespeare's company performed John Webster's dark tragedy *The Duchess of Malfi*, whose titular heroine falls in love with and secretly marries her steward. The action of this play takes place not in the relatively socially liberal, upwardly mobile world of Protestant England, but in the conservative, male-dominated society of Roman Catholic Italy. The marriage and its consequences are explored with sympathy and sensitivity, the tone is tragic, and the disasters that befall the central couple are shockingly moving. There is no hint of comedy, let alone mockery, about the treatment of Antonio, the steward.

To make Malvolio a real person, the actor should try to see him as another Antonio, who clearly believes that he lives in a world in which class is not a barrier to advancement, as was proved to be true time and again throughout the Tudor period. It's true that the key signature of Webster's play is tragic and that of *Twelfth Night* comic, but Shakespeare always blended the masks and animated them so their expressions were constantly changing. If a director finds what is comic in *King Lear*, the tragic aspect will be moving not bathetic. Find Malvolio's tragedy and the comedy will be immeasurably enhanced. Truth is always the way to laughter.

There is a great deal of madness in *Twelfth Night*. People often talk about it as if it was simply a 'revels' play, a light and fickle romp in the spirit of holiday pantomime. Perhaps this is because of the association of its title with the Christmas festival, but for all its laughter and charm it's very much darker than that. Like so many of Shakespeare's plays, it is about what happens to individuals when their picture of themselves prevents them from taking in the reality of the world around them. They act irrationally, lose their sense of proportion, become unbalanced and fail to know themselves. What happens to Malvolio is an example of the consequences of this lack of self-knowledge. He takes himself too seriously, makes enemies by his insensitive handling of others, and this emotional deficit blinds him to the vicious trick played on him by Maria. His vanity and self-importance are too great for him to react sensibly to the forged letter purporting to be from his employer. To Olivia, unaware of the deception, his behaviour seems as crazy as that of a madman. 'Why, this is very midsummer madness,' she exclaims, and perhaps this is what gives Sir Toby the idea for what follows: the imprisonment of the steward in a madhouse cell.

> SIR TOBY. Come, we'll have him in a dark room and bound.
> My niece is already in the belief that he's mad. We may
> carry it thus for our pleasure and his penance till our very
> pastime, tired out of breath, prompt us to have mercy on
> him; at which time we will take the device to the bar and
> crown thee for a finder of madmen.

Deciding how to stage the 'dark room' scene is nearly always a problem for directors. An audience will have divided sympathies when Toby's plan is put into effect. Malvolio is humourless and hard to like, yet the way he is treated seems monstrously unfair and out of all proportion to what he has actually done. So the balance to be struck in staging and playing the scene is a very fine one. The idea of being taken to a dark cell and physically restrained was quite typical of the way the Elizabethan authorities might treat someone they believed to be mad. Attitudes to mental illness were bewilderingly unsympathetic and, to put it mildly, very rough and ready compared to today. They were frightened of madness, and brutal as a result. Any production set in a post-Freudian period is going to experience conceptual difficulties. My own production for the RSC was set in the Elizabethan era (although with Eastern European costumes rather than English), so at least psychological dissonance was not an issue. But the main staging problem anyway is a purely physical one: how much should you see?

The stage directions for Act 4 Scene 2 imply that Malvolio is out of sight of both the other characters and the audience. He is described as speaking from '*within*', and no precise location is given in the Folio text (there is no Quarto text of this play). In an Elizabethan playhouse he might have been speaking from behind a curtained recess at the back of the stage, or from a trapdoor underneath it. A possible staging, then and now, would be to replace the trapdoor with some kind of grille set into the stage floor that allowed only a hand to appear like some small animal pleading on behalf of its owner. That's a powerful image; in fact it's the idea we first started with in rehearsals. However, the more you work on this scene, the more you want to find some way of having the character fully visible on stage. He only has five scenes in the entire play, and it does seem a shame to have him physically absent from one of the most important. My Malvolio had a strong preference for being on the stage rather than under it.

Deciding to have him in full view raises questions because the text makes it clear that he is not able to see his principal tormentor, Feste the Fool, who changes in the course of the scene from being himself to playing a different character. Malvolio is also, according to the text, tied up, so his movement is constrained. Some productions have him in a straitjacket or bound in a wheelchair, which means of course he has to be either blindfolded or have a hat jammed over his eyes, or a bucket or hood covering his head: his eyes cannot see, nor can we see his eyes. But our Malvolio had the most magnificent eyes, huge and highly expressive, the greatest physical asset a stage actor can have. It would have been a pity to cover them. Nevertheless it remains vital to the sense of the script that he cannot see the Fool and that he should be physically restrained in some way. During rehearsal we came up with the idea of him being chained to a post, like the bears in the bear-baiting arenas so popular in Shakespeare's day. It fitted well with the notion of Malvolio's being the victim of a cruel sport laid on for Sir Toby's pleasure. As we discussed it, we remembered the dialogue between Fabian and Toby at the beginning of Act 2 Scene 5, where the audience discovers the reason Fabian has a grudge against the steward: he had reported him to the Countess for organising a bear-baiting on her land: 'You know he brought me out o'favour with my lady about a bear-baiting here.' Sir Toby's instant response is: 'To anger him we'll have that bear again, and we will fool him black and blue.' The whole cast agreed that the image of Malvolio chained to a post was strikingly theatrical, came out of the text, and was typical of Toby's warped and bitter imagination. The next time we worked on the scene, one of the actors suggested that we set it in the dark room itself, that the whole stage should become a cellar to which Feste descended by ladder joining his victim in his prison cell. This would mean that both characters were in darkness unable to see, only to hear each other. There would be no need for any kind of blindfold to cover the eyes for the room would be pitch black.

This all made a lot of sense, and also provided a solution to something that had puzzled us all – why, if Malvolio cannot see Feste and they are not in the same room together, does the Fool bother to put on a disguise of cloak and false beard in order to impersonate Sir Topas the priest (a real character referred to in the play but one who happens not to appear)? Why would it not be enough just to alter his voice? But if they are both stumbling around in the dark together in the same space, then there is some logic to it. Feste could stay beyond his reach when being himself, but come nearer, allowing Malvolio to touch his beard and cloak, when assuming the person of the priest.

These are the moments in rehearsal when actors and director feel the satisfaction of solving practical problems together, when you realise that rehearsing is about finding solutions to what works on stage, and you all experience the craft of shaping narrative and character into stage imagery. It's never about chewing over metaphysical ideas about meaning on an intellectual level. You could say that Malvolio placed in a dark room is a metaphor for his blindness to reality caused by his self-love – but you are better not to say it in a rehearsal room. You cannot act a metaphor.

So it was decided that we would set the scene *in* the 'dark room' specified in the text. This created the problem of how to place Maria and Toby on the stage: they are the 'audience' and present for the first part of the scene. Originally the idea was to have them both very close to Feste egging him on, but instead it was decided to put them at a high window where they could be seen, lit by a tightly focused spotlight, listening to the dialogue down below, smirking at their own cleverness, giggling, kissing and, not to put too fine a point on it, generally getting off on the whole situation. Staging the scene this way also reminded the audience that what was happening between Feste and Malvolio was below ground, subterranean and illicit. It also underlined what a seedy, unsavoury character Toby is; certainly not the lovable rogue, the life-enhancing spirit of mirth that he likes to see himself as. He's closer, perhaps, to being Falstaff's duller and nastier younger brother (if such a character existed). In fact no one in *Twelfth Night* is what they seem or want to seem. Toby is an irresponsible drunken bore who tries to exploit everyone around him, chiefly Maria (well below him in class terms but desperate to better herself), Olivia (off whose money he lives) and, of course, poor Sir Andrew Aguecheek (who believes that he has finally found a friend who understands him). In rehearsal opinions differed about how much, if at all, Toby changes during the baiting of the steward in the dark room. Some thought that his line 'I would we were well rid of this knavery' indicates he's beginning to feel remorse and some guilt, and that the start of a change has begun in him; but others felt he remained, and would always remain, a constitutionally insensitive man who could never be moved by anyone's suffering, let alone Malvolio's. We concluded that the unease expressed in this line, as the humiliation of their victim takes on a darker and more serious complexion, had more to do with worrying about his own skin rather than an awakening sensitivity. He is already in big trouble with Olivia over the night of drunken partying with Andrew (surely not the first evening of that kind), and he must reckon that the trick of the fake letter is bound to be exposed sooner rather than later. He seems to have decided not to take things any further. 'If he may be conveniently delivered,' he remarks, 'I would he were, for I am now so far in offence with my niece that I cannot pursue with any safety this sport to the upshot.'

As the way to stage the scene became clearer, so the way of rehearsing it changed to specific physical experimentation involving work with blindfolds or in blacked-out rehearsal rooms as the actors playing Malvolio and Feste learnt how to play a sighted person who could suddenly no longer see. We explored the kind of fears you would experience such as the danger of sharp objects or falling into a hole in the ground, and the sensation of coming into contact with something unexpected. A discovery that surprised us was how much the human voice changes in those circumstances, becoming higher in pitch and more hesitant and restrained. But by far the most important revelation was how to light the scene, which up till then I had assumed we would play in near total darkness, allowing the audience mere glimpses of the characters, moving like shadows while shrouded in the gloom of the improvised torture chamber. Then someone mentioned the play by Peter Shaffer called *Black Comedy*, in which a sudden power failure causes a group of people in a room to find themselves in total blackout. The clever comic device is to start the play in blackout, with the characters speaking normally as though the lights are on, but then, at the moment of the power cut, to flood the stage with light while the actors play being unable to see anything at all. It was a great idea to steal. Instead of a crepuscular haze we decided to create a square of bright white light exactly centre stage, the walls of the room delineated by the sides of the square. The device worked exceptionally well in performance. Both actors had their eyes wide open, straining to see through the 'dark'. It was instantly clear to the audience by the way the characters moved, stared and listened, that neither could see the other, and every movement and gesture was minutely choreographed. Lighting the scene in this way not only heightened the element of farce but also the cruelty, horror and humour combining in a uniquely Shakespearean way.

Malvolio is not mad in this scene. Nor does he go mad, despite Fabian's nervy suggestion that 'we shall make him mad indeed'. He hangs on desperately to his reason, and the audience should feel respect for his ability to do so. In fact he emerges with his dignity enhanced rather than diminished and humiliated. But there is certainly a 'mad' quality about the 'dark room', with snatches of strange song, the mutating of Feste from Fool to Priest and back again, and the wild, virtually incomprehensible, cod philosophy concerning Pythagoras, wildfowl and the transmigration of souls. The use of bright light to represent darkness seemed strangely consistent with the surreal nature of the whole episode. For this production I treated the play as one primarily about what happens to people when they lose their sense of mental and moral balance, and tried to stress the traditional links between love and madness: to show characters behaving in ways that were extreme, or deluded, uncharacteristic or even slightly 'touched'. This Illyria was a country of baking heat, mad dogs and Englishmen going out in the midday sun. The stage set was whitewashed houses with the background of a perfect, bright blue sky. It conjured up the classic image of a Greek island like Mykonos, but set in the early seventeenth century. The lighting generally was at its most intense when the behaviour was at its most illogical. The 'letter scene' was set at siesta time, and, instead of taking a rest in the cool of his room, Malvolio fantasises about Olivia under the full glare of the sun at midday, his mind wandering off in increasingly bizarre directions until it is horribly vulnerable to the lurid suggestiveness of the fake letter. The watchers were safely in the shade peering out of a second-floor window at the Box Tree Inn ('Get ye all three into the box-tree,' says Maria; we had an inn sign descend from the flying rig above the stage), while the steward believed himself to be alone with his thoughts. The bright white walls of the buildings around him were suggestive of an asylum. Strong light became equated with madness, so in setting the 'dark room' in a square of white light the (earlier) 'letter scene' was evoked, correlating vanity and ambition with the potential for madness. But, as we rehearsed, we never saw Malvolio as in any way mad. The situation might be mad, and the world might be mad, but he was wretchedly and earnestly sane. However, his state of mind in the final scene, when he is led back to Olivia's house into the garish daylight, shielding his eyes from a malignant sun, was another matter. When all has been made clear and his hopes dashed, his humiliation complete, and he leaves the stage with that chillingly famous line, 'I'll be revenged on the whole pack of you!', the audience should ask themselves if, when that revenge comes, it will be the action of a sane man or a mad one.

Othello

TRUTH AND LIES

When we listen to Edmund in *King Lear* or Richard III lying to others, we listen with the knowledge that we have been enlisted, warned, even in a way consulted, because they have justified their motives to us through the intimacy of soliloquy. They trust us with their secret thoughts. With Iago this reaches another level of intensity where his confessional involvement with the audience and the inner emotional chaos it reveals endow us almost with the role of therapist. The actor should make us feel we have advised him and encouraged him on the course he takes; that we are complicit, co-authors of the gathering horror.

It's up to the director to find through rehearsal the ingredients that in performance will capture the improvisational, off-the-top-of-the-head momentum of Iago's campaign of destructive lying. The way he creates doubts in others, especially in Othello, but also in Roderigo (whom he seems at the beginning of the play to be practising on), is by playing up the plausibility of his observations. He points out to Roderigo that Desdemona is much younger than Othello and that Cassio is closer to her in age, and better-looking than her husband. This is exactly the set-up for many comedies of the period – a beautiful young woman married to a powerful older man with whom she becomes dissatisfied after meeting an attractive man of her own age. It's the kind of plot line that audiences at that time would have been used to, a story in which they would have cheered the young lovers on at the expense of the gullible older husband. From the very first line of the play, we are in a world of words that may or may not be conveying truth. We meet Iago, the most convincing liar Shakespeare ever created; and like all great liars he is brilliant at using the truth.

The starting point for any actor playing Iago is to make some kind of measure of the distance between the way he speaks to us and the way he speaks to the other characters. The actor needs to keep in mind that, when he speaks to us, Iago knows that we know the way he speaks to others. Every time he turns to the audience there's an element of *See what I did there?* He is always enjoying the fact that his deceptions are being followed and understood by us, and the fact that we never interrupt implies that we are enjoying ourselves too. Given that to him we are soul-mates, the conclusions he comes to are our conclusions, and his self-revelations could well be our own. Cassio is not deserving of promotion, whereas he is. Iago is twenty-eight (he says he has 'looked upon the world for four times seven years'), and Othello is – what –fifty? Desdemona is barely twenty. Othello is Black, he is white. Othello is gullible and bombastic and emotionally unintelligent, whereas he is shrewd and perceptive like us. So we can see how ridiculous the situation is when it is he who loves Desdemona ('Now I do love her too... partly led to diet my revenge'), and we can all agree, surely, that he deserves her more. The situation needs to be corrected. Besides, the desire for revenge is sometimes honourable, given that Othello has cuckolded him by sleeping with his wife, Emilia. Or at least he tells us he has reason to think so. He defines Cassio for us as an upper-class snob who has never lifted a weapon in anger and now has the job that should be his. What's more, it was given to him by the same arrogant Black man that has had sex with his wife, and he has every right to be, for our entertainment, the hero of his own revenge drama, and we are privileged to be going along for the ride in a first-class carriage.

As an actor, immersion in a role means building a sense of empathy so strong that motivation becomes an almost irrelevant concept. The way the character perceives things is always 'in the moment'; there is no end to the diagnosing of motivation – every thought, every step of the action, is in flux, and is contingent on the relationship between the previous moment and the next. Iago believes himself to be a better person than either Cassio or Othello, which means he thinks we are better people too, because he shares this sense of injustice with us. He does what he does on behalf of all those who have lost jobs to someone with better connections, or who have had to listen to others boasting of their achievements when their own honest toil has passed unnoticed and unremarked, or been patronised by a condescending greeting – *Here comes good old Jack.* Many times in the play Iago is called 'honest'. This word had a different flavour to the Elizabethans in the context of a phrase like 'honest Iago'. It was the way you talked down to servants: it implied loyal subservience with just a dash of stupidity.

Here is the last speech of Act One. It is also the first time Iago addresses the audience directly, the play's first soliloquy. Already all the main narrative ingredients that drive the action forward at breathtaking speed have been established. Iago's resentment at Cassio's promotion; his manipulation of Roderigo's infatuation with Desdemona; the secrecy of Othello's marriage now made public; and her father Brabantio's violent and emotional objection to it proclaimed, overruled and become history. A lot has happened in a very short space. It's time for a pause – and time slows as we enter another dramatic dimension as Iago turns to us and talks first about his 'friend' Roderigo ('a snipe', or dupe) and then about Othello:

> Thus do I ever make my fool my purse:
> For I mine own gained knowledge should profane
> If I would time expend with such a snipe
> But for my sport and profit. I hate the Moor
> And it is thought abroad that 'twixt my sheets
> He's done my office. I know not if 't be true,
> But I for mere suspicion in that kind
> Will do as if for surety. He holds me well,
> The better shall my purpose work on him.

Iago knows we have a little catching up to do, and knows too that, because we are just like him, we will understand the necessary mixture of truth and lies that we've been witnessing in these first hectic minutes of the action. The lie revealed is of course that Roderigo is not his friend but his 'fool'. He's just clarifying casually for us that everything we've seen in his behaviour towards his friend has been plain acting. Of course, he wouldn't spend time with this idiot unless there was something to be got out of it – money, mainly, in this case, but also the fun ('sport') of acting, of pretending to be someone you absolutely aren't. The truth revealed is that he wasn't lying about everything; he really does hate Othello, and not for any reason he'd tell Roderigo – he suspects his boss is sleeping with his wife. It's in this confiding to us something he would never say to anyone else that the actor can find the clue about his character's insecurity, his need for our friendship and the pain of living with jealousy and bitterness. Can the actor find the way to play neediness and self-pity rather than warped evilness? That is the question. Iago lies to everyone except us. Although the phrase 'honest Iago' echoes through the play with increasing irony as circumstance proves constantly the opposite, yet for us, the audience, it's true. And the pain of believing himself to be a cuckold is deeply real. In a later soliloquy he describes it in this way:

For that I do suspect the lusty Moor
Hath leaped into my seat, the thought whereof
Doth like a poisonous mineral gnaw my inwards...

He is in mental pain; we are part of his therapy – we are the only people who can understand why he wants Othello to suffer the same agonies himself.

To sum up Iago's position: Cassio was promoted to a job he is not fit for and one that Iago could do far better. For this Iago blames Othello. Rumours have reached him that Othello has slept with his wife Emilia. He believes himself to be in love with Desdemona, and knows he is much closer to her in age. He believes he deserves her more than Othello. The path he sets out on should make good sense to an audience, and everything about his manner should suggest a frustrated and wounded man merely seeking justice and revenge. Would we begrudge Hamlet a righteous revenge?

We should feel sorry for Iago, and the actor should aim at making us see the other characters through his eyes. He must try to make the audience make the same mistakes as himself, to experience the poisonous taste of jealousy till he is 'evened with him, wife for wife'.

SEX AND CYPRUS

Act 2 Scene 3 tells the story of the first night on the island of Cyprus. After the storm at sea, the destruction of the Turkish fleet, and the happy reunion between the newly-wed husband and wife, Othello and Desdemona, are now making their way to bed:

OTHELLO.   Come, my dear love,
  The purchase made, the fruits are to ensue:
  That profit's yet to come 'tween me and you.

This clearly implies that they haven't yet consummated their marriage. In the play's first scene, Desdemona's father is awoken in the middle of the night and alerted to the secret wedding between his daughter and the Moor with the hysterical and coarse assertion that 'Even now, now, very now, an old black ram / Is tupping your white ewe!' Nothing of the sort was in fact going on: we retrospectively discover that they were not having sex that night. This raises important questions for the director and actors in creating an internal backstory. What, in fact, *were* they doing?

The apparent lack of sex on their wedding night might indicate a fragility in their relationship, something that makes it precarious and

vulnerable, prone to disruption. It would be a bad mistake to stage
Othello's first entrance with him hastily pulling on clothes, let alone
with Desdemona cowering in the background wrapped in a blanket, as
I've seen done. Despite its being the middle of the night, he should be
fully clothed and she nowhere to be seen, as her absence from the original stage directions indicate. However it would be just like Iago with
his gnawing jealousy to have assumed they were indeed 'making the
beast with two backs', in his colourful phrase. But when we get to
Cyprus, Shakespeare wants to surprise us with the idea that they have
not yet had sex. Why? Did they try and fail? There is no direct textual
evidence that they may have talked through that first night in Venice
until disturbed, but Shakespeare seems to want to imply it. A director
could of course cut the line 'The purchase made, the fruits are to ensue'
and show them both appearing in the earlier scene half naked and
wrapped in bedclothes, but Shakespeare apparently chooses to emphasise that they have remained chaste with each other, a thought that
remains in the air until Othello groans to his wife's corpse: 'Cold, cold,
my girl, / Even like thy chastity.' It's likely that in that line Shakespeare
is simply opposing the idea of 'chastity' to the infidelity he has accused
her of, and, if the two actors need to locate the point in the action where
their characters have first, and for the only time, made love, it is, without question, after the exit that follows Othello's words, 'That profit's
yet to come 'tween me and you'.

   During their absence from the stage a lot happens, the most telling
part of which is a conversation between Iago and Cassio that conjures
up a taste of the action behind the bedroom door:

> IAGO. … Our general cast us thus early for the love of his
>   Desdemona – whom let us not therefore blame; he hath
>   not yet made wanton the night with her, and she is sport
>   for Jove.
> CASSIO. She's a most exquisite lady.
> IAGO. And I'll warrant her full of game.
> CASSIO. Indeed she's a most fresh and delicate creature.
> IAGO. What an eye she has! Methinks it sounds a parley to
>   provocation.
> CASSIO. An inviting eye; and yet methinks right modest.
> IAGO. And when she speaks is it not an alarum to love?
> CASSIO. She is indeed perfection.
> IAGO. Well: happiness to their sheets!

And so the drinking begins.

That they were not making love on the wedding night in Venice, but are doing so now in Cyprus (as Iago tries to make Cassio uneasily, lustfully, jealously imagine), is crucial to the psychic energy of the play. In Venice Othello had stood before the leaders of the state and defended his marriage as a true meeting of minds, a union of souls:

> She loved me for the dangers I had passed
> And I loved her that she did pity them.

This describes empathy and mutual understanding, not lust. And when they consummate their love in Cyprus, it is to the accompaniment of riot, violence and the heady chaos of drunkenness. The key signature of their marriage has changed from dignity to disgrace. It's as if the lovemaking that we don't see has charged the atmosphere with instability and a touch of madness. Cassio has changed from being a trusted companion to an unpredictable trouble-maker – everything that Iago wants him to seem if his lies are to transmit their malicious infection into Othello's brain. A context has been created that conjures doubt out of contentment and prepares the ground in which the seeds of sexual jealousy can be sown. Cassio's diminishing seems to prove that Iago is right to have resented his promotion; it makes Othello doubt his own judgement – if Cassio is capable of causing a riot on an island recently saved from invasion, what else might he not be capable of? Cuckolding his commander-in-chief? Maybe. Iago made Cassio imagine Othello and Desdemona in bed together, then he got him drunk and reduced him to a shameful supplicant; at the same time Iago can now paint a picture to the world of the great general as a sexual supplicant to a devious wife who casts an erotic spell over her husband.

> Our general's wife is now the general. I may say so in this
> respect, for that he hath devoted and given up himself to the
> contemplation, mark and denotement of her parts and graces.

In other words, he's *addicted to her body and will do anything she wants.*

Iago is now in the perfect place to suggest to Cassio that he asks Desdemona to get his job back for him. Her pleading to her husband on behalf of Cassio will strengthen Othello's preparedness to believe in her infidelity. Bringing us back into his confidence, Iago assures us:

> His soul is so enfettered to her love
> That she may make, unmake, do what she list,
> Even as her appetite shall play the god
> With his weak function.

He tells us, his co-conspirators, he can now suggest to Othello

> That she repeals him [Cassio] for her body's lust.
> And by how much she strives to do him good
> She shall undo her credit with the Moor –
> So will I turn her virtue into pitch
> And out of her own goodness make the net
> That shall enmesh them all.

In setting up the lie that Cassio and Desdemona are secret lovers, any production has to move carefully to establish a balance between Iago's credibility and Othello's gullibility. If Iago is too obviously a 'bad' person, then Othello becomes too obviously a stupid one, and he is very far from stupid. Pride, innocence, a nature forged in battle rather than a connoisseur of human relationships, a deep sense of honour, a tendency to be bombastic in his self-expression, which might be a symptom of cultural insecurity – all these and many others might help explain to the audience why he succumbs to Iago's lies.

However, one element totally outside of character needs to be thrashed out in the rehearsal room: the timescale. This was discussed in the section on Time in Part One, but is worth repeating here, so important is it to the psychology of the play. Simply put, since Desdemona and Cassio arrive in Cyprus on separate boats, and there is only one night on the island when they could have slept together, and that night was the night she consummated her marriage to Othello, the idea that she and Cassio are having an intense sexual relationship makes no sense at all. The double time scheme was a device Shakespeare often used, but most noticeably in *Othello*. The trick he plays on the audience is to make references to days, weeks or months having passed so as to enhance credibility, but also to enhance dramatic tension by creating a feeling of events moving very fast. Audiences don't notice, and academics say it's only of minor relevance, but to the actor building a realistic character existing in real time and space it matters deeply. So Othello cannot believe his wife has committed adultery, nor can the actor playing Iago be expected to seriously be attempting to make him believe she has. The use of a double time scheme, so obvious from a close and detailed study of the text, is at odds with the modern tendency for director and actor to develop in rehearsal a complete and coherent backstory to the action seen on the stage. In the case of this play at least, the only alternative to simply ignoring the issue and relying on the fact that the audience probably won't notice, is to think of Iago as persuading Othello that

Desdemona was sleeping with Cassio *before* her marriage and wishes to continue doing so *after* it. In the morality of Elizabethan England this would have been regarded as just as bad as marital infidelity, if not worse. The stain of losing her virginity before marriage would render a woman little better than a whore in the perception of most people, and that is exactly how Othello, once in the grip of jealousy, begins to perceive and describe her. These sensibilities make the director confront one of the biggest issues in moving Shakespeare from the late Renaissance into the modern world: the need to make the audience believe that characters who look like us can think like Elizabethans.

King Lear

THE MADNESS OF KING LEAR

Sometimes a production's interpretation of a play can hinge on a single pivotal moment. Here are two examples. Director and actor may decide together that Iago never intends that Othello should kill Desdemona; his purpose is simply to make Othello feel the same maddening jealousy that afflicts him. Then imagine that in working on *King Lear*, both the director and the actor want to challenge the convention that Lear goes mad. In the case of *Othello*, it's possible to chart several moments when, as Iago's poison works, the possibility of Othello murdering Desdemona crystallises in his mind until it becomes an inevitability. Iago has gone with the flow of Othello's jealousy, following where it leads, and ultimately suggesting the means to the end: 'Do it not with poison, strangle her in her bed – even the bed she hath contaminated.' But with *King Lear*, the moment of deciding whether he has finally gone mad or not arrives with a sudden rush: an entrance, following a long absence from the stage, in which everything about him has changed. He appears as the perfect image of a man whose wits have shattered, the very essence of a mad man. Or not?

In rehearsal this climactic moment is profoundly connected to the discussions and decisions surrounding the well-known dialogue between Lear and his youngest daughter, Cordelia, in the opening minutes of the play. Most directors conclude that the 'madness' of the King is on display from the word go, that a mental instability is implied in the very idea of dividing his kingdom between his three daughters, and that it is manifested in the bizarre notion that the best bit will go to the daughter making the most loving speech, although paradoxically those bits seem to already have been decided on.

It's important for the director to have fully absorbed that it was the most extraordinary thing for a king to 'retire'. This kind of abdication of power was virtually unheard of; you lost your power when you died, not before. You never gave it away. Lear has enjoyed power for so long he has come to think of it – both the power and the country – as his, rather than as an attribute of the office of King and his position at the head of the state.

After Goneril and Regan have played along, spouting their conventional endearments, he turns to Cordelia, and in a single phrase delivers to the actors and director a backstory of favouritism, bitterness, jealousy and jaw-dropping emotional illiteracy that may serve as the psychological key to the entire play: 'Now, our joy...' Novels could be written about such a father's relationship with his daughters, in which this clumsy insensitivity has shaped their personalities from childhood. Here it kick-starts the terrible unravelling of all their lives.

Ten lines then follow which light the fuse for the tragic explosion:

> ... Although our last and least; to whose young love
> The vines of France and milk of Burgundy
> Strive to be interested. What can you say to draw
> A third, more opulent than your sisters? Speak.
> CORDELIA. Nothing, my lord.
> LEAR. Nothing?
> CORDELIA. Nothing.
> LEAR. Nothing will come of nothing, speak again.
> CORDELIA. Unhappy that I am, I can not heave
> My heart into my mouth.

What is he hoping for? This contrived and unnecessary game for thrones, displaying publicly his favouritism, could be some kind of crazy attempt at a joke, or some deeply serious need for his beloved youngest child to tell the world how much she loves him, or any complex mix of the two. There is insensitivity and neediness on display but, worse, there is the revelation that he does not know her, and, for a man of power and pride, that this should be so publicly revealed is humiliation of epic proportions. How, the director must ask the actor, does the lack of self-knowledge, mentioned by his elder daughters at the end of the scene, and his lack of insight into the nature of others, lead to madness – if that is what it is – when he enters crowned with weeds and flowers at Dover?

It begins as a rage arising like a storm, an expression of his incredulity at Cordelia's words, or rather her lack of them. But Cordelia must know, every bit as well as her older sisters, the limits of her father's self-knowledge. So in the 'nothing' exchange she must be seen to be trying to tell him something, not just perversely crossing him; trying to show him the ridiculousness of the game. I think she should say it with a hesitant smile, not looking sullen or defiant, as if she is trying to make him get her point, beautifully expressed as being unable to 'heave / My heart into my mouth'. But he does not understand, and lack of emotional intelligence combines with monumental pride and offended dignity to become an uncontrollable anger, a tempest that washes away all sense of nuance, all possibility of sensitivity. So in this rush of rage the fatal decisions are made: Cordelia's rejection, the banishment of Kent, the division of the kingdom between two unstable queens and his creation of the 'hundred knights', the very symbol of power without responsibility. Even in this whirlwind of terrible decision-making, the actor needs to feel a sense of panic in the character, a fear of instability and an awareness of losing control, being swept by the waves of emotion into a dangerous sea in which he cannot row back for fear of losing face.

So Lear's journey towards madness begins in anger at Cordelia's (to him) incomprehensible behaviour, and builds through his rejection by Goneril and Regan into the cosmic raging on the heath in the face of the storm. At the end of Act 1 Scene 5, after his eldest daughter's refusal to house him and his hundred rowdy knights, one of those key moments occurs, where a director should attempt to make time stand still, to hold the audience gripped by an awareness of significant change, as Lear, within an absolute stillness and as quietly as the actor dares, says:

> O let me not be mad, not mad, sweet heaven!
> Keep me in temper, I would not be mad.

What should be shocking is the element of self-awareness the line implies; shocking because this is a man who 'hath ever but slenderly known himself'. The delivery should imply that this sudden shaft of self-knowing light would be truly terrifying to the man.

He perceives how madness might come not just from the outrageous unfairness of his treatment by his own flesh and blood, but also from the jolt of understanding that he had committed a terrible wrong, made a ghastly mistake. Here the way words change meaning over time is significant to the acting of the moment. Nowadays we talk of someone having a 'bad temper' meaning they get angry easily – *temper* and *anger* are synonymous. But back then, 'temper' meant stability, meant being well balanced, and to 'lose your temper' was to lose control. Temper was calm; anger was storm. So the word further implied *sanity* as opposed to the 'madness' of rage. Temper is not anger; it is what controls the anger. Madness is losing control, and the actor playing Lear should consider that maybe this is where *fear* enters the equation. Lear is angry not only at injustice, but because he is frightened suddenly by his loss of power, loss of love, loss of security, but most of all he is frightened of being alone. This is why he wants to be constantly surrounded by a hundred men, men who admire him, respect him, defer to him, validate him, and give him the illusion that he is still King in his own mini-kingdom, where he can enjoy acclamation without the grind of work.

The director and actor need to chart the references to madness from this point until the stage direction which in the Quarto text reads quite simply: '*Enter Lear mad*'.

>Act 3 Scene 2:
>My wits begin to turn.

>Act 3 Scene 4:
>The tempest in my mind
>Doth from my senses take all feeling else,
>Save what beats there, filial ingratitude.

Here again is the frightening sense of awareness that the actor must mine to uncover incredulity, shock, the feeling of uncontrolled alteration. Do people who are going mad see it that clearly? It's usually others who gradually become aware of it. In Act 3 Scene 4 towards the end, Kent observes that 'His wits begin t'unsettle'. In Act 3 Scene 7 Regan calls him 'the lunatic King'. On her return from France, Cordelia gently laments that 'he was met even now / As mad as the vexed sea'. Gloucester states baldly in Act 4 Scene 6: 'The King is mad.'

These are some of the references, but perhaps the most significant is the comment of the unnamed 'Gentleman' in Act 4 Scene 7, who observes of Lear's recovery as he wakes from sleep to find himself in the forgiving presence of his youngest daughter: 'the great rage / You see is killed in him.' This confirms for me that what the actor looks for in playing King Lear on the way to his 'mad' entrance are the various stages, types and qualities of anger. They find which lines express the frightened anger, which the humiliated anger, which the ignorant anger, which the proud, which the confused, the petulant, even the satiric; and by identifying the shades and colours, they give shape and texture, variety and nuance to the performance, and maybe they can even isolate which type of anger is the pure rage against the dying of the light. The anger at mortality.

So what is the big change after the long absence of Lear from the stage? What is it that defines the actual madness of that moment, 'Enter Lear mad'? I think it is that, earlier, the rage had a focus. Even in the craziness and zaniness of the 'hovel scene', his anger has a satiric purpose, articulating outrage at a world that had such people as Goneril and Regan in it. It even, in the storm, gives birth to the arrival of a kind of socio-political awareness: 'Poor naked wretches...' But when he arrives on stage dressed in rags and weeds, that focus and sense of purpose has gone, and Shakespeare brilliantly captures the broken speech patterns and random subject matter of a fragmented mind. And yet, as has often been observed, it is in these speeches that objective wisdom and empathy about the world around him take the place of subjective, selfish fury at his own situation.

Some entrances are more difficult than others and I find 'Enter Lear mad' very difficult indeed! The text demands that he has physically changed, yet there must be a connection to the man we last saw six scenes ago being led away from his place of shelter, fleeing for his life. So much has happened in those intervening scenes, and an atmosphere of mad and random violence has taken over the play. It seems to me that the transformed Lear somehow has to both reflect and inhabit this atmosphere. An internal backstory has to be invented about what the character has been doing, and who has been with him, if anyone. Of the characters we last saw him with – Gloucester, Edgar, Kent and the Fool – at least two have been otherwise engaged, and one of them (the Fool) disappears from the play entirely. These missing links are common in Shakespeare, but often there is some kind of textual evidence around which an unseen narrative can be constructed. Not in this case.

Actors who have played King Lear tell me they have relished the half-hour or so they are able to spend in their dressing rooms to rest, shower, change costume and generally prepare themselves for the climactic final stages. But when I discussed the possibilities with Corin Redgrave, who was playing the title role in our RSC production, we decided that, after quickly changing into his ragged clothes and coronet of weeds, he should sit in the wings and watch the intervening scenes: the torture and blinding of Gloucester; the murder of the servant who tries to intervene; the fatal wounding of Cornwall; the meeting between Edgar (pretending once more to be someone else) and his father; the bizarre attempted suicide from the non-existent Dover cliff; and Gloucester's 'survival' of his 'fall' to meet his son again in yet another disguise on the imaginary beach. Our thinking was that these remarkable episodes create the essence of the madness that possesses Lear on his crucial entrance. Corin, who was himself an extraordinary actor, was able to use these extraordinary visions of a world gone mad to feel his way into the state of mind of one whose psyche is shattered by both the cruelty and the devotion of which human beings are capable. The base for acting 'madness' was awareness, not just of the wrongs done to him, but of the wrongs he himself had committed; wrongs that had led to this hurricane of violence, chaos and heartbreak.

This, of course, was not a conventional backstory; it was more an impressionistic way of retaining the mood of the play and an example of how the central responsibility of every actor is to reflect that mood. It reminds us that character is something born of the play, not added into it. It is the objective, selfless act of storytelling, not the subjective pride of performing. Corin was a selfless actor, all his choices being inspired by the impulses of those around him. In this production I think we got close to the ideal of an ensemble where every actor's primary aim is to help their fellow actors be better.

So – back to that entrance. When you read the 120 lines of Act 4 Scene 6 that constitute the 'mad scene', it is likely that you will first hear them in your head as the wailing of a miserable and demented man, cries of sorrow at the wretchedness of life and the hypocrisy of the world. But the more you rehearse it, the less it seems to work as a deranged lament. What emerges instead is the black, wry humour of a disinhibited mind, of a man who's perceived the truth and for the first time in his life is able to speak it freely with more of a dark chuckle than a helpless wail.

To begin with, Corin and I realised that staggering about the stage agitated, wild-eyed and ranting felt pointlessly generalised. We found that stillness and a calm voice could be mesmeric. After all, there are plenty of opportunities to represent the Royal Shouting Company!

'Blow winds and crack your cheeks!' had invited the bringing out of the vocal big guns; but that is expressive of a blind raging at the gods, at the unearthly random force of Nature. Here, near the end of the play, the mood is different: earthy, knowing, amused:

> Thou, rascal beadle, hold thy bloody hand;
> Why dost thou lash that whore? Strip thine own back,
> Thou hotly lusts to use her in that kind
> For which thou whipp'st her.

There is the quiet, bitter humour that we found: a deep sanity about the society that Lear once ruled, a sanity which had been obscured by the inherited power to punish, gilded with the flattery of those around him, especially his daughters who 'told me I was everything'. Something has opened Lear's eyes in the time between the flight from the hovel and his entrance crowned with weeds. It may be as simple as having been alone, with space to think for the first time in his life. We know that being alone and thinking was not something he wanted to do. He wanted to surround himself with a hundred sycophantic mates, hunting and drinking, unburdened by reflections on the injustices he had presided over and barely noticed. But I think he knew it all along, and his observations in his 'madness' don't come as shocking revelations: they emerge as truths he always felt but never bothered to face. Poverty leads to crime, and the rich buy 'justice':

> Through tattered clothes great vices do appear;
> Robes and furred gowns hide all. Plate sin with gold,
> And the strong lance of justice hurtless breaks;
> Arm it in rags, a pigmy's straw does pierce it.

His madness is really crazy laughter at how stupid he has been to have wasted his power letting corruption thrive, making his elder children full of jealousy and rejecting the only two people who could have helped him find a better way: Kent and Cordelia.

So Corin just stood quietly centre stage, musing on the irony of a world in which wealth could buy power and justice, smiling at the absurdity of it all, until, like a wild and naughty child, he suddenly bolted from those sent to help him in a manic game of 'catch me if you can'. About a year after his last performance, Corin had a massive stroke while addressing a demonstration in support of a group of travellers being evicted by the police from a patch of land. He suffered an almost total loss of memory. When I visited him in hospital shortly before he died, I asked him what he could remember about being Lear. 'Nothing,' he replied. 'Just a storm in my mind.'

The storm in Lear's mind goes through many stages, but, at the end, as he wakes to find his youngest daughter present, forgiving, loving and calm, he seems at last to have escaped the rage that has tormented him and must, surely, have pre-dated the decision to give up his throne. True, he has not achieved much self-knowledge, but I think it was beginning to arrive, and that precisely was the problem.

In a future production I would explore with the actor a backstory something like this. Lear is over eighty and has begun to realise that he lacks the strength, wisdom, skill, will and, above all, time to even begin to engineer the social changes needed to bring better justice, fairness and compassion to a corrupt, greedy and barbaric nation. He knows that Cordelia has a good mind, a kind heart, and a profound honesty of purpose. However, he's clever enough to realise that making her sole Queen, would generate such bitterness and resentment from her sisters that every moment of her time would be spent dealing with the emotional fallout, making it impossible for her to concentrate on the business of government. So his plan is to appease the ambitions of Goneril and Regan by dividing the country between the three of them. What is vital is that he has left the most important part (not the most beautiful part) to Cordelia. It is the part nearest France, and she is about to marry a Frenchman. It is the part with the highest concentration of people, the most economically significant in terms of trade, agriculture and industry. Most importantly, we can imagine it as the dominant political area, whose stability has the greatest influence on the nation as a whole. All he requires of her, in the piece of political theatre that begins the play, is a simple statement of love and a promise to rule with diligence and ensure peace with France.

This thesis may be full of contradictions, but the rehearsal room is a place where you face contradictions, some of which need to be resolved and some embraced. I think it's important to credit Lear with a purpose, albeit one which he handles incredibly badly. Some would argue that a backstory like the one I've suggested above is simply not playable by the actors. Maybe not, but you have to start from somewhere. Lear loves the country he is giving up; he is not a bad man; he knows he is 'crawling toward death'; he feels guilty about his failures as a leader – but hopes that someone else (Cordelia in this dynastic world) will put them right. His 'madness' begins with his inability to control the unresolved personal and political issues of a long reign, to sit down quietly with the heir he most trusts and sort out a viable plan. But, as the Fool says, he became old before he became wise. The 'madness of King Lear' is a mental storm (for which the actual storm is the perfect metaphor) of unresolved contradictions, mainly the contradictions between love and guilt, which, if you think about it, is true of all four major tragedies. Macbeth, Hamlet and Othello all go 'mad' in a way, and all are driven primarily by fear – the exact nature of which needs to be carefully analysed: fear of retribution; fear of failure; fear of chaos; or simply that pulsating beat of anxiety that plagues us all as life appears to spiral out of our control?

The Tempest

THE STORM

The Tempest begins with a storm at sea. A lot of things that go on in a rehearsal room would look incredibly silly to a fly on the wall, especially the noises a director or stage manager might make to represent sound effects that will be present in performance but haven't yet been created by the sound designer. Things like going '*Ring-ring!*' to indicate a telephone, or '*Bang!*' for any loud noise, or knocking on the table to provide a cue for the Porter in *Macbeth*. But perhaps the most bizarre are the range of vocal improvisations that stand in for a storm. The two most famous storms in Shakespeare are the magically engendered typhoon that opens *The Tempest*, and the storm on the heath in *King Lear* that darkly shadows the onset of his madness. Both present the same problem for a director. The problem is: how do you create an effective storm on stage while still being able to hear the actors? Whatever the style of production, the balance between the human voice and the sound effects is tricky. In my production of *Lear* for the RSC, I used recorded sounds of wind and thunder alongside the visual effect of rain, with real water coming from two rows of pipes situated up in the lighting rig. The sound effects were reasonably easy to manipulate, punctuating the dialogue with thunder during brief pauses and dropping to lower levels of wind only under the text. The problem came with the rain, because the machine that pumped the water at high pressure through the pipes above the stage itself made an extremely loud noise that bore no relation either to thunder, wind or rain, but only to a pump which, in order to work, had to be operating constantly throughout the scene. It was this noise alone that made the voices almost impossible to hear. So great was this problem that after a couple of performances in which Lear might as well have been *miming* 'Blow winds and crack your cheeks!' I had to reluctantly cut the rain. I don't know how many other directors have found this an issue – in non-naturalistic productions there are many imaginative ways to create the impression of rain without high-pressure pumping systems, but in naturalistic ones, rain needs to look like rain. (Maybe the technology is better now?)

By the time I came to direct *The Tempest* at Birmingham Rep, I'd learnt my lesson about stage rain: imagine a simple wooden platform about ten feet square suspended by thick hemp ropes at each corner. As characters come and go, the platform moves, swaying slightly like the deck of a ship on a swelling sea. There is near silence, except for an eerie, distant, song-like sound, evoking siren voices trapped within a restless wind. The characters all focus on something that appears to be taking shape behind the audience and speak to each other in hushed whispers, clear and crisply articulated. Then, at a certain moment in the dialogue, the wind suddenly swells, climaxing in a huge explosion that sends some reeling off the platform, while others are wrenched up into the air. Some regroup, the dialogue continues, and the same sequence repeats twice more, each time with greater violence. What you see on the page is terrified men shouting at each other, trying to be heard over the cacophony of a massive storm at sea. But I could not think how to do this, while still allowing the audience to hear every word. Sometimes, as a director, your own limitations force you to be creative, but it must always be in service of the text. And the text of this scene is brilliant: it's all about the absurdity of class and privilege in a situation of extreme natural disaster where men are truly equal in the profoundest possible way. It shows how people reveal their true characters in a crisis and serves as a key signature for the whole play.

The Tempest is unusual in Shakespeare's work as it set entirely in one place, an island. It's almost unique because it not only observes Aristotle's supposed rules concerning Unity of Place, but also of Time and Action as well. It seems to cry out for a rich, detailed and exotic design, but what the island actually looks like appears to depend on the character of the observer. For instance, to the bitter and cynical duo of Sebastian and Antonio it is a desert, but the optimistic and gentle Gonzalo describes it as a lush paradise. How do you design a set that mutates according to the personality of whoever is looking at it? The cynic and the optimist will always see the world in different ways, so what the audience see must somehow accommodate different points of view. Maybe Shakespeare was using the idea of an isolated island simply to explore the notion that life is what you make it, that there are always 'glass half-empty' and 'glass half-full' types? Positive and well-intentioned people will see the island's beauty and potential, whereas the embittered and fearful will experience it as a wasteland far from civilisation. I think you have to try to imagine the beauty and terror of the New World as the first Europeans found it, but to fill the stage with dense jungle, deserted beaches and the panoramic views of an uncultivated and virgin country would be to swamp the language that itself conveys so brilliantly the variety of human perceptions about that world. In a way, my perfect *Tempest* would be an 'in-the-round' production – a circle of sand surrounded by an audience – and every time a character described some physical aspect of the place, they would speak while looking through and beyond the audience, who would never know exactly what the character 'saw' beyond their own capacity to imagine landscape from the spoken word. Shakespeare's Hamlet observes that 'there is nothing either good or bad but thinking makes it so'. Working with and stimulating the audience's visual imagination is one of his great ideas. The best known and most direct statement of this comes in the opening speech of *Henry V* when the Chorus suggests to the spectators in the Globe that they let the actors 'On your imaginary forces work'. Too much literal physical representation can only act as a barrier to the pictorial element in the language. Visual restraint in the design brings the actor into sharper focus, so that their speech can better create pictures in the minds of the listeners, an intense and individualised gallery. This inner visualisation is central to the rehearsal process, because a huge part of the actor's job is to make their audience see as well as feel. As the blinded Gloucester says in *King Lear*: 'I see it feelingly.'

THE BACKGROUND

Cymbeline and *The Winter's Tale* are the two plays usually grouped with *The Tempest* as 'Late Romances', and all the evidence points to *The Tempest* being the last, written around 1610 or 1611. There seems to be a purpose behind them as a group, as if Shakespeare was in the mood to write old tales with happy endings for reasons that could have been commercial or personal or both or neither. All three plays feature royal children separated from their roots and brought up in a state of nature. In *The Winter's Tale*, Perdita, the daughter of a king and queen, is being raised by shepherds in a rural farming community in Bohemia; Guiderius and Arviragus, the lost sons of King Cymbeline, live in a cave in the Welsh mountains; and in *The Tempest*, Miranda, the daughter of a duke has been brought up by her father on a mysterious island somewhere off the North African coast. In all three situations these children are being raised in an environment entirely free of influences from city or court. There seems to have been a revival of interest in stories of this kind towards the end of Shakespeare's career, but whether he began this trend or went with its flow is impossible to say. Despite the happy endings, a strong element the first two of these plays have in common is the theme of sexual jealousy. *Troilus and Cressida* handled that emotion with bitter, black satire; *Othello* with heart-breaking tragedy; and *The Merry Wives of Windsor* through pure farce. In *Cymbeline* and *The Winter's Tale* Shakespeare returned to it as the motor of a central tragicomic plot. Why this should be, we'll never know, but the obsession of Leontes that his new baby daughter is the bastard child of his best friend, and the conviction of Posthumus that his wife has been unfaithful to him, both nearly result in tragic rather than happy endings.

There is little about jealousy in *The Tempest*; here the return to romance may have been prompted by something else that was part of the zeitgeist. There was a growing sense during Shakespeare's lifetime of the opportunities and challenges created by the discoveries in the New World. Accounts by people like Richard Hakluyt and Thomas Harriot had been widely circulated, and the romantic associations of new territory open to colonisation were creeping into the national consciousness in dreams of fresh beginnings, pure ways of living and escape from what was perceived to be the sullied decadence and disappointments of the old world. The astonishing daring of those setting sail across a dangerous and uncharted ocean to make new lives for themselves in an unknown land was colouring the British collective imagination. So it shouldn't be surprising that this spirit of adventure lies in the background of Shakespeare's last and most magical play. It may be a cliché to think of *The Tempest* as a kind of farewell to the theatre, but that doesn't mean it's not true. Having produced on average two plays a year for twenty years while continuing to function as both actor and theatre manager, he may have considered himself written out. He was famous, well off, and loved and respected by his colleagues, and, possibly, he was ill. There is internal textual evidence of a goodbye, and as he'd never cast himself in a leading role before, he may have felt this was his last chance. I like to think of him as Prospero, which is sentimental perhaps, but not impossible.

What has long been recognised is that there may be a direct connection between the play and certain publications known as the 'Bermuda pamphlets' describing the wrecking of a ship on the Bermuda islands in 1609. The facts as described in the pamphlets are as follows. (The relevant extracts are supplied in both the old and new Arden editions of the play). In May 1609 a fleet of nine ships with five hundred colonists on board under the command of Sir Thomas Gates and Sir George Somers set out to strengthen the colony at Virginia, which had been left under the governorship of John Smith. But on 25 July the *Sea Venture*, which carried both Gates and Somers, was separated from the rest of the fleet by a storm and, being driven towards the coast of the Bermudas, the crew were forced to run their ship ashore. Then near the land, to quote from one of the eye-witness accounts, the ship 'fell in between two rocks, where she was fast lodged' and would not budge. All on board got safely to the beach and also managed to save a good portion of the ship's fittings and stores. All the other ships in the fleet, bar one, made it to the mainland of America. Eventually those shipwrecked were able to set out for Virginia the following May. They arrived safely, and the story of their adventure was carried to England in the autumn of the same year. Everyone had assumed the *Sea Venture* was lost, so the revelations of the crew's safety and their strange experiences on the island must have made a deep impression on the public, especially as many tales of the shipwreck were distributed and later published. Shakespeare could easily have read these accounts when they were circulating in manuscript form before being printed: as source material it would have been very different from the usual historical chronicles, medieval poetry and Italian novellas that fuelled his imagination for most of his writing life. This story was more daily newspaper than Boccaccio or Seneca.

As with *Hamlet*, a major and highly significant change is made to the source material. The location of the island is shifted from the Atlantic Ocean to the Mediterranean Sea. Although the exact spot is never specified, we must assume it is somewhere between Tunis on the north coast of Africa and Naples on the west coast of Italy, simply from internal evidence in the text (Gonzalo remarking that they had been shipwrecked on their way back from the wedding of the King's daughter in Tunis). There is a reason why it's worth knowing this background when preparing to rehearse *The Tempest*, because the changes Shakespeare made to the story in the pamphlets illuminate his purpose. Had Ben Jonson decided to use the same material he would probably have kept to the social composition of the real group of castaways, seamen and artisans of all types headed for a new life of opportunity. Jonson's plays have very few aristocratic or courtly characters, and he would have been fascinated by the interaction of the different middle-class types thrown together in a high-pressure situation. Shakespeare, though, nearly always deals with the world of the court, and his interest lies in what happens when that world is deposited in the wilderness. The court's servant figures, Stephano and Trinculo, take up with the island's slave, Caliban, and plan a revolution that is comically unrealistic, while two of the court's aristocrats, Antonio and Sebastian, plan to murder the King of Naples. Meanwhile Prospero orchestrates the action on his island stage, a magician director with a mixed cast of spirits and men.

THE MAGIC ISLAND

The small family unit who live on the magic island that has no name consists of three characters – a man, his daughter, and an adopted son – plus Ariel, who, being an 'airy spirit', is not strictly speaking part of the family. The man is an exile called Prospero, once the Duke of Milan, but now banished here by his brother, who became Duke in his place. His daughter is called Miranda, and was three years old at the time of expulsion. The third character is Caliban, the sole inhabitant of the island until the arrival of Prospero and Miranda twelve years before the beginning of the action. Who is Caliban? We learn from the text his mother was the witch Sycorax, and his father a devil! Ways of exploring what this means exactly to the actor make for interesting rehearsal-room debate. Imagining the son of a devil and a witch as a natural character is a real challenge to anyone trained in the methods of Stanislavsky.

We learn that at some unidentifiable moment in the past Caliban attempted to rape Miranda, and his dealings with his adoptive father prior to that traumatic event are the basis for creating a believable relationship between the two men. Caliban's mother seems to have been the kind of witch who practised black magic with the ability to control and command lower spirits and minor devils. Prospero, on the other hand, is a magus: a self-taught man who practises discipline and piety, and who has gained the ability to control the natural world. The term normally applied to this kind of power was 'holy magic'. His years of study, as understood by Elizabethan scholars, would concern the harmonic relationships between the worlds of the intellect, the heavens, and nature (the elements). He is both a magician and a Christian holy man, and he is partly inspired by the real-life astrologer John Dee, who died in 1609, a few years before *The Tempest* was first performed. Cornelius Agrippa had already written a highly influential book called *Occult Philosophy* (1533) in which he states: 'It is in no way irrational that it should be possible for us to ascend by the same degrees through each world to the same very original world itself, the Maker of all things, and First Cause, from whence all things are and proceed.' This belief hovers throughout Shakespeare's life on the edge of his society's intellectual horizon. Prospero is the only human character in the entire canon who can actually perform supernatural magic. Puck, Oberon and Titania are fairies, and the witches in *Macbeth* diabolical spirits.

Since the attempted rape, Caliban has been reduced from son to slave, but the description of the original bond between him and his teacher, father, and now master, is one of the most moving speeches in the play. It is a rich and extraordinary backstory, deeply human, which the actor can draw on and will find far more accessible than those of monster and magician.

> CALIBAN. This island's mine by Sycorax, my mother,
> Which thou tak'st from me. When thou cam'st first
> Thou strok'st me, and made much of me; wouldst give me
> Water with berries in't, and teach me how
> To name the bigger light and how the less
> That burn by day and night. And then I loved thee
> And showed thee all the qualities o'th' isle:
> The fresh springs, brine pits, barren place and fertile.
> Cursed be I that did so!

This describes a relationship both tender and mutually beneficial, far from the angry bitterness that characterises most of their exchanges in the play. It must somehow still be there: this father-figure was kind and gentle and needy, and Caliban came to love him. Here is the starting point. Caliban did a terrible thing that he continues to be punished for, but has that original love vanished completely or is it only buried under layers of anger and shame? This is how the rehearsal room differs from the lecture hall. A teacher might begin a course of lectures and seminars on *The Tempest* by considering the relationship between Prospero and Caliban as equivalent to colonising master and native slave: the play is often discussed in the context of the emerging colonialism of the period. Another thematic approach might involve patriarchal assumptions about teenage daughters in Elizabethan society and make comparisons between the relationships of Prospero and Miranda with other fathers and daughters such as Capulet and Juliet, Egeus and Hermia, or Shylock and Jessica. Other themes might involve attitudes towards marriage and virginity or (the most often discussed concept around *The Tempest*) nature and nurture. These are all fascinating subjects that directors should certainly be concerned with, and think hard about, during preparation while always remembering that, as far as the rehearsal room is concerned, you can't act a theme. The job of theatre is to make sense of character and narrative, and let the audience discuss the 'themes' over dinner. Then they can talk about whether or not Caliban represents Prospero's bestial side and Ariel his angelic one.

Irrespective of such debates, Prospero takes a long time to tell Miranda the story of how they came to be on this lonely island in the first place. Scenes of exposition are notoriously difficult: things are being said simply to let the audience know the plot rather than driving it forward. But after the excitement of the tempest itself, which is all action, this lengthy conversation between father and daughter is packed with psychological drama and is one of the few chances we get to find out who this duke-turned-magus really is. Powerful magician he may be, but the nervy and sometimes muddled way he speaks as he tells his story should make us wonder if he is actually conflicted about what happened to him, even the validity of his deposition. I think a sense of his brother's point of view should gradually emerge, perhaps even the thought that Antonio did the right thing in deposing his elder brother. If this can be established in the playing, then Prospero's journey from preparing revenge to embracing forgiveness becomes more understandable. Is his jagged language a sign of latent guilt? Or perhaps moral confusion? The facts he outlines to his daughter are simple: he wanted to pursue a life of mystical and alchemical study. To do so, he delegated the running of the state to his brother. If a country's prime minister, or president, decided to take an Open University course on quantum physics and persuaded his brother to run the government for him while he studied, we would be somewhat amazed and understandably a little shocked. What Prospero did was bizarre, to say the least. The more morally confused he appears as the story emerges, the greater the interest in discovering more about his brother, Antonio, and the greater the build in dramatic tension as an encounter between the two brothers grows closer. But an actor might equally feel that the timescale the magus Duke has set himself – four hours to showdown, much to do, and uncertainty about the outcome – is quite enough to account for his scrambled and irritable state of mind. As ever, the range of interpretive choice is huge.

Let us return for a moment to the contrast between the university seminar room and the theatre rehearsal room, and develop the thought that there are many academics who caution against the whole idea of making too much fuss over inventing backstories for Shakespeare's characters, of creating psychological profiles or even emotional prehistories. Their view is that it is unhelpful and irrelevant for students to expect this kind of theatre to be in any way naturalistic, and that imagining individual motivations is beside the point. Many see their job, while preparing students for a degree in literature, as exploring the social processes that create the characters and conflicts and, by understanding them, to make comparisons with those of our own times. This is directly and fascinatingly opposite to the instincts of most theatre practitioners. The rehearsal-room mentality is tuned to helping the actor inhabit a life other than their own and to get inside a character they feel the need to know as much about as they possibly can. Why did Antonio need the help of a Neapolitan army to get rid of his brother? Wouldn't a few well-armed and well-paid men have done the job just as well and with much less public awareness? How did Prospero, who had removed himself from worldly political affairs, come to know about the plotting between Antonio and King Alonso?

The director and the actors can invent answers to questions like these that the text doesn't provide. Clearly they were irrelevant to the author, who was writing a play, not a novel, and was concerned with storytelling in a theatre, not the privacy of the page. But these kinds of question that float outside the text and have no real life outside the rehearsal room are the questions that help an actor develop character, because they are part of the imaginative process of becoming someone else. In the second scene of *The Tempest* Prospero gives us a lot of backstory, but the gaps he leaves and his way of telling are themselves informative. He tells Miranda (and us) that he was loved by the people of his state. I have said above that characters in Shakespeare always tell the truth, but, of course, it is always their own truth – the way they see things. Could the mention of a Neapolitan army be his way of implying that the merest hint of any harm coming to him would have led to a popular uprising that would have needed an army to put down? Does a needy and arrogant man emerge from that thought? If, despite his immersion in study, he nevertheless knows about the political relationship developing between the King of Naples and his younger brother in Milan, doesn't that suggest that he had his spies with ears to the ground on his behalf? Does a crafty and slightly hypocritical man begin to appear? But there can be no question that he was wronged, for otherwise the story of the banished Duke, who has the powers and opportunity to take revenge but who chooses instead to forgive, is muddied. Can an audience feel comfortable being asked to side with a needy, crafty, arrogant and hypocritical magician? Do we need the audience to be comfortable? Whether we do or not, we need to be affected by him, we need to care, because, if we don't, the play will have no emotional impact in the theatre.

When, in the rehearsal room, we try to put ideas into action, how do we draw boundaries between the possible and the impossible? I'm talking about intellectual ideas, concepts, themes, social philosophy and political arguments. For instance, in *The Tempest* the following issues are all somewhere present and all could be discussed, almost infinitely, in the seminar room:

1. Patriarchy: the history of fathers and daughters.

2. Historic perspectives on the place of marriage in society.

3. The balance between Nature and Nurture in the upbringing of children.

4. Colonialism and the settlement of new territory between 1400 and 1900.

5. Ideal forms of government.

6. Relations between indigenous people and newcomers.

7. Renaissance courts and Machiavelli.

None of these ideas can be either expressed or explored in the abstract in a production. They can only be present through specific relationships between characters and the individualised realisation of character. Any of the ideas on the above list only have any meaning through character conflict and the emotional tension created by it. The actions and choices of the characters *are* the story; narrative is character in action.

The state of being in the moment is basic to all acting, and to give flesh and purpose to this idea is to find ways of helping actors capture the feeling of individuals being driven by their own natures. That implies creating the palpable sense that those individuals are in the constant process of discovering their own natures. So there is a kind of circularity at work that is set in motion by the characters being placed in dramatic situations, an extreme state not unlike heat being applied to a test tube full of chemicals. This is true of all narrative theatre that operates through the naturalistic representation of the world, and is a source of energy. It is especially important in Shakespeare because his poetic language requires huge amounts of emotional energy to make it work. His writing had injected complex emotional truthfulness into the form of rhetorical language, and that established a new set of demands on the work of the actor. *The Tempest* is a good play in which to see this process at work. The magic island is like a giant test tube presided over by a master alchemist who is himself unsure of the nature of his ingredients or the precise purpose of his experiment. The characters trudge round and round the island cauldron, heated and stirred until ready to be transmuted into something better (or, at least, more interesting) than they were. The play is a very special case, as the vital ingredient of magic makes the human elements subject to an overall control that is limiting their free will, making them subject to factors that don't normally exist in their lives; the most important of these factors being that they are constantly under the observation of an invisible master. Prospero really *is* playing God.

In fact the relationship between free will and an all-powerful authority figure can begin to make the whole play look like a religious metaphor. We often question why, if there is a Divine Creator, He lets certain bad things happen, and we might equally well ask why Prospero creates a situation in which a murder could occur, when he is only too familiar with the worst side of his brother's nature. This is the kind of situation where naturalistic acting impulses have to be squared with the contrivances of non-naturalistic dramatic conflict. Shakespeare wants a certain scene to happen, so we must provide Prospero with a motive: most likely that he needs to prove to himself that his brother is still the same person who organised his expulsion from his dukedom. This is not really typical of the realistic dilemmas that Shakespeare's plays often throw up because in this case magic is involved, and we know that Shakespeare cared deeply about motive and was in the vanguard of making motive's inner workings the very heartbeat of the new theatre. However, when academics talk of schemes and themes, practitioners must think in terms of character, action and logic.

MAGIC AND MORALITY

The moral language of *The Tempest* is located in a strange no-man's-land between magic and religion. The narrative depends heavily on coincidence, and its plotting is broadly schematic. For Prospero, welcome events happen by 'providence divine' or 'accident most strange', by 'bountiful fortune' or a 'most auspicious star'. We have a rich late-Renaissance cocktail of religion, fortune, chance, astrology and magic. So it is vital for directors and actors to work at understanding a culture in which religion and magic were completely interwoven in most people's minds. The Elizabethans' grandparents would have believed literally that wine became the blood of Christ in church during Mass; and they would have believed in the capacity of witches, in their role as Satan's servants on earth, to maliciously affect events. On the most basic level the vast majority would take for granted the regular interventions of an all-powerful and all-seeing God. That Prospero's language accommodates both religion and a belief in magic is to say no more than that religion was magical, and that magic could be godly or satanic.

For his last solo play, and for only the third time (not counting ghosts), some of Shakespeare's characters are either non-human or not fully human. Following the fairies in *A Midsummer Night's Dream* and Hecate in *Macbeth*, we have Caliban and Ariel, an 'airy spirit'. For the actors playing these two characters, creating a realistic backstory is devilishly difficult. How are we to imagine Sycorax, Caliban's mother, or his father, at one point described as 'the devil himself'? The name 'Sycorax' is no help as it appears to be Shakespeare's own invention and is not found elsewhere. The mythical Circe, who may be the inspiration, was, in legend, born in Colchis, which was a region inhabited by the Coraxi tribe – creating the name Circecorax which he may have adjusted to Sycorax. But the name is the easy part. How does a modern actor make sense of the ethereal, the supernatural being, when belief in the existence of the supernatural isn't shared by most people today? How do you even begin to approach plays whose world view is so alien and with which we feel little or no empathy?

I think it's important to be very clear about the exact nature of these underlying assumptions: this matters in rehearsal whether the production puts this understanding on display or not. *The Tempest* is an extreme case, and it's impossible to conceive of a production of it in which the magic is not real – it couldn't possibly make any sense, whereas in the *Dream* you could just about construct a scenario in which the fairies were being dreamt by the others. This matters for the same reason the actor playing Hamlet has to accept that his character believes in some form of life after death even if he himself does not.

I once did a production of *Macbeth* set in a future, post-apocalyptic world where superstition had returned to medieval levels. By various means I tried to convey the idea that, despite what the characters thought, the supernatural did not in fact exist. Hecate was played as a nurse who convinced three gullible teenagers (the 'witches') that she was a goddess in a kind of mini-cult. Whether the audience ever understood this backstory (which obviously has no support from the text whatever) I don't know, but the idea made no kind of sense at all, and I suspect many members of the cast were quietly deeply sceptical about it. But at least we had interesting discussions during rehearsals about the nature and intensity of belief in the supernatural amongst the characters, and how much their own belief or lack of it affected their motives, actions and reactions that propelled the events of the play.

So understanding the underlying assumptions of people in the late sixteenth and early seventeenth centuries is simply about getting to a starting point with the acting decisions that make sense of the play. Playing Miranda and Ferdinand as indifferent to their elders' preoccupations about sex before marriage would contradict what they actually say. The only way the actors could do it would be to play against the text by somehow signalling to the audience that they did not mean what they said, imposing modern irony and subtext where it was not intended and thereby distorting the sense and weakening the emotive force. Just as a painter learns to draw naturalistically in order to give their work foundation and integrity before creating purely abstract paintings, so for a director and cast the heart of their approach to staging Shakespeare should lie in the relationship between the created stage world and the human beings that inhabit it without dissonance, contradiction or irony.

If this is beginning to sound like an argument for always setting the plays in the author's own period it most certainly isn't. All Shakespeare's plays inhabit hybrid, invented worlds anyway, which is what gives us the licence to create imaginary worlds of our own – a palimpsest of old and new. There is very little historic authenticity in his works (there is a striking clock in *Julius Caesar*, for example); what is authentic is the reality of the characters that people them. In that reality the old and new Elizabethans sometimes are shockingly similar. The focus in rehearsal is motive: why do the characters behave the way they do; who are they; what do they want; what are they prepared to do to get it? A director should always examine the contrasts between Shakespeare's actual world and his stage world. For example, Polonius has very little Viking in him (the play is notionally set in eleventh-century Denmark), but he probably strongly resembled Queen Elizabeth's chief minister, Lord Burghley. Prospero is no charlatan alchemist like John Dee, but may be a subtle glimpse of Shakespeare himself. These intertwining realities are ingredients in the cocktail of character.

It was Shakespeare's friends and fellow company members in the King's Men who changed the face of dramatic literature. Their decision to publish his complete works seven years after his death in order to 'keep the memory of so worthy a friend and fellow alive' meant that twice the number of the plays he wrote are known to us than would otherwise have been – including *The Tempest*, which they placed at the very beginning of their book. His place in history was cemented by their labour of love and respect. And, of course, his place in the theatre too. But why was it left to them? Would he have overseen the project himself had he lived longer? Would he have followed his friend and fellow playwright Ben Jonson, who took such pride in and suffered much ridicule for publishing his 'works' in a Folio edition? We will never know how deep Shakespeare's personal interest in the survival of his plays in print was, although we do know of the massive change in the importance and profile of theatre during his lifetime.

But is worth stating again and again – amongst those of us whose job is to move his work from words on paper to actions on a stage – that he lived and breathed theatre as an actor who wrote plays. He was also a member of Elizabethan and Jacobean society, and as such a much heard and significant social commentator. How should this inform the rehearsal room in the case of *The Tempest*? Once again, using information from Frank Kermode's excellent Arden edition of the play, we need to remember that debate about the opportunities, responsibilities and plain danger of the New World must already have been part of the national conversation for many years. The particular events of shipwreck and survival surrounding the story of the *Sea Venture* and its crew must have been well known to Shakespeare from the published pamphlets and private letters that recorded the saga in great and absorbing detail and provided the starting point for his play. He believed the whole point of theatre was to hold a mirror up to nature, but in the case of *The Tempest*, it might be a mistake to see it as part of a colonialist discourse, if only because such a discourse had not really got started, and ideas of usurpation and disenfranchisement were nothing like as current and important as ideas about the tensions between concepts of Nature and Nurture, Nature and Art, the figure of the Noble Savage, and the myth of the Golden Age. Along with this went re-readings of Ovid in the light of the new discoveries, and the complex interactions between the early settlers and the Algonquin Indians of the eastern seaboard of North America.

Can a transference of preoccupations between his time and ours ever illuminate a play like *The Tempest* for a modern audience? In the same way that the relationship between Caliban and Prospero is multilayered and contradictory, so the exchanges of ideas about human empathy between settler and native were fraught and confused. In the group of 'Last Plays', *The Tempest* is the one with the most documentary significance to the theatre audience of the day; but of greater importance would have been its exploration of broader themes such as reconciliation, forgiveness, redemption and virginity before marriage. We can't make a modern audience feel the same way about these things, but we can make them feel their importance to the characters involved, in whatever period a production is set.

Returning to the role of backstory – where do we draw the line? Is the writer's own biography something that may be relevant? At the time of writing this play, Shakespeare was involved with his own elder daughter's settling into marriage and the rearing of children; in the same way, Prospero seeks to frame and fix Miranda's future, to an extent that would seem excessively controlling and domineering today. But both Shakespeare and Prospero are using their 'art' for the last time. Both are on the verge of sacrificing the power which that art has given them. In rehearsal I remember encouraging the actor playing Prospero to imagine how his life would be if he were never to set foot on a stage again, never to feel that rush of adrenalin, hear the applause, experience the power to move and touch large numbers of people at the same time. Shakespeare was leaving the world that gave him power and influence and fame: how easy was that for him? But he was giving up the pressure as well. I've known many actors who, on reaching a certain age, have been only too willing to give up the 'magic' of theatre, the effort and strain and risks of live acting for the comfortable, lucrative and relatively undemanding world of the screen.

THE ART OF FORGIVENESS

Many allegorical interpretations have been offered for *The Tempest*, some political, some autobiographical and some religious. Many of these are fascinating, none are provable, any may or may not inspire an interesting production. At the heart of the play is a fascination with the contrast between Art and Nature at a time when the word 'art' had a far broader meaning than it does now. In the early seventeenth century it described learning that encompassed magic and science, rather than a narrow application to the idea of creativity. This has to be understood in an intellectual context where the concepts of 'art' and 'science' were virtually interchangeable. Specifically, the story is to do with Prospero's art and Caliban's nature. Caliban can be seen as the key character in the play, the natural man against whom the cultivated man was measured. Elizabethan explorers had been fascinated by their close encounters with the native peoples of the New World, both on the West Indian islands and on the mainland of America. It is highly unlikely that Shakespeare did not read or hear reports of these encounters. But whereas many accounts stressed the innocence and honesty of the natives, Shakespeare resists any easy contrasts between the goodness of the primitive and the decadence of the sophisticated. Caliban's nature has resisted nurture, the nurture offered by his father figure; his mother possessed an evil natural magic, which was the opposite of Prospero's benign magic. But in contrast to this the genteel world of nurture, that is meant to generate civilised behaviour and is represented by the ship-wrecked courtiers, is also the world in which the malice of men like Antonio and the guilt of men like Alonso breed. Just like the real events of 1609, a group of men are cast away but, at the same time, saved. It's a fruitful island with a temperate climate; nature will provide. This new world presents a theatrical backdrop in which redemption or damnation, forgiveness or revenge, are equally balanced possibilities.

For me there is something ritualistic about the play. However the island is designed, the theme of the transmutation of revenge into forgiveness needs to hit the audience with force and clarity. The magic island reconciles the conflicts of the past and purges Alonso's guilt. It also offers redemption to Sebastian and Antonio. But the really significant emotional progress is made by Prospero himself, who learns to subdue his anger to his reason and step beyond revenge to forgiveness. The struggle between reason and emotion is central to Shakespearean psychology. In Elizabethan thinking it is often referred to as the tension within every individual between wit (reason) and will (emotion) and is linked to the injunction that mankind's first duty is to 'know thyself'. This conflict forms the basis of much of the drama. In *King Lear* there is, for example, Regan's acidic comment on her father's character that 'he hath ever but slenderly known himself'. Macbeth, gripped by the horror of the murder he has committed, says: 'To know my deed, 'twere best not know myself.' And in *The Merchant of Venice* there's Antonio's lament that 'I have much ado to know myself'.

In one of Shakespeare's earliest plays, *Titus Andronicus*, he had pictured a world in which pure will and raw emotion dominate the characters' actions, and revenge becomes not only morally satisfying but somehow honourable too. Twenty years later in his last play the desire for revenge is repressed, and wit or reason create the conditions for forgiveness to triumph, and honourable behaviour to be redefined. Shakespeare had changed, and so had his society.

Human morality triumphs over power in *The Tempest* – specifically over the power of magic. The desire for revenge is overtaken by the need to forgive. At the beginning of the final act Prospero has a conversation with Ariel: an actual conversation, not orders, praise or argument. For a brief moment they cease to be servant and master and talk to each other. The extended moment only lasts for fourteen lines of text, but it is a pivotal point in the play with a crucial choice to be made: either it is a moment of profound inner change or the affirming of a change that has already happened. Having reported on the wretched state of Alonso and his party, Ariel concludes:

> Your charm so strongly works 'em
> That, if you now beheld them, your affections
> Would become tender.
> PROSPERO.   Dost thou think so, spirit?
> ARIEL. Mine would, sir, were I human.
> PROSPERO.   And mine shall.
> Hast thou, which art but air, a touch, a feeling
> Of their afflictions, and shall not myself
> (One of their kind, that relish all as sharply,
> Passion as they) be kindlier moved than thou art?
> Though with their high wrongs I am struck to th' quick,
> Yet with my nobler reason 'gainst my fury
> Do I take part. The rarer action is
> In virtue than in vengeance. They being penitent,
> The sole drift of my purpose doth extend
> Not a frown further.

So one choice for the actor playing Prospero is to show the audience that he is experiencing a radical and life-changing moment of insight, and suddenly, in the moment of Ariel's beautiful line, grasps the barren nature of revenge and is flooded with the spiritual need to forgive. But he could perhaps, alternatively, be putting into words a realisation that may have been forming during the course of the day, since the storm and the arrival of his enemies onto the island; it could even be that an intellectual battle between revenge and forgiveness has been going on inside him for years. Unusually in key Shakespearean moments, I think this decision amounts to a straightforward binary choice. Whether that is true or not, it is certainly a moment of change because the deadly option would be to deliver the speech as a sage: sermonising, speaking spiritual wisdom from a lofty high moral position while standing, staff in hand, on his rocky pulpit. It's moments like this throughout the plays that define the quality of a production. The full quality of the moment will of course also depend on other decisions made about Prospero's character, but good acting is about precision of thought, which means that the process of Prospero's thinking through the speech needs to be crystal clear. Either could work. The force of revelation can be powerful theatre, but so too can the dawning understanding – through the very act of speaking – of something previously only half-known by the speaker. In other words, as I have constantly stressed in this book, the articulation of thought into language.

Shakespeare realised that watching characters getting to know themselves can inspire audiences to want the same thing, to aspire to better self-knowledge, and by aiming for that to understand others better. Caring about others takes you out of the morbid loop of self-reflection and into the creative thinking that each of us is an 'other' to everyone else. The cliché that nobody is an island can lead us to mentally sail to other islands, both near and distant, and discover that we are not alone and never can be alone. Theatre is the medicine we need to take us on countless journeys of exploration, and that itself is a kind of magic.

Part Three

THREE
CASE STUDIES

The Merry Wives of Windsor, Richard III and A Midsummer Night's Dream

A director of Shakespeare must look thoughtfully at two worlds – the one we are surrounded by, and the one that surrounded Shakespeare – and use the periods of preparation and rehearsal to explore the mental and emotional highways that connect them, and how to time-travel between them. With the help of design, light, sound and music, an original and unique world will emerge with its own hybrid style, but it will only contain substance if that world also exists in the mind of the actor. That's the director's main job: to finesse the connection between Renaissance language and modern thought.

But here comes a secret. As far as an audience is concerned (and to be frank, as far as the community of theatre critics is concerned), there are three ways directors make their mark. Firstly, by mastering the orchestration of moving pieces of scenery in smooth and magically protean ways accompanied by lights and music: in other words, great scene changes. Secondly, by choreographing the movement of large numbers of actors around the stage space in original, dramatic and meaningful ways. Thirdly, by inventing surprising translocations of the play in time and place that work to illuminate its themes and meaning.

If all three of these factors are present, and provided the actors have spoken clearly, audibly and intelligently, then great acclaim will go to the director. A director may also get praised for casting good actors, yet seldom for the quality of the acting. And, I suppose, what more could you ask for? Yet every actor and every director knows that the heart and soul and secret of the rehearsal process is the chemistry – or alchemy – created between an enlightened objectivity (director) and an emboldened subjectivity (actor). This creative relationship takes place in a bare space with bleak lighting and no costumes – the rehearsal room – and what is born from this, if the work is good, should be enough to put before an audience and make wonderful theatre. But I realise this austere vision of dramatic interaction can seem pious and puritan, and although as a director I have always aspired to a minimalist approach, this may well have as much to do with my own limitations as with any lofty ideal. Sure, the centre of a director's work is with the actors and the text, to which sound, light, music, costume, and stage architecture can be beautiful adornments – even if 'I loved the set' is the last compliment most directors want to hear. The truth is, though, that a great designer can make a director's reputation. I was lucky in two productions at the RSC, early in my career, to have a great designer, Bill Dudley. Our collaborations on *Richard III* and *The Merry Wives of Windsor* were in no way austere or minimalist. *Richard III* was set in a medieval cathedral rendered in exquisite detail, while *The Merry Wives* was played on a roundabout of 1950s interiors inspired by Ealing comedies and Giles cartoons.

The Merry Wives is Shakespeare's most middle-class and suburban play. In fact the only other of his plays that I can think of that has such a complete absence of the upper, aristocratic and ruling class is *The Taming of the Shrew* (at least the 'play-within' part). Falstaff in *The Merry Wives* is arguably an aristocrat fallen among shopkeepers, and that situation provides the meat of the comedy, but the provenance of his 'knighthood' remains obscure and therefore dubious. We take from the *Henry IV* plays a sense of his exclusion from courtly life, although no element in the plot of *The Merry Wives* specifically links him to those events. Is his story in this play somehow meant to take place after the end of the second part of *Henry IV* and before his reported death in *Henry V*? Or perhaps before either play, or some time in between? We don't know and actually don't care. *The Merry Wives* is self-contained and floats in a parallel universe. This was one of the reasons I felt happy relocating the period in which the play is set and searching for transhistorical meanings free from the presence of actual historic events.

It seemed to me that the so-called 'new Elizabethan age' in England following the coronation of the young Queen in the mid-1950s was a perfect reflection of the stress and strain caused by the emerging class mobility at the time of the first Elizabeth, especially in the mid-1590s, when *The Merry Wives* was written. The aristocracy was becoming impoverished and turning to trade for finance and to the increasingly wealthy middle class for marriage, a trend reflected, as we have seen, in the comedy of Malvolio's aspiration to marry Olivia, and the Duchess of Malfi's tragedy. One of the really funny ideas in *The Merry Wives* is how panic-stricken the resolutely middle-class Page is at the idea of his daughter Anne marrying Fenton, her penniless social superior, when only a generation earlier he would have been delighted. The world of a fallen Falstaff fused in my mind with the world of the posh protagonist in the Ealing comedy *I'm All Right Jack*. Falstaff misunderstands his time. He believes his breeding, or assumed breeding, gives him automatic access to the beds of the bourgeoisie. He reckons without their newfound self-confidence and pride, their moral strength built on financial security. The first sign in my production that sought to establish the similarities between the two Elizabethan ages came when the lights went up on what the audience took to be a row of Tudor cottages in the 1590s, until TV aerials rose slowly from the roofs of what were in fact mock-Tudor villas in suburban 1950s Windsor.

My view of the two central women, Mistresses Page and Ford, was absolutely clear: they were witty, confident wives secure in their marriages, capable in their actions, and not remotely subservient to their husbands – but not necessarily particularly nice. These women think Falstaff is absolutely ridiculous – a complete and utter joke. It is really quite easy for them to come out on top, given the depth of the sleazy knight's self-delusion. They never have a moment's doubt about what he deserves or how to deliver his well-earned humiliation. The fact that they are not in any way conflicted about, let alone tempted by, the situation, allows the play, uniquely in Shakespeare, to be a classic farce rather than a darkly tortured comedy like *Twelfth Night* or *Troilus and Cressida*. The world they lived in was one of late-fifties suburban affluence, a post-war life of 'You've never had it so good' optimism framed by pseudo-Elizabethan black beams and new cars. Bill Dudley's sets revolved around the large Stratford stage, dancing in and out of sight, suggesting at one moment semi-detached houses furnished with sofas, bay windows, cocktail cabinets and radiograms, and the next, a roadhouse, The Tudor Garter Inn, with wood panelling in fake mahogany, a dartboard and a bar with gleaming pumps. Shallow and Slender arrived on stage in an open-topped Morris Minor driven by Simple and presided over by the iconic figure of the Michelin man, a consumerist marketing deity of the age. When they received their fateful letters from Falstaff, the wives were seated under a pair of huge hairdryers, which meant they had to shout the contents at each other, bizarre but necessary in a way that seemed to emphasise these women were not conventionally jolly and warm-hearted but somehow spiky, tasteless and just a little cruel.

As I said earlier, the play stands so apart from the *Henries* that you could conclude Falstaff and his companions are not even the same characters (or maybe just pale shadows of the originals) dumped in a land and zeitgeist totally unfamiliar to them, as if the move from the Boar's Head to the Garter Inn had rendered them sadly vulnerable: out of place and out of time. Falstaff especially seems stranded, unaware that he doesn't know the new rules of this new society. His language is rich and garrulous but without the edge, wit and irony of the man who had beguiled a prince. We played him as a pub bore, a soaked anecdote-spewer, with a touch of Terry-Thomas to add grit and a whiff of danger.

Because the world of the production was so clearly defined, rehearsals were easy. The actors felt contained, protected, and therefore liberated to explore and exploit the very specific social language of 1950s Windsor. The fact that the text is almost entirely in prose helped, as we didn't have to spend hours unravelling complex verse. All uses of 'thou' were changed to 'you' on day one, and more time was spent working out gags with cocktail cabinets than wrestling with iambic pentameters. It is a very unusual play within the canon; it doesn't feel like any other, but in one aspect alone it has a whole group of cousins: *The Winter's Tale*, *Othello*, *Troilus and Cressida* and *Cymbeline*. Why? Because at the centre of the plot is the issue of sexual jealousy. This theme has to be taken seriously for the comedy to work – there is nothing remotely funny going on as far as Mr Ford is concerned. His jealousy is the absolute centre of the action. If the audience don't believe in it, they won't believe in the story, and so the play won't be funny: with the exception of *The Comedy of Errors*, it's the only one of Shakespeare's 'Comedies' (to use the Folio's description) that really has to be funny. The essence of a sexually jealous man is that everything he sees and hears seems to confirm his suspicions. In one scene of the production, as Ford was tearing his house apart searching for Falstaff, he ripped down the curtains drawn across the bay window to find staring back at him the 1959 Tory party election slogan, YOU'VE NEVER HAD IT SO GOOD. It was the final straw leading to total breakdown. I did sometimes worry that in thinking up the character's backstories during rehearsals, we had made them all Tory voters just to get that gag in. To Ford, it was as if the world was laughing at him – the dupe, the cuckold – and at that moment the kitsch Swiss cuckoo clock on the living-room wall struck the hour: CUCKOO – CUCKOO – CUCKOO! Ford at that moment was quite literally being driven mad by jealousy, just like Othello or Leontes. Knowing that he has no cause to be jealous allowed the audience to laugh because it was a moment framed by farce. Knowing that Othello has no cause might make one weep. The concept expressed by a brilliant set and cast made the production work, and so stands as a cheerful contradiction to everything I believe about the centrality of language, especially verse, to the directing and playing of Shakespeare.

*

So what about a *Richard III* set entirely in Worcester Cathedral? Bill Dudley and I chose a medieval setting because our starting point was the relationship between this early play of Shakespeare's and the great cycles of mystery and miracle plays that were fading memories during the writer's youth. Richard seemed to me a direct descendant of the Vice figure in these plays – wicked yet beguiling; fascinating, seductive and deadly. At least, this is Richard's starting point, but his tragedy is to develop a conscience, or at least a terrifying sense of self-consciousness that also forms a bridge from the ritualistic, allegorical past to the emerging, psychologically realistic present that Shakespeare was helping to create. The set was directly modelled on the interior of the chapter house in Worcester Cathedral, linking the play to the roots of medieval religious drama. For me, the central character's mental progress from mythical mask of evil to vulnerable self-awareness shaped the story. Analogies with figures such as Hitler or Stalin seemed pointlessly superficial; nor did I want to lose the significance of the actual historical moment, the change from late medieval to early modern with its own particular relevance to now.

All through this book I've avoided, on the whole, referring to specific actors by name because this isn't an autobiography or a book of theatrical anecdotes, but in the case of *Richard III* that's not possible, because Antony Sher gave one of the most astonishingly brilliant Shakespearean performances of our time, one that is burnt into the memory of anyone who saw it. The production has its place in theatre history as a result of that performance, and the remarkable set that housed it. Tony wrote an excellent book called *Year of the King*, recording in detail the rehearsal process and his evolving thinking about the role: it's worth a read.

The first thing we discussed was the physical appearance of the character. Tony had come up with the idea of playing Richard on crutches, which he had a lot of experience with having spent the previous year on them after snapping his Achilles tendon while playing the Fool in *King Lear*. During our rehearsal period he fiendishly lifted weights in the local gym to build his upper body strength while letting his legs grow weak. The result was an amazing ability to speed about the stage with his feet barely touching the ground, looking like a demented half-man, half-spider creature from a horror movie, bringing gasps from the audience. Then there was the issue of the famous crookback. In the first week of rehearsal we were invited to the RSC wardrobe department to find that all the humps from previous productions had been lined up for our inspection. We were invited to choose between Ian Holm's hump, Alan Howard's hump, Norman Rodway's hump, and several others. We politely said that we would like our own hump. In fact we got three – specially made at huge expense. For all my insistence that a director's first and last duties are reverence for the text and grappling with the polarities of poetry and realism, sometimes plain old theatrical magic (trickery is probably a more honest word) is hard to beat. Here's why there were three. Hump number one was worn the majority of the time. It was very light, made from some kind of hard foam rubber, and contributed to Tony's ability to be incredibly agile and fast. Hump number two was a masterpiece. In researching I had discovered that in medieval coronations and royal weddings kings and queens stripped naked to the waist as they knelt before the high altar. There is no wedding or coronation in the play, but I invented and inserted, just before the interval, a ceremony that combined both. In procession, and to the accompaniment of grandiose Gothic music, Richard and Anne moved slowly downstage under the Gothic arches of the set and between the Gothic tombs that were a permanent feature, halting at the last possible moment and, turning their backs to the audience, knelt before the Archbishop and were stripped to the waist. The effect of seeing Richard's deformed back in the flesh was electric. To this day I'm not sure exactly how it was made, but it was spectacularly realistic. Remember that at this stage of the play, roughly halfway through, Richard's capacity for evil has not yet had full expression; he has murdered his way to the crown but bizarrely retained both his impish humour and our guilty relish at his actions, clothed as they are in the garments of a consummate actor, and one we don't want to stop watching. The sight of his pitiful nakedness forced the audience to consider his humanity, not his 'villainy', to take into account what he had endured rather than what he had inflicted, and even to pity him.

The third hump was the one he died in. The night before his final battle Richard dreams he is visited by the ghosts of those he has murdered. As he speaks to the audience in soliloquy for the last time, he discovers in himself emotions that are completely new to him and should provoke another surge of that pity that may have been stirred by the sight of his naked back:

> I shall despair. There is no creature loves me,
> And if I die, no soul shall pity me.

The rawness and simplicity of those lines that express his vast and terrifying loneliness, his awareness that love is a real thing in the world and how closely related to pity it is, are the words of a man who was never loved from the moment of his birth, who was cursed by his own mother, and now faces death with no faith to sustain him. I didn't want to show that death at the hands of Richmond as the climax of a savage single combat. The context of the cathedral setting, as well as the ghost of the religious drama of the Middle Ages that haunted the production, needed an event that was more ritualistic than a brutal and prolonged fight to the death. So the staging was like this: the most famous line in the play, 'A horse, a horse, my kingdom for a horse!' echoed around the auditorium from loudspeakers as the audience stared at a totally empty stage shrouded in mist. Then from the very back of the stage the tiny stumbling figure of Richard appeared, not only horseless but without his precious crutches, his life support, his superpower, his identity. Almost crawling, he made his way to the front of the stage, seeming to silently plead with the audience for their help, a lame spider, a crippled toad. The contrast with his first appearance, also from the very back of the stage, when he had seemed to float and skim over the surface towards us was heart-breaking. Then he fell to his knees and began to pray silently, hands clenched, eyes staring in terror and lips moving in frantic imprecations to a stranger God. Richmond appeared holding a shining silver sword, not by the hilt, but by the top part of the blade as if carrying a crucifix to an exorcism. He moved slowly, stopping immediately behind Richard and raised the sword, grasping the hilt in both hands, like Hamlet poised unseen behind Claudius; then came a brief moment of total stillness before he plunged it into his back. Actually into hump number three, which had a carefully designed slit in it constructed to receive exactly a third of the blade's length. Richmond removed his hands leaving the sword buried in the crumpled body as the lights faded to a pinpoint of light.

I was so taken by this *coup de théâtre* that it was some days after the first performance that I realised this probably would not have been a fatal blow: real-life accounts of the King's death at Bosworth had him being hacked to bits by about half of Richmond's army in a sea of mud. But hey! This was THEATRE, and no one complained. Like *Hamlet*, *Richard III* is a lot about acting, acting in the improvised theatre of life. Richard loves acting; it's as if he's fully absorbed Hamlet's renowned piece of directorial wisdom, that a man may smile and smile, yet still be a villain. It seems hilarious to him how easy it is to fool people, and how amusing it is to experience up close how vanity leads directly to gullibility. This dramatic self-consciousness makes him charismatic to audiences: he realises they are more entertained by audacious, immoral and plain wicked behaviour than they would be by displays of goodness, kindness, piety and charity. I suggested to Tony that he thought of the audience as a thousand selves, a meeting of the Richard III Fan Club. He is loved by no one in the play, but he could be loved by everyone in the audience. Charisma is nothing without love as its reward.

The productions of *The Merry Wives* and *Richard III* essentially worked because both were held together by a controlling idea that came from the spirit of the play and helped to develop its meaning and purpose. They were both stagings that helped an audience understand why the play existed. They were also good examples of how the collaboration between director and designer should work. In both cases I put a single simple idea into Bill's head, and he turned it into a brilliant physical representation of that idea. For *Richard* it was the medieval mystery plays, for *Merry Wives* the Ealing comedies of the 1950s. But there is a cautionary tale here for directors: to inspire a designer your simple idea has to be a good one – it has to be a meaningful one.

*

For the third time in three years Bill Dudley and I were put together on a project by the RSC for the main stage: *A Midsummer Night's Dream*. In those days the *Dream* was a play directors at Stratford were terrified of. Peter Brook's 1970s 'Chinese Circus' version had been so groundbreaking and become so famous a piece of theatre history that it cast a very long shadow, and almost no RSC director wanted to go anywhere near it. The few productions that did go on were damned by comparison. But Bill and I were on a roll, so it was felt we should go for a hat trick. The problem was I didn't have an idea, let alone a good one. I was at the stage where what qualified as an 'idea' in my head was dominated by design; I hadn't yet learnt that the PLAY was the idea, the TEXT as unlocked in the rehearsal room was the treasure, and if you didn't have an IDEA, then just ask for a bare stage and dress the actors in either Elizabethan or modern clothes or an invented fashion, and get on with discovering through hard work with the language and the narrative and the characters what *Shakespeare's* idea was. But then I didn't know what directing really was. I told Bill I wanted to set it in the 1930s, for no better reason than that I liked the 1930s. But woods know no period and 80 per cent of the play is set in the woods. I could have just suggested trees, but that didn't seem to me enough of an idea: it had no 'concept'.

In my own garden there was a rope hanging from a tall tree that my children and their friends would swing on for hours, and beside it in the lower branches a little wooden tree house in which they would play. I told Bill I wanted the stage to be filled with hundreds of ropes with a variety of diameters, some as thick as tree trunks and some the size of creepers, and, among the ropes, little tree houses where Puck could perch and Titania have her bower.

Why did I have this idea? Something about childhood? Something personal and therefore, by definition, 'artistic' and 'conceptual'? It connected with my life, but had no connection with the play. I'm not sure I'd even read the play particularly thoroughly and was nowhere near being inside the text. I had to go and work abroad shortly after the initial design meeting and wasn't due to return until the day before rehearsals began. But Bill and I said we'd talk by phone as he worked on my idea, and anyway we were a proven team – we were going for the hat trick!

When I saw the model for the set, it was nothing like the idea we had discussed. But it was a beautiful work of art. The concept was that as the lovers entered the woods, the night-time habitat of the world of Titania and Oberon, they shrank to the same size as the Fairy King and Queen and their minions. Consequently the stage was filled with huge flowers, some of them twenty feet tall, and gigantic leaves that swooped out of the wings, bending towards a mossy ground with huge mushrooms straight out of *Alice in Wonderland*. High up, nearly touching the lighting rig, was a massive spider's web stretching the width of the stage. Bill, showing me the model, pointed out where all the access points would be for the actors to climb the flowers, slide down the huge leaves and swing between the strands of the web. I had realised that my vision of ropes and wooden tree houses had no intrinsic meaning, that it did not come from the play; but neither did this. Visually it was a stunning idea but totally disconnected from the text. Besides, big stage acting requires that the actors have as much size and status as possible within the space, not that they be dwarfed by the set. A further practical difficulty was that the structures needed to represent the flowers, the leaves and the web could not properly fit into the rehearsal room, so working on the movement that related to their use was always approximate at best.

So our director/designer partnership didn't achieve the hat trick. The production wasn't a success. The set was brilliant on its own (in fact it got a round of applause on the Press Night before a word in the woods was spoken), but my use of it was poor. I failed to exploit it because I didn't believe in it.

I think it was that experience that turned me into a design minimalist and forced me to understand that the way to do Shakespeare is to put the text and the actor first. The thrill of discovery while exploring that wonderful world of words is like nothing else in theatre, like nothing else in life.

EPILOGUE

There is no right or wrong way to be a good theatre director: there are things to aim for and things to avoid, but ultimately the job is to respond to the actor and try to be as many different kinds of director as there are actors in the cast. An actor once said to me that 'faster and louder' was the best direction they'd ever had. Some actors like just a little direction, others like a lot, but that changes according to the project or the part, or even whether a scene is in poetry or prose. There is no process that can be described as 'how to do Shakespeare'. If the stage is small, one kind of acting is possible; if large, something different is needed. Many actors wish never to have to experience going on a stage at any point in their careers and hope the screen will always be their creative home. I've simply tried to point out not only how Shakespeare's plays are different from other texts in their demands, emotionally and technically, but also how they are the same when it comes to searching for truth and the reflection of humanity in the mirror of art.

These considerations (technique and truthfulness) may not necessarily be such a basic foundation for other practitioners as they are to me, but they are values I feel worth holding on to, and they are explored in the rehearsal room, which is what I hope this book has been all about. Stunning design, brilliant lighting and glorious costumes may all, at one time or another, be important, but it is the interaction between director and actor that truly makes the difference.

As I said at the beginning: stage acting is demanding, and actors need to be brave people to want to do it. Good direction is about giving them the courage they need to step out of the darkness into the stage light, and into the imaginations of expectant strangers whose lives might be changed by the act of living theatre.

INDEX

*Page numbers in **bold** indicate a play's extended discussion*